Biblical Interpretation Then and Now

Biblical Interpretation Then and Now

Contemporary Hermeneutics in the Light of the Early Church

David S. Dockery

BAKER BOOK HOUSE
Grand Rapids, Michigan 49516

Copyright 1992 by
Baker Book House Company
P. O. Box 6287
Grand Rapids, MI 49516-6287

Printed in the United States of America

Library of Congress Cataloging-in-Publication Data

Dockery, David S.
Biblical interpretation then and now : contemporary hermeneutics in the light of the early church / David S. Dockery.
p. cm.
Includes bibliographical references and indexes.
ISBN: O-8010-3010-2
1. Bible—Criticism, interpretation, etc. I. Title.
BS500.D63 1992
200.6'01—dc20 91-44120

Unless otherwise noted, Scripture references are from the Holy Bible, New International Version. Copyright © 1973, 1978, 1984 International Bible Society. Used by permission of Zondervan Bible Publishers.

To *Lanese*

whose constant joy and
faithful love has deeply
enriched my life

86221

Contents

Acknowledgments

Numerous people have been extremely helpful in the course of my work on this book. My interest in the early church can be traced to my studies with B. K. Lackner, James Leo Garrett, and William Countryman. Those who awakened me to the vast world of contemporary hermeneutics include Lenore Langsdorf, Robert Longacre, Daryl Schmidt, and James Duke. My students in the hermeneutics classes and my colleagues at The Southern Baptist Theological Seminary also greatly challenged, informed, and improved my work. To each of these, and to many others, particularly Richard Melick for his perceptive and helpful input, I wish to offer my deep appreciation. The shortcomings of this work, however, should not reflect negatively on any of them, but largely whatever good is found here can be traced in some degree to them.

Readers will quickly note that this work is dependent on previous contributions by Richard N. Longenecker, E. Earle Ellis, Karlfried Froelich, Willis A. Shotwell, Robert M. Grant, Rowan A. Greer, R. P. C. Hanson, Karen Jo Torjesen, Maurice F. Wiles, Gerald Bonner, and Anthony C. Thiselton among others. The book is not so much a creative venture plowing new ground as it is an up-to-date synthesis and summary of numerous previous works, not unlike the hermeneutical work of Theodoret of Cyrus in the fifth century (see chap. 5). It is intended to be an introduction to the history of biblical interpretation for beginning students and a review for others who have traveled this ground before. Because it is an introductory survey, almost all references (whenever possible) are to English sources and English translations.

I wish to offer my appreciation to the people who made this work possible. I thank Jim Weaver and Allan Fisher and the staff at Baker Book House for their faithful encouragement and careful editorial work. More importantly I wish to thank my wife, Lanese, and our three sons, Jonathan, Benjamin, and Timothy, who patiently encouraged me and prayed for me at every stage of this work. Without their sacrificial love and support this book would not have come to fruition.

I offer this book with the hope that our Lord, who has redeemed us, will be honored and his people will be helped in the task of reading, understanding, and ultimately obeying his written Word.

Soli Deo Gloria

Abbreviations

AB	Anchor Bible
ACW	*Ancient Christian Writers*
AJP	*American Journal of Philology*
AJT	*Anglican Journal of Theology*
ALUOS	*Annual of the Leeds University Oriental Society*
ANF	*Ante-Nicene Fathers*
ATJ	*Asbury Theological Journal*
Aug	*Augustinianum*
AugSt	*Augustinian Studies*
BAGD	Bauer, *A Greek-English Lexicon of the New Testament and Other Early Christian Literature*, ed. Arndt, Gingrich, and Danker
Bib	*Biblica*
BibSac	*Bibliotheca Sacra*
BJRL	*Bulletin of the John Rylands Library*
BNTC	Black's New Testament Commentaries
BZNW	*Beihefte zur Zeitschrift für die neutestamentliche Wissenschaft*
CanJTh	*Canadian Journal of Theology*
CBQ	*Catholic Biblical Quarterly*
CBTEL	*Cyclopedia of Biblical, Theological and Ecclesiastical Literature*
CH	*Church History*
CHB	*Cambridge History of the Bible*
CHLGEMP	*Cambridge History of Later Greek and Early Medieval Philosophy*
CPhil	*Classical Philology*
CQ	*Classical Quarterly*
CQR	*Church Quarterly Review*
CR	*Classical Review*
CSR	*Christian Scholars Review*

CT	*Christianity Today*
CTJ	*Corcordia Theological Journal*
CTM	*Concordia Theological Monthly*
CTR	*Criswell Theological Review*
DBR	*The Dictionary of Bible and Religion*
DLGTT	*A Dictionary of Latin and Greek Theological Terms*
DTC	*Dictionnaire de théologie catholique*
EBC	*Expositor's Bible Commentary*
EDT	*Evangelical Dictionary of Theology*
EP	*The Encyclopedia of Philosophy*
EQ	*Evangelical Quarterly*
ExT	*Expository Times*
GLCC	*Great Leaders of the Christian Church*
GNC	Good News Commentary
GNT	The Greek New Testament
GOTR	*Greek Orthodox Theological Review*
GTJ	*Grace Theological Journal*
HBD	*Harper's Bible Dictionary*
HDAC	*Hasting's Dictionary of the Apostolic Church*
HDB	*Hasting's Dictionary of the Bible*
HDCG	*Hasting's Dictionary of Christ and the Gospels*
HJG	*Historisches Jahrbuch der Gorresgellschaft*
HNTC	Harper's New Testament Commentaries
HSCP	*Harvard Studies in Classical Philology*
HT	*History and Theory*
HTR	*Harvard Theological Review*
HUCA	*Hebrew Union College Annual*
IBD	*Illustrated Bible Dictionary*
ICC	International Critical Commentary
IDB	*Interpreter's Dictionary of the Bible*
IER	*Irish Ecclesiastical Record*
IJT	*Indian Journal of Theology*
Int	*Interpretation*
ISBE	*International Standard Bible Encyclopedia*
ITQ	*Irish Theological Quarterly*
JAAR	*Journal of the American Academy of Religion*
JANESCU	*Journal of the Ancient Near Eastern Society of Columbia University*
JBC	*Jerome Bible Commentary*
JBL	*Journal of Biblical Literature*

JE	*The Jewish Encyclopedia*
JETS	*Journal of the Evangelical Theological Society*
JPhil	*Journal of Philology*
JQR	*Jewish Quarterly Review*
JR	*Journal of Religion*
JRH	*Journal of Religious History*
JRomSt	*Journal of Roman Studies*
JSJ	*Journal for the Study of Judaism*
JSNT	*Journal for the Study of the New Testament*
JTC	*Journal for Theology and the Church*
JTS	*Journal of Theological Studies*
LLA	*Library of Liberal Arts*
LPGL	Lampe, *Patristic Greek Lexicon*
LSGEL	Lidell and Scott, *Greek-English Lexicon*
MLN	*Modern Language Notes*
NAC	New American Commentary
NASB	New American Standard Bible
NCB	New Century Bible
NCE	*New Catholic Encyclopedia*
NDLW	*A New Dictionary of Liturgy and Worship*
NDT	*New Dictionary of Theology*
NIC	New International Commentary
NIDCC	*New International Dictionary of the Christian Church*
NIDNTT	*New International Dictionary of New Testament Theology*
NIV	Holy Bible: New International Version
NLH	*New Literary Theory*
NovT	*Novum Testamentum*
NPNF	*Nicene and Post-Nicene Fathers of the Christian Church*
NSHERK	*New Schaff-Herzog Encyclopedia of Religious Knowledge*
NTS	*New Testament Studies*
ODCC	*Oxford Dictionary of the Christian Church*
PhT	*Philosophy Today*
PQ	*Philosophical Quarterly*
PRS	*Perspectives in Religious Studies*
RAug	*Recherches Augustiniennes*
RB	*Revue Biblique*
RBen	*Revue Bénédictine*
REAug	*Revue de études Augustiniennes*
RevEx	*Review and Expositor*

RevQ	*Revue de Qumran*
RJ	*Reformed Journal*
RS	*Religion Studies*
RSR	*Recherches de science religieuse*
SBLDS	Society of Biblical Literature Dissertation Series
SBLMS	Society of Biblical Literature Monograph Series
SC	*Second Century*
SJT	*Scottish Journal of Theology*
SO	*Symbolae Osloenses*
ST	*Studia Theologia*
StEvan	*Studia Evangelica*
StPat	*Studia Patristica*
StPhil	*Studia Philonica*
SVTQ	*St. Vladimir's Theological Quarterly*
SWJT	*Southwestern Journal of Theology*
TB	*Tyndale Bulletin*
TBT	*The Bible Translator*
TDNT	*Theological Dictionary of the New Testament*
TE	*Theological Educator*
ThT	*Theology Today*
TNEB	*The New Encyclopedia Britannica*
TNTC	Tyndale New Testament Commentaries
TPAPA	*Transactions and Proceedings of the American Philological Association*
TS	*Theological Studies*
VC	*Vigilae Christianae*
VE	*Vox Evangelica*
VT	*Vetus Testamentum*
WBC	Word Bible Commentary
WDCT	*Westminster Dictionary of Christian Theology*
WTJ	*Westminster Theological Journal*
ZKT	*Zeitschrift für Katholische Theologie*
ZNW	*Zeitschrift für die neutestamentliche Wissenschaft*
ZPEB	*Zondervan Pictorial Encyclopedia of the Bible*

Introduction

That any of the writers of the early church wrote with the idea someone would later read their writings with the purpose of examining the continuity, discontinuity, and hermeneutical developments from one time period to the next is doubtful. The apostles and the church fathers wrote for their churches and against their opponents, both to advance and to defend the Christian faith as they interpreted it. Even though the articulation of their faith was influenced by their context, culture, tradition, and presuppositions, all shared a common belief in the Bible as the primary source and authority for the Christian faith.

Studying and interpreting the Bible was natural for members of the early Christian community, having inherited the practice from late Judaism. Virginia Stem Owens has suggested that studying literature developed from the practice of studying and interpreting the Bible:

> We in fact got the whole idea of literature as something to be taught and studied because we already developed the habit with the Bible, the central text of Western civilization. At least ever since that category of teachers called rabbis sprang up in the first century and compiled the Midrash, a collection of rabbinical commentary on the Hebrew scriptures, we have been gnawing away at texts, chewing the gristle, sucking the marrow from the bones that are words.[1]

It is true that, from the beginning, Christian interpretation of Scripture has inherited the approaches to interpretation found in the writings of both intertestamental Judaism as well as that of the contemporary Graeco-Roman world. From this dual heritage, Christian interpretation adopted characteristics of extreme literalism and extreme fancifulness—the first resulting from an unquestioning belief in the divine origin, nature, and

1. Virginia Stem Owens, "Fiction and the Bible," *RJ* 38 (July 1988): 12.

authority of the Scripture, word by word; and the latter developing from a desire to discover a deeper meaning hidden in the Bible, or to sanction certain practices either not mentioned or even contradicted by the written Word. Because of this heritage there is an observable continuity with the hermeneutical methods of the rabbis and Philo as well as the followers of Plato and Aristotle. Yet, a discontinuity is also evident as early Christianity attempted to break with Judaism and the surrounding Graeco-Roman religions to establish its uniqueness.

This book traces the developments in early Christian interpretation, noting both continuities and discontinuities. The study will begin with Jesus and observe the developments to the time of the historic Council of Chalcedon (A.D. 451). In order to observe these developments, the discussion will note the influences, philosophy, theology, and tradition that influenced each period. We shall also see what responses or reactions were triggered by interaction with previous approaches. Through this method, we shall be able to observe continuity, diversity, and development in early Christian interpretation.

At the outset certain key terms must be defined. Other important terms are defined or described in the glossary. By "Scripture" we mean the Old Testament and the New Testament, the sixty-six canonical books accepted by the church. While we will refer to the significance of the canon to matters of interpretation, the concept of an approved canon will be accepted as a historical given. *Hermeneutic* derives from *hermeneuein* (Luke 24:27; Acts 8:35) and means to interpret, explain, transpose into another language, or bridge a gap. When we use the term in the singular, *hermeneutic,* it refers to the general theory of interpretation applied to various literature—legal, biblical, medical, philosophical, historical. The plural usage, *hermeneutics,* in our study refers to special approaches focusing upon the interpretation of the biblical materials. *Hermeneutical* means of or pertaining to the interpretation of Scripture. While contemporary discussion of hermeneutics makes an important distinction between exegesis and hermeneutics, there was little or no difference in these ideas during the time period under consideration: the early church and the patristic period through the middle of the fifth century. I have chosen to use the words *exegesis* and *hermeneutics,* as well as *exegetical* and *hermeneutical,* interchangeably.

We may now direct our attention further to the need for this study. As we have noted, hermeneutics concerns itself with the developing principles and rules for a proper understanding of texts, including the Bible. This work concentrates upon the understanding of the Bible in the early Christian church and seeks to discover the significance of these approaches for contemporary hermeneutical discussion. One of the central concerns in contemporary theology and biblical studies has been the interest in hermeneutics. Hans-Georg Gadamer, in his magnum opus, *Truth and*

Method, says, "Nowhere is the debate of the contemporary hermeneutical problem so lively as in the area of protestant theology."[2] In *How to Read a Book,* Mortimer J. Adler says, "The problem of reading the Holy Book—if you have faith that it is the Word of God—is the most difficult problem in the whole field of reading."[3]

The current discussion includes many trends, theories, and approaches that cause the student or experienced scholar to experience a certain degree of bewilderment. Several recent studies that have traced these trends include Donald K. McKim, ed., *A Guide to Contemporary Hermeneutics* (Grand Rapids: Eerdmans, 1986); Terence J. Keegan, *Interpreting the Bible*(New York: Paulist, 1985); Robert K. Johnston, ed., *The Use of the Bible in Theology* (Atlanta: John Knox, 1985); D. A. Carson, "Hermeneutics: A Brief Assessment of Some Recent Trends," *Themelios* 5:2 (January 1980): 12–20; I. Howard Marshall, ed., *New Testament Interpretation: Essays on Principles and Methods* (Grand Rapids: Eerdmans, 1975); David Alan Black and David S. Dockery, eds., *New Testament Criticism and Interpretation* (Grand Rapids: Zondervan, 1991); and Grant Osborne, *The Hermeneutical Spiral* (Downers Grove, Ill.: InterVarsity, 1991). This work attempts to look at the present by looking at the past, the approach being to employ a historical examination of the use of the Bible in the early church to elucidate the contemporary hermeneutical task in order to help us unfold the meaning of Scripture for the contemporary reader.

The major contribution of this work is its reflection on the principles and framework in which the biblical writings were interpreted by different groups and individuals at various times in early Christian thought. The principles reflect the methodology by which the language of biblical revelation was scrutinized so that it yielded insight into God's plan of redemption and its ramifications for the life of the Christian community. We shall see how biblical interpretation determined theology and also how theology shaped biblical hermeneutics. It will be noted that not only theology, but also philosophical presuppositions and hermeneutical concepts taken over from the literary culture of the surrounding world were often developed into new, creative paradigms of interpretation. In order to do so, we will draw from the observations concerning development and paradigmatic advancement of Peter Toon, Jaroslav Pelikan, and Thomas Kuhn.

Pelikan has reminded us that development includes not only change and diversity but also continuity. Thus our use of the term *development* is not equivalent with a traditional scientific or biological concept of evolution. Development includes broader ideas than the simple to the complex,

2. Hans-Georg Gadamer, *Truth and Method,* ed. Garrett Borden and John Cumming (New York: Sheed and Ward, 1975), 473.

3. Mortimer J. Adler, *How to Read a Book* (New York: Simon and Schuster, 1940), 288.

or the basic to the advanced, as has been noted by C. F. D. Moule in *The Origin of Christology*.[4] We shall consider, in this regard, such questions as, Is it possible that development does not necessarily advance? Does the development have continuity? If it does have some degree of continuity, often expressed as unity and diversity, what is the central thought within the continuity?

Most scholars will acknowledge some form of development both in the biblical revelation and in Christian theology. Sometimes this is referred to as "advancement in religion," emphasizing the evolving human thought; or "theological development," emphasizing both the human and divine aspects of theology; or "progressive revelation," primarily focusing upon the divine overview; of human understanding.

Various models of development have been constructed in order to characterize what is meant by the idea of development. Models of development include (1) contextual, (2) syllogistic, (3) innovational, and (4) inherent advancement. Each of these, to various degrees, is present in the early church's hermeneutical developments. A contextual model seeks to account for change by the circumstantial and contextual nature of the interpretation. A syllogistic model maintains that innovations may appear in later formulations, but in reality, these are more precise explications and applications of what was already implicit in earlier statements. With this approach, an analogy can be drawn to syllogism in which what appears to be an innovation in conclusion is really only the logical deduction already contained in the major and minor premises and is a new development only in the sense that it has not been explicitly seen to be the case before. A third model emphasizes the innovations in the growth of interpretation and minimizes any connections with the foundational core. The final model, inherent advancement, can be illustrated by the example of a growing plant and its relation to the original seed; it argues that genuine growth involves innovations of structure and expression. The stalk, leaves, and flower or fruit of a plant are more than mere reproductions of the original seed, yet the growth is always controlled and judged by what is inherent in the seed itself. Based on these models, we shall note the different varieties of development present in the early church's hermeneutical perspectives.

The uniqueness of this study involves not only the comparison of the hermeneutical debate in the early church with the contemporary issues in modern hermeneutical theory, but primarily the synthetic overview of the patristic approach to Scripture. There is no shortage of works on particular individuals or groups, but there is a need to see the broad picture of

4. See C. F. D. Moule, *The Origin of Christology* (Cambridge: Cambridge University Press, 1977).

the early church's hermeneutical perspectives. Coupled with this overview of the church's hermeneutics are matters of the relationship between Scripture and tradition. How are the methods of interpretation related to early church creeds and councils? Aloys Grillmeier observes that "the study of the use and understanding of scripture would be of the greatest significance" for the whole of patristic theology.[5] This observation provides much of the motivation for the present work.

In the past few years, there have been several studies on the history of interpretation in general, or patristic interpretation specifically. Each of these has built upon and advanced the classic work by Frederick W. Farrar, *History of Interpretation.* These recent studies include Moisés Silva, *Has the Church Misread the Bible?: The History of Interpretation in the Light of Current Issues;* Karlfried Froehlich's brief survey in *Biblical Interpretation in the Early Church;* John Rogerson's and Barnabas Lindars's contributions in *The Study and Use of the Bible;* Rowan Greer's section in *Early Biblical Interpretation;* and the initial section of Robert M. Grant's overview, *A Short History of the Interpretation of the Bible.* Yet, much of the recent work in hermeneutics has briefly surveyed or passed over the patristic contributions. For instance, the work of Jack B. Rogers and Donald K. McKim, *The Authority and Interpretation of the Bible: An Historical Approach,* makes a significant contribution to the history of the church's use and understanding of the Bible, yet it devotes only 34 of 471 pages of text to the early church. Likewise, W. G. Kümmel, in *The New Testament: The History of the Investigation of Its Problems,* gives only 6 of 461 pages of text to the early church period as he discusses problems in the history of New Testament interpretation. While volume 1 of *The Cambridge History of the Bible* covers many of the major areas clearly and competently, it does not deal with the less significant persons or provide a picture of development and continuity in the early church. There is a need for a synthesis on the early church comparable to the excellent work of Beryl Smalley, *The Study of the Bible in the Middle Ages* (2d ed.). The scope of this work is not as thorough as Smalley's work, yet we hope it is an initial contribution toward that end. The unique contribution of this book is its overall summary and synthesis of early church interpretation and its attempt to relate the insights of the early church to the current trends in hermeneutics.

There have been at least three different approaches to patristic hermeneutics. The first concentrates on describing how the text of Scripture is assimilated by the theology of the early church. Characteristically, this approach has concluded that exegesis in the early church is, in reality, eisegesis, reading the meaning of a passage into Scripture rather than a

5. Aloys Grillmeier, *Christ in the Christian Tradition,* vol. 1, *From the Apostolic Age to Chalcedon (451),* trans. John Bowden, 2d ed. (Atlanta: John Knox, 1975), 34.

reading of the meaning out of Scripture. This approach views the early church's interpretation as a major misunderstanding of the Bible. A second approach to patristic hermeneutics is a descriptive method that does not seek to evaluate the correctness or validity of the interpretations. The first approach sees exegesis subsumed under theology, while the role of theology is neglected in the second. The third approach focuses upon the methods, more than the content, of the early church interpreters. The strengths of the third approach enable us to see the relationship between Christian exegesis and its Hellenistic and Jewish sources, as well as the relationship between the various Christian perspectives. The first approach asks, Have the patristic exegetes rightly understood Scripture? The second asks, What was their understanding of the meaning of Scripture? The final approach asks, What methods and principles did they use to interpret Scripture? In our examination, we shall focus upon the third question, while not neglecting the first or second.

We have mentioned that our study will begin with Jesus' own interpretation of the Old Testament Scriptures. Included in this discussion of "christological hermeneutics" will be the use of Scripture by the apostles, as well as a brief discussion on the influence of Jewish hermeneutics.

We will next consider the apostolic fathers and the apologists. This will include the work of Clement, Ignatius, Justin Martyr, Irenaeus, and Tertullian, especially as they reacted to heresy. In this period we shall also examine the role of tradition, the rule of faith, and its relationship to biblical interpretation. The next major period begins a formulated approach to hermeneutics beyond the functional and authoritative methods previously practiced. During this time period, from the middle of the second century to the middle of the third century, biblical exegesis developed into an art and a science. The background of allegorical interpretation and its influence on the school of Alexandria will be closely examined. Our analysis will focus on the brilliant and creative work of Origen. A halfway step between the Alexandrians and the Antioch school, largely influenced by theological concerns, is found in the exegesis of the later Alexandrians, including Athanasius and the Cappadocian fathers.

Our next period locates the beginning of historical and contextual hermeneutics in the Antiochenes of the late fourth and early fifth centuries. We shall analyze their reaction to and rejection of allegory, their understanding of typology, and the role of authorial intention. Our discussion will concentrate on John Chrysostom and Theodore of Mopsuestia. A final period features the contributions of Jerome, Augustine, and Theodoret of Cyrus, all fifth-century exegetes. In this chapter we shall observe the movement toward a catholic and canonical synthesis that had some characteristic strengths and weaknesses of the previous approaches. While this book will interact with numerous early church representatives, it will concentrate mainly on Justin, Irenaeus, Origen, Chrysostom, Augustine, and Theodoret.

Our final section will employ the early church as a window through which insight may be gained for the contemporary discussion. Contemporary trends and approaches that will be surveyed include (1) authorial-intent hermeneutics, (2) textual hermeneutics, and (3) reader-approach hermeneutics. We shall conclude by observing the significance of the early church's hermeneutical approaches for understanding the contemporary hermeneutical debate. This final aspect of the work is one of the unique features of the book.

That questions are still raised concerning the meaning of biblical texts is not surprising. People wonder if there is more involved in understanding the text than just a literal reading. With these thoughts in mind I have addressed the subjects outlined with the idea that the use of the Bible in the early church may shed some light on the reading of that same Bible in the latter part of the twentieth century. The contemporary discussion of hermeneutics has centered on the issues of the relevance and contemporization of Scripture for modern men and women. The process whereby Scripture was interpreted and appropriated for the purpose of explicating the Christian faith in the early church should prove helpful for illuminating our contemporary work in biblical interpretation.

1

The First Century: The Beginning of Christian Hermeneutics

From the beginning of the Christian movement, the early believers shared the Holy Scriptures of the Jews. Following the example of Jesus, these believers held that Scripture was first and foremost the authoritative, inspired Word of God. Indeed, not only did the earliest church inherit its Scriptures from the Jews, it also inherited various methods of interpretation and interpretations themselves. The interpretation of the Jewish Scriptures by the earliest church, however, included an additional factor that stamped a new meaning upon Scripture: the life, death, and resurrection of Jesus. In this chapter, we shall lay the foundation for our study by examining briefly how Jesus and the apostles interpreted the Old Testament.

Jesus and Christological Hermeneutics

Jesus and the Old Testament

The New Testament account of the ministry of Jesus maintains that Jesus himself instructed his followers to show that his life and ministry fulfilled Scriptures.[1] Although Jesus interpreted the Scriptures in a manner

1. John Rogerson, Christopher Rowland, and Barnabas Lindars, *The History of Christian Theology*, vol. 2, *The Study and Use of the Bible*, ed. Paul Avis, 3 vols. (Grand Rapids: Eerdmans, 1988), 3–5; Donald Guthrie, *New Testament Theology* (Downers Grove, Ill.: InterVarsity, 1981), 955–57.

similar to his contemporary Jewish exegetes, there also was novelty in his method and message.

This new method was a christological reading, meaning that Jesus read the Old Testament in light of himself. For example, in John 5:39–40, it is recorded that Jesus said: "You diligently study the Scriptures because you think that by them you possess eternal life. These are the *Scriptures that testify about me*" (italics added). And in John 5:46: "If you believed Moses, you would believe me, for *he wrote about me*" (italics added). On the Emmaus road Jesus said, "How slow of heart [you are] to believe all that the prophets have spoken! Did not the Christ have to suffer these things and then enter his glory? And beginning with Moses and all the Prophets, he explained to them what was said in all the Scriptures concerning himself" (Luke 24:26–27).

Jesus understood the Old Testament christologically, and it is from him that the church derives its identification of Jesus with Israel. In the temptation narratives (Matt. 4:1–11; Luke 4:1–13), Jesus' own estimation of his status and calling is reflected in his answers from Deuteronomy 6–8. In this Old Testament passage Moses, following the forty years of wandering in the wilderness, exhorted Israel toward wholehearted obedience and continued faith in the divine provision for them. It was a time of hunger and testing, preparatory to a special task, in which God disciplined his nation Israel (Deut. 8:5), to teach them to worship only the true God. Jesus, at the end of the forty days, accepted afresh his messianic mission and his status as Son of God, seeing himself in some sense as the new Israel, succeeding where the old Israel had failed.[2] His belief in his forthcoming resurrection after three days seemed to be motivated both by the promises of Israel's resurrection (cf. Hos. 6:2) and by seeing himself in light of the Jonah story (cf. Jon. 1:17; Matt. 12:40). He observed his own experiences prefigured in the psalms of vindication and suffering, used both by individual Israelites and by corporate Israel (Pss. 22, 41, 42, 43, 118).[3]

R. T. France sums up the evidence of the synoptic Gospels in these words:

> He uses persons in the Old Testament as types of himself (David, Solomon, Elijah, Elisha, Isaiah, Jonah) or of John the Baptist (Elijah); he refers to Old Testament institutions as types of himself and his work (the priesthood and the covenant); he sees in the experiences of Israel foreshadowings of his own; he finds the hopes of Israel fulfilled in himself and his disciples, and sees his disciples as assuming the status of Israel; in deliverance by God he sees a type of the gathering of men into his church, while the disasters of Israel are foreshadowings of the imminent punishment of those who reject

2. John W. Wenham, *Christ and the Bible* (Downers Grove, Ill., InterVarsity, 1973), 106–8.
3. Cf. Matt. 21:42; 23:39; 26:38; 27:46; Mark 12:10; 14:18, 34; 15:34; Luke 13:35; 20:17.

him, whose unbelief is prefigured in that of the wicked in Israel and even, in two instances, in the arrogance of the Gentile nations.[4]

In all these aspects of the Old Testament people of God, Jesus saw foreshadowings of himself and his work. This resulted in opposition from and rejection by the majority of the Jews, while the promises concerning Israel were partially fulfilled in the new Christian community. The history of Israel had reached its decisive point in the coming of Jesus. The whole of the Old Testament pointed to him. He embodied the redemptive destiny of Israel, and in the community of those who belong to him that status and destiny are to be fulfilled.[5]

Because Jesus saw himself as the representative of Israel, words originally spoken of the nation could rightly be applied to him, and because Jesus is the representative of humankind, words spoken originally by the psalmist can be fulfilled by him (cf. John 13:18; 15:25; 19:28). For Jesus, the key to understanding the Old Testament was located in his own life and work, for everything pointed to himself. The New Testament writers, following the pattern of Jesus, interpreted the Old Testament as a whole and in its parts as a witness to Christ.[6]

This is not the place to evaluate the question of the relationship between the Jesus of history and the picture presented of him in the Gospels. It would be most surprising, however, if the new and radical way in which the earliest Christians interpreted the Jewish Scriptures was entirely their invention and owed nothing to Jesus himself.[7] The gospel tradition indi-

4. R. T. France, *Jesus and the Old Testament: His Application of Old Testament Passages to Himself and His Message* (London: Tyndale, 1971), 75.

5. Ibid., 76; cf. Matthew Black, "The Christological Use of the Old Testament in the New Testament," *NTS* 18 (1971): 1–14; Morna D. Hooker, *Studying the New Testament* (Minneapolis: Augsburg, 1979), 70–92.

6. The literature on the way the New Testament writers use the Old Testament is numerous and varied in its approach, but the overall christological emphasis is generally accepted. See D. L. Baker, *Two Testaments, One Bible: A Study of Some Modern Solutions to the Theological Problem of the Relationship Between the Old and New Testament* (Downers Grove, Ill.: InterVarsity, 1976); E. Earle Ellis, "How the New Testament Uses the Old," in *New Testament Interpretation*, ed. I. Howard Marshall (Grand Rapids: Eerdmans, 1975), 199–219; Darrell L. Bock, "Evangelicals and the Use of the Old Testament: Part 1," *BibSac* 142 (1985): 209–23; idem, "Evangelicals and the Use of the Old Testament in the New: Part 2," *BibSac* 142 (1985): 306–19; D. A. Carson and H. G. M. Williamson, eds., *It Is Written: Scripture Citing Scripture. Essays in Honour of Barnabas Lindars* (Cambridge: Cambridge University Press, 1988); Klyne Snodgrass, "The Use of the Old Testament in the New Testament," in *New Testament Criticism and Interpretation*, ed. David Alan Black and David S. Dockery (Grand Rapids: Zondervan, 1991); Robert B. Sloan, "Use of the Old Testament in the New Testament," in *Reclaiming the Prophetic Mantle*, ed. G. L. Klein (Nashville: Broadman, 1992).

7. Robert H. Stein, "The Criteria for Authenticity," in *Gospel Perspectives: Studies of History and Tradition in the Four Gospels*, ed. R. T. France and David Wenham (Sheffield: JSOT, 1980),

cates that Jesus viewed his mission as a fulfillment of the Scriptures and in a way that ran counter to the assumptions and expectations of his closest followers as well as his opponents.[8] We can content ourselves with C. K. Barrett's words: "The gospel story as a whole differs so markedly from current (i.e., first-century) interpretation of the Old Testament that it is impossible to believe that it originated simply in meditations of prophecy; it originated in the career of Jesus of Nazareth."[9]

It is not surprising that in providing different pictures of Jesus' life, the biblical writers saw that at almost every point his life had fulfilled the Old Testament. His birth had been foretold (Isa. 7:14 = Matt. 1:23; Mic. 5:2 = Matt. 2:6); as had the flight to Egypt (Hos. 11:1 = Matt. 2:15); the slaughter of the innocent children by Herod (Jer. 31:15 = Matt. 2:18); and his upbringing in Nazareth (cf. Matt. 2:23). The overall impact of his ministry had been described (Isa. 42:1–4 = Matt. 12:17–21), as well as his use of parables in his teaching (Isa. 6:9–10; Ps. 78:2 = Matt. 13:14–15, 35). The message of Jesus' passion is filled with allusions to the Old Testament, including accounts of the triumphal entry into Jerusalem (Zech. 9:9 = Matt. 21:5), the cleansing of the temple (Isa. 56:7; Ps. 69:9 = Matt. 21:13), and the events surrounding the cross (John 19:24, 28, 36–37).[10]

The question that faces us for the purposes of our study is, How did Jesus interpret the Old Testament so that this christological hermeneutic developed? The answer to this question requires us to look carefully at the Jewish approaches to biblical interpretation before and during the time of Jesus' life.

225–63. We concur with Stein: "Finally it should be pointed out that if by the use of these various criteria certain sayings in our Gospels can in fact be demonstrated as being authentic and this in turn can establish a continuity between the historical Jesus and the kerygmatic Christ, there is then no *a priori* reason to be skeptical about the general portrait of Jesus found in our Gospels. On the contrary it would then be clear that the burden of proof lies with those who would reject the authenticity of the gospel materials rather than with those who accept their authenticity. We can say this in another way using the terminology of the law court. If by the criteria discussed above the authenticity of certain sayings and motifs in the Gospels can be demonstrated which establish a continuity between the Jesus of history and the Christ of faith, then we should assume that the other sayings and motifs in the Gospels are 'innocent until proven guilty,' i.e. a saying in the Gospels purporting to come from Jesus is true (authentic) until proven false" (263). For a full discussion of this matter and bibliographic survey, see Craig Blomberg, *The Historical Reliability of the Gospels* (Downers Grove, Ill.: InterVarsity, 1987).

8. Rogerson, Rowland, and Lindars, *The Study and Use of the Bible*, 5.

9. C. K. Barrett, "The Interpretation of the Old Testament in the New," *CHB*, 1:405.

10. Cf. R. T. France, "The Formula-Quotations of Matthew 2 and the Problem of Communication," *NTS* 27 (1981): 223–51; Homer A. Kent, Jr., "Matthew's Use of the Old Testament," *BibSac* 121 (1964): 34–43; Donald Juel, *Messianic Exegesis: Christological Interpretation of the Old Testament in Early Christianity* (Philadelphia: Fortress, 1988).

Jewish Approaches to Biblical Interpretation

Jewish interpreters, no matter how diverse their hermeneutical methods, found agreement on several common points. First, they believed in the divine inspiration of Scripture. Secondly, they affirmed that the Torah contained the entire truth of God for the guidance of humanity. The texts, for the Jew of the first century, were extremely rich in content and pregnant with plural meanings. Richard N. Longenecker illustrates this with quotations from the rabbis:

> From the school of R. Ishmael (second-generation Tannaim, c. A.D. 90–130) we have the maxim: "Just as the rock is split into many splinters, so also may one biblical verse convey many teachings" (b. Sanhedrin 34a). Bemidbar Rabbah, the most recent of the pentateuchal Midrashim, dating no earlier than the eleventh or twelfth century A.D. in its codified form, expands this to insist, based on the numerical value of *dgl* ("standard") in Cant. 2:4, that the Torah "can be expounded in forty-nine different ways" (Num. R. 2.3) and based on the value of *yayin* (wine), that "there are seventy modes of expounding the Torah" (Num. R. 13.15f).[11]

Thirdly, Jewish exegetes, because of their view that the text contained many meanings, considered both the plain or literal meaning and the implied meanings. Lastly, they maintained that the purpose of all interpretation is to translate the words of God into life, thus making them relevant for people in their own particular situations.

Traditionally, four hermeneutical methods have been considered the primary alternatives for studying the exegetical practices behind the New Testament writers. However, we shall consider the typological along with the literal, allegorical, pesher, and midrash, a total of five approaches.[12] It is helpful to be reminded that these classifications may not have always been consciously considered categories for early Jewish interpreters. R. Loewe rightly notes that in dealing with a system that thinks more wholistically, functionally, and practically than it does analytically, that stresses precedent more than logic in defense of its ways, any attempt at classification inevitably goes beyond that system's explicit statements as to its own prin-

11. Richard N. Longenecker, *Biblical Exegesis in the Apostolic Period* (Grand Rapids: Eerdmans, 1975), 19.

12. Cf. Barry Ray Sang, "The New Testament Hermeneutical Milieu: The Inheritance and the Heir" (Ph.D. diss., Drew University, 1983), 1–38. Longenecker regularly speaks of a typological correspondence as well in *Biblical Exegesis,* though he considers only the four traditional categories. The most important work in the area of Jewish hermeneutics in recent times has been done by Jacob Neusner: e.g., *Invitation to Midrash* (San Francisco: Harper and Row, 1989).

ciples.[13] Nevertheless, as others have suggested, the Jewish treatment of Scripture falls rather easily into one or the other of these five categories.

Literal

Rabbinic literature contains a number of examples where the Scriptures were understood in a straightforward fashion, resulting in the plain, simple, and natural meaning of the text being applied to the lives of the people, particularly in observing the deuteronomic legislation. The interpretation often was extremely literal, as the comments on Deuteronomy 6:7 by the School of Shammai illustrate. Deuteronomy 6:7 reads,

> Impress them [the commandments] on your children. Talk about them when you sit at home and when you walk along the road, when you lie down and when you get up.

The comments from Shammai note that "in the evening all should recline when they recite the shema, but in the morning they should stand up, for it is written, 'And when you lie down and when you rise up.'"[14] Again, on the treatment of the "stubborn and rebellious son" in Deuteronomy 21:18–20, a strict literalism is found in the commentary:

> If either of them [the parents] was maimed in the hand, or lame or dumb or blind or deaf, he cannot be condemned as a stubborn and rebellious son, for it is written, "Then shall his father and mother lay hold on him"—so they were not maimed in the hand; "and bring him out"—so they were not lame; "and they shall say"—so they were not dumb; "this our son"—so they were not blind; "he will not obey our voice"—so they were not deaf.[15]

The literal interpretation was considered foundational for all other hermeneutical developments. As S. Lowy comments, "the Rabbis considered the plain interpretation of the laws, based mainly upon a literal understanding, as being of equal value with 'things which even the Sadducees agree upon,' and these should therefore be learned in elementary school."[16]

Jesus occasionally adopted the literal approach, particularly with regard to moral questions. In instruction concerning human relationships three examples can be offered. Mark 7:10 (Matt. 15:14) reports Jesus rebuking the Pharisees with straightforward explications from Exodus 20:12, "Honor your father and your mother" and from Exodus 21:17, "Anyone who curses his father or mother must be put to death." Regarding

13. R. Loewe, "The 'Plain' Meaning of Scripture," in *Papers of the Institute of Jewish Studies, London*, ed. J. G. Weiss (Jerusalem: Hebrew University Press, 1964), 140–85.

14. Mishnah Berakah 1.3.

15. Mishnah Sanhedrin 8.4.

16. S. Lowy, "Some Aspects of Normative and Sectarian Interpretation of the Scriptures," *ALUOS* 6 (1966–68): 131.

marriage and divorce questions, he answered in Mark 10:7 (Matt 19:5) with a literal quotation from Genesis 2:24, "For this reason a man will leave his father and mother and be united to his wife, and the two will become one flesh." Since God had spoken quite plainly on these foundational concerns, Jesus also interpreted them in a straightforward manner.

Midrash

Midrash was the term designating the normal way that the rabbis and Pharisees interpreted Scripture. Renee Bloch goes so far as not to regard midrash as a specific method of exegesis but rather as rabbinic exegesis in general. She defines midrash as "an edifying and explanatory genre closely tied to scripture, in which the role of amplification is real but secondary and always remains subordinate to the primary religious end, which is to show the full import of the work of God, the Word of God."[17] Bloch notes five major characteristics in her description of this approach: (1) its foundation is in Scripture; (2) it is homiletical; (3) it seeks to clarify the meaning of the text; (4) it attempts to contemporize the Scripture being considered; and (5) it seeks to discover the basic principles inherent in the legal sections, with the aim of solving problems not dealt with in Scripture (*halakah* = having reference to the full range of hermeneutical devices involved), or it sets out to find the true significance of events mentioned in the narrative sections of the Pentateuch (*haggadah* = focused reference to the type of material treated).[18] The ongoing discussion of midrash has raised the question whether it is a literary genre or a hermeneutical method. For our purposes midrash has the meaning of commentary, particularly with the idea of making Scripture contemporary in order to apply it to or make it meaningful for the interpreter's current situation.[19]

Midrashic syllogism is found also in the teaching of Jesus. In the Sermon on the Mount, Jesus employed the midrash principle of moving from light to heavy.[20] "If you then, though you are evil, know how to give good gifts

17. Renee Bloch, "Midrash," in *Approaches to Ancient Judaism: Theory and Practice,* ed. W. S. Green, trans. Mary Howard Callaway, Brown Judaic Studies 1 (Missoula, Mont.: Scholars, 1978), 29.

18. Ibid., 33. Point 2 of the listing assumes the validity of Bloch's understanding of the synagogue Targum as the basis for rabbinic haggadah. Also see Birger Gerhardsson's useful descriptions in *The Testing of God's Son* (Lund: Gleerup, 1966), 14, and Daniel M. Patte, *Early Jewish Hermeneutics in Palestine,* SBLDS 22 (Missoula, Mont.: Scholars, 1975), 315–19.

19. E. Earle Ellis, *Prophecy and Hermeneutic in Early Christianity* (Grand Rapids: Eerdmans, 1978), 151–62; cf. idem, "Midrash, Targum and New Testament Quotations," in *Neotestamentica et Semitica,* ed. E. Earle Ellis and M. Wilcox (Edinburgh: T & T Clark, 1969), 61–69.

20. Rabbi Hillel, whose teaching preceded the rise of Christianity by a generation or two, is considered the author of the seven basic principles of midrashic or rabbinic exegesis. Hillel was considered "the Prince" over the assembly. For the history and background of this tradition, see Emil Schurer, *The Jewish People in the Age of Jesus Christ (175 B.C.–A.D. 135),* rev. and

to your children, how much more (*posoi mallon*) will your Father in heaven give good things to those who ask him" (Matt. 7:11). Similarly in Luke 12:28, Jesus applied the parable of the foolish rich person with the following illustration, "If that is how God clothes the grass of the field, which is here today, and tomorrow is thrown into the fire, how much more (*posoi mallon*) will he clothe you, O you of little faith!"

Jesus confounded the Pharisees with Scripture by using their own hermeneutical principles. When they objected to his disciples plucking and eating grain on the Sabbath, he alluded to the time when David ate the Bread of the Presence in the house of God, an act unlawful yet permitted in this case because of the greater importance of the life of David, Israel's anointed king, and, by analogy, argued that "the Son of Man is the Lord even of the sabbath" (Mark 2:25–28).[21] Jesus' use of midrash was basically apologetical, used in the context of debate. His ingenious treatment of Scripture befuddled his opponents on their own hermeneutical ground.

Pesher

Since the discovery of the Dead Sea Scrolls in the middle of the twentieth century, another hermeneutical method common among Judaism has come to our attention. This approach, known as pesher, is usually described as an exegetical method or collection of such interpretations (*pesharim*) that suggests that the prophetic writings contain a hidden eschatological significance or divine mystery that may be revealed "only by a forced and even abnormal construction of the biblical text." F. F. Bruce, in his detailed work on the texts of the Qumran community, has discovered that pesher often involved manipulation of textual intricacies and can be

---

ed. Geza Vermes and Fergus Millar (Edinburgh: T & T Clark, 1973), 363. Schurer suggests that Hillel was the father of Gamaliel, who was the teacher of Saul of Tarsus (the apostle Paul). The seven principles ascribed to him include:

1. *Qal wahomer:* what applies in a less important case will certainly apply in a more important case.
2. *Gezerah shawah:* verbal analogy from one verse to another; where the same words are applied to two separate cases it follows that the same considerations apply to both.
3. *Binyan ab mikathub 'ehad:* building up a family from a single text; when the same phrase is found in a number of passages, then a consideration found in one of them applies to all of them.
4. *Binyan ab mishene kethubim:* building up a family from two texts; a principle is established by relating two texts together; the principle can then be applied to other passages.
5. *Kelal upherat:* the general and the particular; a general principle may be restricted by a particularization of it in another verse; or conversely, a particular rule may be extended into a general principle.
6. *Kayoze bo bemagom 'aher:* as is found in another place; a difficulty in one text may be solved by comparing it with another which has points of general (though not necessarily verbal) similarity.
7. *Dabar halamed me'inyano:* a meaning established by its context.

21. Other examples of this approach are Matt. 10:25; 12:5–7; Mark 12:26; John 7:23; 10:34–36. See C. F. D. Moule, *The Birth of the New Testament* (New York: Harper and Row, 1966), 65–66.

frequently described as "atomistic interpretation."[22] There was a close relationship between pesher and midrash that is difficult at times to distinguish.[23] Isaac Rabinowitz offers a more specific understanding of pesher: "a literary composition which states in ordinary language the realities thought to be presaged (i.e. prefigured or portended) by the words of some portion of the Hebrew Bible, words regarded whether as already fulfilled or as still awaiting fulfillment."[24]

Rabinowitz's argument is built upon the accepted consensus of the connection between pesher and dream interpretation as found in Genesis 40:5–22; 41:8–18 and Daniel 2:1–45; 4:4–27; 5:5–17, where the word *pesher* was actually used and always within the context of dream interpretation. It is believed that pesher as used in these Old Testament sources provides the foundation and background for its meaning in Qumran literature. In both settings, the dream or prophecy was perceived to contain a divine mystery which required interpretation, whether by Joseph, Daniel, or the Teacher of Righteousness. Pesher, therefore, was a form of interpretation whose solution could be reached only through divine revelation. We can distinguish pesher from midrash by understanding midrash as a contemporizing treatment of Scripture that sought to make God's Word relevant to the present circumstances and ongoing situations, whereas pesher looked upon the biblical material from the standpoint of imminent apocalyptic fulfillment. We can describe midrash as "this has relevance to this" while pesher is "this is that."[25] The question that we must address is, How did Jesus employ pesher exegesis?

Longenecker believes that Jesus used both literal and midrash approaches on occasion, yet his most characteristic interpretation of Scripture was pesher.[26] In Jesus' first recorded exposition (Luke 4:16–21), he

22. F. F. Bruce, *Biblical Exegesis in the Qumran Texts* (Grand Rapids: Eerdmans, 1959), 14.

23. William H. Brownlee, *The Midrash Pesher of Habakkuk,* SBLMS 24 (Missoula, Mont.: Scholars, 1979), 25.

24. Isaac Rabinowitz, "Pesher/Pittaron: Its Biblical Meaning and Its Significance in the Qumran Literature," *RevQ* 8 (1973): 219–32. Additional helpful discussions are found in Elieser Slomovic, "Toward an Understanding of the Exegesis in the Dead Sea Scrolls," *RevQ* 7 (1969): 3–15; Joseph A. Fitzmyer, "The Use of Explicit Old Testament Quotations in Qumran Literature and in the New Testament," *NTS* 7 (1961): 297–333.

25. Karl Elliger, *Studien zum Habakuk-Kommentar vom Toten Meer* (Tübingen: Mohr-Siebeck, 1953), 155, comments, "Seine Auslegung grundet sich also nicht auf den Text allein, sondern in noch starkerem Masse und im entscheidenden Punkte auf eine besondere Offenbarung." Cf. Geza Vermes, "The Qumran Interpretation of Scripture in its Historical Setting," *ALUOS* 6 (1966–68): 90–97; Longenecker, *Biblical Exegesis,* 38–45, who questions drawing too sharp a distinction between pesher and midrash.

26. Longenecker, *Biblical Exegesis,* 70–75; cf. James D. G. Dunn, *Unity and Diversity in the New Testament: An Inquiry into the Character of Earliest Christianity* (Philadelphia: Westminster, 1977), 91–93.

read and interpreted Isaiah 61:1. After reading the text, he rolled up the scroll, handed it to the synagogue attendant, and sat down to speak, claiming, "Today this scripture is fulfilled in your hearing." John 5:39–47, which we mentioned earlier, also explicitly states this fulfillment theme. Longenecker provides examples that indicate all four Gospel writers believed that Jesus viewed the Old Testament from the perspective of his own ministry, that the fulfillment theme was a definite element in his teaching, and that he often treated selected biblical texts in a fashion that we have called pesher. If we had only the two passages cited, it would be possible to claim that Jesus himself gave impetus to the fulfillment theme and the pesher approach to Scripture in the early church.[27]

Allegorical

The most prominent practitioner of allegorical exegesis among first-century Jewish interpreters was Philo of Alexandria, a contemporary of Jesus whose major work was simultaneous with the earliest days of the church. For Philo, Scripture had two levels of meaning: (1) the literal and (2) the underlying meaning. This underlying meaning was recovered only through allegorical exegesis which, according to Harry A. Wolfson, means "the interpretation of a text in terms of something else, irrespective of what that something else is."[28] Although allegorical exegesis was widespread among Jews of the first century, it was not dominant in Palestine. There seems little evidence of allegorical exegesis in the New Testament, and none to support such usage by Jesus.[29] There was usage of allegory in Jesus' parables, but no example of an allegorical method of interpretation.[30]

27. Longenecker, *Biblical Exegesis,* 70. Other examples include Mark 12:10 (=Ps. 118:22); Mark 14:27 (=Zech. 13:7); Matt. 11:10 (=Mal. 3:1/Isa. 40:3); Matt. 13:14 (=Isa. 6:9); Matt. 15:8 (=Isa. 29:13); Luke 22:37 (=Isa. 53:12); John 13:18 (=Ps. 41:9); John 15:25 (=Ps. 35:19); Mark 12:36 (=Ps. 110:1).

28. Harry A. Wolfson, *Philo I* (Cambridge: Harvard University Press, 1968), 115, 134; cf. Carl Siegfried, *Philo von Alexandria als Augsleger Alten Testaments* (Jena: Duft, 1875), 168–70; Irmgard Christiansen, *Die Technik der allegorischen Auslegungswissenschaft bei Philon von Alexandrien* (Tübingen: Mohr, 1969), 134; Jean Danielou, *Philon D' Alexandaire* (Paris: Librairie Artheme Fayard, 1958), 129–38. More detailed analysis of allegorical hermeneutics with reference to Philo is found in the work of Burton L. Mack, "Exegetical Traditions in Alexandrian Judaism: A Program for the Analysis of the Philonic Corpus," *StPhil* 3 (1974–75): 71–112. I shall consider this subject more carefully with amplification in chapter 3.

29. Cf. A. T. Hanson, *Studies in Paul's Technique and Theology* (London: SPCK, 1974), 159–66; for a different approach, see Rudolf Bultmann, *Theology of the New Testament,* trans. Kendrik Grobel (New York: Scribners, 1955), 108–21.

30. Hans-Josef Klauk, *Alegorie und Allegorese in Synoptischen Gleichnistexten,* Neutestamentliche Abhandlungen, 19 (Munster: Aschendorf, 1977), 354–55, emphasizes the distinction between "allegorizing" as a method and "allegorical elements" in the parables; Mikeal C. Parsons, "'Allegorizing Allegory': Narrative Analysis and Parable Interpretation," *PRS* 15 (1988): 147–64.

Typological

Typological exegesis seeks to discover a correspondence between people and events of the past and of the present or future.[31] The correspondence with the past is not necessarily discovered within the written text, but within the historical event. This approach can be distinguished both from prophecy, where the text functions only, or primarily, as a prediction of the future, and from allegorical hermeneutics, where the correspondence is found in the hidden meaning of the text and not in the history it presents. Typological exegesis does not ignore the historical meaning of a text, but begins with the historical meaning.[32] Typological exegesis then is based on the conviction that certain events in the history of Israel prefigure a future time when God's purposes will be revealed in their fullness.[33]

Jesus is recorded as pointing out typological correspondences between earlier events in redemptive history and circumstances connected with his person and ministry. Longenecker suggests three examples where Jesus invoked this correspondence theme: (1) Matthew 12:40, where Jesus paralleled the experience of Jonah and his own approaching death and entombment; (2) Matthew 24:37, where the relationship was drawn between the days of Noah and the days of "the coming of the Son of Man"; and (3) John 3:14, where Jesus connected the elevation of the serpent in the wilderness to his own approaching crucifixion.[34] In each case, "Jesus viewed these Old Testament events as typological, pointing forward to their fulfillment in his person and ministry—not just analogies that could be drawn for the purpose of illustration."[35]

Apart from the literal usage of the Old Testament for moral injunctions, the other approaches to the Old Testament Jesus used have an obvious

31. Dunn, *Unity and Diversity,* 86. Because of the abuses in the usage of typology by post-Reformation exegetes, many people tend to ignore the typological method. But when carefully defined and distinguished from allegorical exegesis, it can be and should be considered a separate exegetical category for both Jewish and Christian interpreters of the first century. Extensive discussion of typological hermeneutics will be offered in chapters 2 and 4. The most complete work on the subject to date is Richard M. Davidson, *Typology in Scripture: A Study of Hermeneutical TYPOS Structures,* Andrews University Seminary Doctoral Dissertation Series, 2 (Berrien Springs, Mich.: Andrews University Press, 1981); also see David S. Dockery, "Typological Exegesis: Beyond Abuse and Neglect," in *Reclaiming the Prophetic Mantle,* ed. G. L. Klein (Nashville: Broadman, 1992).

32. D. S. Russell, *The Method and Message of Jewish Apocalyptic* (London: SCM, 1964), 283–84, offers the following examples of typological events within the Old Testament that regularly find correspondence in the New Testament: (1) paradise (Isa. 11:6–8); (2) the exodus and the wilderness wanderings (Isa. 43:16–21); (3) David (Isa. 11:1); (4) Moses (Deut. 18:15–18).

33. Cf. Leonhard Goppelt, *TYPOS: The Typological Interpretation of the Old Testament in the New,* trans. Donald H. Madvig (Grand Rapids: Eerdmans, 1982), 61–208.

34. Longenecker, *Biblical Exegesis,* 34.

35. Ibid.

christological reference. No one single image or pattern, no one motif or theme can adequately express this concept, yet what is emphasized throughout the New Testament is that numerous themes, images, and motifs of revelation and response are fulfilled in Jesus Christ. The note of Philip's jubilant words, "we have found [him]" (John 1:45), was echoed by the Gospel writers as the way to interpret the Old Testament events, pictures, and ideas. It was not so much one fulfillment idea, but a harmony of notes presented in a variety of ways by different hermeneutical methods.[36] The teaching of Jesus and his hermeneutical practices became the direct source for much of the early church's understanding of the Old Testament. The church appears to have taken Jesus' own interpretation of Scripture and its themes as paradigmatic for their continued exegetical endeavor. We must now direct our attention to the apostles' hermeneutical practices before beginning our concentration on the postapostolic church.

The Apostles and Christological Hermeneutics

In the record of the missionary preaching of the apostles in Acts, the apostles' eyewitness testimony concerning the mighty acts of God was always accompanied by a word of Scripture that shed light on the age (Acts 1:21–22; 2:32; 3:15; 5:32; 10:41; 13:31). From the very beginning, the apostolic witness of the New Testament was linked to the prophetic witness of the Old Testament in order to evoke faith through the witness of the Spirit (Acts 2:33; 5:32). Certainly diversity is evident in the apostolic testimony, but the common element in the church's preaching was the lordship of Jesus Christ. The central point in the church's preaching was the heavenly lordship of Jesus Christ. He had been put to death as Messiah, and was also raised as Messiah (1 Cor. 15:3–4), ready at God's right hand to be the agent of his kingdom (Heb. 1:1–3). Thus the renewal of the preaching of Jesus after his crucifixion carried with it a statement concerning his own person and function, and reception of the message involved acknowledgment of Jesus as the exalted Lord and allegiance to him. This greatly influenced the church's reading of its Scriptures, the Old Testament, and had literary consequences for the development of the New Testament. By reading the Old Testament in this fashion, the church preserved the christological approach that it learned from Jesus. In this section we shall examine the usage of Scripture by four writers of the New Testament outside the Gospels: Luke (Acts), Paul, Peter, and the author of Hebrews.

36. F. F. Bruce, *New Testament Development of Old Testament Themes* (Grand Rapids: Eerdmans, 1968), 20–21. When one accepts the Gospel presentations as authentic, there is a continuity which is expressed in Jesus preeminently in the history of salvation. Cf. Baker, *Two Testaments, One Bible;* Carson and Williamson, eds., *It Is Written.*

Luke

We have considered the Gospel writers' understanding of the Old Testament as it was presented through the voice of Jesus himself.[37] Now we turn to the early church's message in Luke's work known as the Acts of the Apostles. Luke's work is not only a history of the early church but also an apologetic for its existence based on the revelation of God in the Old Testament. Both Jesus and the Scriptures testified to the witness of the Spirit. It was the Spirit who continued to direct the early church in its christological interpretation of the Old Testament.[38] To account for the beginning of this most original and fruitful process of rethinking the Old Testament, C. H. Dodd suggests the church needed a creative mind: "The gospels offer us one [Jesus]. Are we compelled to reject the offer?"[39]

One obvious factor is that the Old Testament passages in Acts are set entirely within Jewish contexts, with the one exception of Paul and Barnabas at Lystra (Acts 14:15). The dominant portion of the quotations and allusions occur in chapters 1–15. This indicates that it was only among Jews that such a direct appeal to the Old Testament would have been appreciated or understood.[40]

Literalistic and midrashic modes of exegesis are present in Acts (Acts 3:25 = Gen. 12:3; Acts 2:25–28 = Ps. 16:8–11/Ps. 110:1),[41] but what appears to be most characteristic are pesher and typological approaches.[42] These

37. This is not meant to deny that the Gospel writers are theologians and interpreters in their own right. In fact the portraits that we have of Jesus and their interpretation of Jesus, while historical, are shaped by the Gospel writers' theological purpose. Current redaction criticism has helped us to see that the Gospel writers were creative in their adaption and communication of the material of and about Jesus. See I. Howard Marshall, *Luke: Historian and Theologian* (Grand Rapids: Zondervan, 1970); Grant Osborne, "Redaction Criticism," in *New Testament Criticism and Interpretation*, ed. David Alan Black and David S. Dockery (Grand Rapids: Zondervan, 1991).

38. Longenecker, *Biblical Exegesis*, 79; cf. Gerd Luedemann, *Early Christianity According to the Tradition in Acts* (Philadelphia: Fortress, 1988). Recent New Testament scholarship has vigorously debated the Lukan purpose and aims. John B. Polhill has provided an up-to-date discussion of the debate in *Acts*, NAC (Nashville: Broadman, 1992).

39. C. H. Dodd, *According to the Scriptures: The Sub-Structure of New Testament Theology* (London: Nisbet, 1952); see also Robert Sloan, "'Signs and Wonders'" A Rhetorical Clue to the Pentecost Discourse," *EQ* 63 (1991): 225–40.

40. William Barclay, "A Comparison of Paul's Missionary Preaching and Preaching to the Church," in *Apostolic History and the Gospel*, ed. W. Ward Gasque and Ralph P. Martin (Grand Rapids: Eerdmans, 1970), 165–75.

41. Richard N. Longenecker, *Christology of Early Jewish Christianity* (London: SCM, 1970), 32–35.

42. Behind these approaches are the hermeneutical presuppositions of (1) corporate solidarity, (2) correspondences in history, (3) eschatological fulfillment, and (4) messianic presence. Cf. Ellis, "How the New Testament Uses the Old," in *New Testament Interpretation*, ed. I. Howard Marshall (Grand Rapids: Eerdmans, 1975), 212–14.

approaches, coupled with concepts of corporate solidarity and correspondences in history, provide a way to understand the biblical message and history from a christocentric or christological perspective.

In Stephen's defense of the expansion of Christianity, given prior to his martyrdom at the hands of the Jewish authorities, he took what Jesus said about the prophets serving as types of his own ministry and suffering and reshaped them into a finished typology by giving them special application to Moses (Acts 7:17–43). The Mosaic period served as a model for the new age since Moses referred to himself as a type of the future deliverer (Acts 7:37 = Deut. 18:15). In the new age, the fulfillment of the promises made to the nation of Israel was inaugurated. Moses' actions, like those of Jesus (Acts 2:22) and the apostles (Acts 4:30), were accompanied by signs and wonders (Acts 7:36). Like Jesus, Moses became "a man powerful in speech and action" (Acts 7:22 = Luke 24:19) and likewise, was rejected by his people (Acts 7:27), though God gave him the honor of being a deliverer of his people. The description given of Moses has led Leonard Goppelt to offer the following conclusion: "By crucifying Jesus the present generation has completed what their fathers did to Moses, the prototype of the redeemer, and to all the prophets who predicted the coming of Christ" (Acts 7:51–52).[43]

Further examples could be offered, but this one chapter (Acts 7) illustrates how the early church preserved the typological and pesher approaches that Jesus taught and modeled for them, thus shaping their interpretation of the Old Testament as the basis of their preaching of salvation. For the earliest believers, this meant that the living presence of Jesus, through his Spirit, was to be considered a determining factor in all their biblical exegesis and also that the Old Testament was to be interpreted christologically. W. D. Davies has noted that there existed the expectation that the coming of the Messiah would make plain the enigmatic and obscure in the Torah.[44] Such an expectation seems to have developed into a basic conviction among the earliest believers, as evidenced by their hermeneutical approaches. We shall find the same thing in the other groups of New Testament Scriptures.

Paul

As the church and its missionary endeavors grew, there was bound to be a need to continue contact and consultation with the new churches. These practical concerns were handled by sending letters, and so the internal

43. Goppelt, *TYPOS*, 122; cf. David John Williams, *Acts*, GNC (New York: Harper and Row, 1985), 114–30.

44. W. D. Davies, *Torah in the Messianic Age and/or the Age to Come* (Cambridge: Cambridge University Press, 1952), 84–94.

life of the church included written correspondence. Apostolic instruction by letter produced a type of writing for which there are few ancient parallels. The letter of Christian instruction was in fact almost as distinctive a Christian contribution to literary types as the written gospel.[45] The idea of collecting these letters and preserving them for posterity developed after the letters had been written. When Paul wrote his letters, there were no Christian books. His library was the Old Testament, and his interpretation of those Scriptures must now be considered.

The way Paul used Scripture was not exactly identical with the way it was used in the Gospels. Yet, Paul generally shared the current exegetical presuppositions and attitudes toward Scripture.[46] His own experience and background would lead us to expect this. Furthermore, Dodd has shown a commonality among Paul and the rest of the New Testament writers in their use of the Old Testament.[47]

The consensus among Pauline scholars recognizes that Paul understood the Old Testament christologically and that he worked from two primary presuppositions: (1) the messiahship and lordship of Jesus, as validated by the resurrection and witnessed to by the Spirit and (2) the revelation of God in the Scriptures of the Old Testament.[48] Paul's starting point was the scriptural text in its context. Longenecker has insightfully observed, "While the early Christian leaders at Jerusalem characteristically began with Jesus as the Messiah and moved on to an understanding of the Old Testament from this Christocentric perspective, Paul usually started with the text itself and sought by means of a midrashic explication to demonstrate Christological significance."[49]

This is not to suggest an extreme dichotomy between Paul and Jesus nor to elevate one approach as superior to another, but only to point out that the Pauline approach to the Old Testament varied to some degree from that practiced by Jesus and the earliest Jewish Christians. Most likely, the variety can be traced to differences in training, differences in the ideological environments confronted in the missionary enterprise, and dif-

45. Although this statement is true in the strict sense of letters composed for a didactic purpose, the format and style of Paul's letters follow conventional patterns known to us from methods of letter-writing in the Hellenistic world. Four parties were involved: the author, the secretary, the messenger, and the recipient. See the discussion in Ralph P. Martin, "Approaches to New Testament Exegesis," in *New Testament Interpretation*, ed. I. Howard Marshall (Grand Rapids: Eerdmans, 1975), 220–51; also David E. Aune, *The New Testament in Its Literary Environment* (Philadelphia: Westminster, 1987), 158–225.

46. E. Earle Ellis, *Paul's Use of the Old Testament* (Grand Rapids: Eerdmans, 1957).

47. Dodd, *According to the Scriptures*, 22–23.

48. Cf. Ellis, *Prophecy and Hermeneutic*, 3–22; Longenecker, *Biblical Exegesis*, 104–7.

49. Longenecker, *Biblical Exegesis*, 105.

ferences in personal spiritual experiences.[50] Recognizing these variations, let us look at some examples from the writings of the apostle.

Paul manifested such a wide range of the various uses of the Old Testament that we cannot give special treatment to his particularities. It is significant to note that, for Paul, the Old Testament was credible only when it was believed to be the Word of God, whose authority must be reverenced (Rom. 3:1–2; 7:12, 14; Gal. 3:17).[51] It is also apparent that the large majority of Paul's Old Testament quotations and allusions are found in the four major books: Galatians, Romans, and 1 and 2 Corinthians, and moreover, half of these occur in Romans.[52]

At times it is difficult to discern exact allusions and conflated ideas from the Old Testament because biblical language is found throughout the Pauline corpus. The Old Testament, notes E. Earle Ellis, "was for Paul not only the Word of God but also his mode of thought and speech" and thus parallels of language are inevitable.[53] Like the usage in Acts, the dominant usage by Paul in the four major books can be traced to the hypothesis that, in one way or another, these communities primarily had Jewish audiences or were affected by some Jewish teaching.[54]

The apostle's usage of the Old Testament demonstrated the influence of his rabbinic training. Thus the apostle primarily read the Scriptures from his midrashic heritage. The seven principles of midrash interpretation attributed to Hillel are apparent in several places in Paul's letters. The idea of "light to heavy" (rule 1) is expressed in his argument in Romans 5:12–21. Romans 4:1–12 (which brought together Gen. 15:6 and Ps. 32:1) demonstrated the concept of analogy (rule 2), comparing Abraham, David, and the Christians in Rome. The other rules or principles are evident, but one more illustration should suffice. The idea of context (rule 7) is exemplified in Romans 4:10 where Abraham was accounted righteous before his circumcision and in Galatians 3:17 where God's promise was confirmed 430 years before God gave the law. As with Jesus, Paul interpreted the moral passages of the Old Testament commandments (Exod. 20) quite literally as he applied them to various ethical issues. He quoted Leviticus

50. Particularly see S. Kim, *The Origin of Paul's Gospel* (Grand Rapids: Eerdmans, 1982). See also Gunther Bornkamm, "The Revelation of Christ to Paul on the Damascus Road and Paul's Doctrine of Justification and Reconciliation," in *Reconciliation and Hope*, ed. Robert Banks (Grand Rapids: Eerdmans, 1974), 90–103.

51. See Barrett's discussion of this point, "Interpretation of the Old Testament in the New," *CHB*, 1:393–94, 407–8; also George Eldon Ladd, *A Theology of the New Testament* (Grand Rapids: Eerdmans, 1974), 376–95.

52. See the introductory comments in C. E. B. Cranfield, *A Critical and Exegetical Commentary on the Epistle to the Romans*, 2 vols., ICC (Edinburgh: T & T Clark, 1975–79), 1:24–27; Leslie C. Allen, "The Old Testament in Romans I–VIII," *VE* 3 (1964): 6–41.

53. Ellis, *Paul's Use of the Old Testament*, 10.

54. Longenecker, *Biblical Exegesis*, 112.

19:18, "love your neighbor as yourself" (Rom. 13:9; Gal. 5:14), as the overarching principle from the Old Testament teaching.

Paul also employed Scripture typologically (Rom. 5:12–21; 1 Cor. 15:20–22; Gal. 3:10–12; 1 Cor. 10:1–11).[55] In Romans 5:14, the typological concept produced a tension which broke through the typological method.[56] Paul's point in this exposition was that the world and history of the first Adam stand over against those of the last Adam, and have been overcome by the latter.[57] Adam is designated a type of the one to come.[58]

The most obvious usage of typological exegesis found in Paul's writings is 1 Corinthians 10:1–11. Paul used the typology concept to interpret the events in the Corinthian church in the light of Israel's experiences in the wilderness.[59] The punishment of God's ancient people that followed their disgraceful practices was seen as a prefiguration of judgment on those who abused the Lord's Supper.[60] The typological method was employed to expound the analogous relationship of concrete historical Old Testament events, in the sense of the past prefiguring present or future eschatological happenings.[61]

Contrary to Richard M. Davidson, who understands typology in a cause-and-effect relationship, Paul used the concept to mean that after the fact one saw a correspondence between earlier biblical events and the current situation.[62] Paul did not understand the events surrounding the exodus as prophetic of the Corinthian situation; rather they should be understood as divinely given instruction. Granted they prefigured, but they did not demand further fulfillment.[63]

55. See the discussion in Walter C. Kaiser, Jr., *The Uses of the Old Testament in the New* (Chicago: Moody, 1985), 103–21; Goppelt, *TYPOS,* 127–52; Gordon D. Fee, *The First Epistle to the Corinthians,* NIC (Grand Rapids: Eerdmans, 1987), 441–50.

56. H. Muller, "Type," *NIDNTT,* 3:906.

57. Ernst Käsemann, *Commentary on Romans,* trans. G. W. Bromiley (Grand Rapids: Eerdmans, 1980), 142–43. Käsemann is correct to note that "typology fundamentally presupposes history." Although it is difficult to distinguish between analogy and typology, the description of this passage as analogy seems insufficient.

58. Cf. Matthew Black, "The Pauline Doctrine of the Second Adam." *SJT* 7 (1954): 170–79; William Barclay, "Romans V.12–21," *ExT 70* (1958–59): 132–35.

59. Muller, "Type," 905.

60. C. K. Barrett, *First Epistle to the Corinthians,* HNTC (New York: Harper and Row, 1968), 218–27. It is possible that Paul was quoting an existing Exodus midrash, though with some modification (see Barrett's discussion, 220–21); see also Wayne A. Meeks, "And Rose Up to Play: Midrash and Parenesis in 1 Cor. 10:1–22," *JSNT* 16 (1982): 64–78.

61. Fee, *First Corinthians,* 441; Charles H. Talbert, *Reading Corinthians* (New York: Crossroad, 1987), 62–65.

62. Davidson, *Typology in Scripture;* for a contrasting view, see Leonhard Goppelt, *"Typos," TDNT,* 9:246–59.

63. Fee, *First Corinthians,* 443; Ellis, *Paul's Use of the Old Testament,* 126–35; see also the discussions in A. T. Hanson, *Jesus Christ in the Old Testament* (London: SPCK, 1965), 11–16; G. R. Beasley-Murray, *Baptism in the New Testament* (Grand Rapids: Eerdmans, 1973), 181–85; James D. G. Dunn, *Baptism in the Holy Spirit* (Philadelphia: Westminster, 1977), 125–26.

The question regarding Paul's usage of allegorical and pesher interpretation has brought many diverse responses. Some scholars, such as James D. G. Dunn and Longenecker, see 1 Corinthians 9:9–10, Galatians 4:22–31, and 2 Corinthians 3:7–18 as examples of a form of allegorical interpretation.[64] Others, among them A. T. Hanson, reject any idea that Paul used allegorical interpretation.[65] The issue at stake is the important distinction between allegory and the allegorical method of interpretation. Allegory is a continuous metaphor which already includes in itself the intention of having more than one point. Allegorical interpretation, on the other hand, is an attempt to find a hidden meaning quite different from the intended or historical one. Like Jesus, Paul used allegory to communicate his story, but did not seem to adopt outright an allegorical methodology.[66] The most debated of the Pauline passages is Galatians 4:22–31. It will be helpful for us to view briefly this passage. The verb *allegoreo* (to say an allegory) occurs in Galatians 4:24 in a participle form, translated "which things are figurative." Paul is comparing Hagar to Sarah, the old covenant with the new.[67]

The two women represented the two covenants. One was from Mount Sinai, bearing children for slavery; she was Hagar. Paul compared Mount Sinai with the present Jerusalem, symbolizing bondage to the law. He then contrasted it with the Jerusalem that is above, which is free and is our mother (Gal. 4:26). Longenecker is correct in his observation that Paul is adopting a rabbinic methodology to "counteract in particular the Judaizers' application of this Jewish motif which argued in effect that Paul's teaching is the elemental while theirs is the developed."[68] The context was obviously triggered by polemical debate and was strongly circumstantial.[69] Like Jesus, Paul adopted an approach similar to the allegorical method for both apologetical and polemical purposes. Yet, in this instance, allegory was really an elaborate piece of typology. Paul's use of *allegoreo* should not be interpreted in light of third-century Alexandrian exegesis which was bound up with philosophical ideas alien to Paul.

Finally, a word must be said about Paul's usage of pesher. Ellis notes more than twenty occurrences of Pauline pesher. One of the clearest examples, found in Ephesians 4:8, involves a textual variant that has a definite bearing on the interpretation of the passage.[70] Ephesians 4:8 is a reference to Christ's ascension and triumphant procession based upon Psalm

64. Dunn, *Unity and Diversity,* 90–91; Longenecker, *Biblical Exegesis,* 126–29.

65. Hanson, *Studies in Paul's Technique,* 159–66, 169–200.

66. Colin Brown, "Parable," *NIDNTT,* 2:751–56.

67. E. Earle Ellis, "A Note on Pauline Hermeneutics," *NTS* 2 (1955–56): 131–34.

68. Longenecker, *Biblical Exegesis,* 128.

69. For discussions of the background situation in Galatia, see Hans Dieter Betz, *Galatians,* Hermeneia (Philadelphia: Fortress, 1979); F. F. Bruce, "Galatian Problems: The 'Other' Gospel," *BJRL* 53 (1970–71): 253–71.

70. Cf. Ellis, *Paul's Use of the Old Testament,* 144.

68:19, a psalm associated with Pentecost in the synagogue calendar. The Old Testament passage presented a picture of a victorious king ascending in triumphant procession, attended by a long train of captives, receiving tribute from his subjects. Psalm 68 reads, "When you ascended on high, you led captives in your train, you received gifts from men." Ephesians 4:8 says, "When he ascended on high, he led captives in his train and gave gifts to men."

Undoubtedly, Paul has adopted a Targum reading that speaks of "giving" gifts rather than the Hebrew text which speaks of the Lord as receiving them.[71] The passage in Ephesians is not a direct quotation from the Hebrew text and represents an example of pesher exegesis, which, according to Dunn, exemplifies "that the sense of the text is significantly modified by means of altering the text form."[72] From these observations we can posit that Ephesians 4:8 offers a christocentric explanation of what God is doing in history distinct from the setting and situation described in the psalm.[73]

Paul's apostolic qualifications were unique and therefore his understanding of the Old Testament could not be directly related to the teaching and example of the historical Jesus. He was, however, well schooled in the rabbinic tradition of Old Testament interpretation; yet he had been confronted by the exalted Lord himself, and that encounter brought about a change in his view of the Old Testament. Now he viewed the Scriptures from the pattern of redemptive history grounded in the life, death, and resurrection of Jesus of Nazareth.

Peter

The writings of the apostle Peter are not as voluminous as Paul's or Luke's, yet his importance in the early church is unquestioned.[74] Peter frequently used a typological approach to the Old Testament that served as an excellent means of assuring the church of its salvation. His basic state-

71. For evidence that this has happened, see R. Rubinkiewicz, "Psalm LXVIII.19 (=Ephesians IV.8): Another Textual Tradition or Targum," *NovT* 17 (1975): 220; Ellis, *Prophecy and Hermeneutic,* 178.

72. Dunn, *Unity and Diversity,* 92.

73. Hanson, *Studies in Paul's Technique,* 171, says, "One could construct the major part of Paul's Christology from his Psalms quotations alone. . . . His use of the Psalter thus enabled Paul to be supremely Christocentric in his exegesis of scripture—we might even say cross-centered."

74. Although his importance is unquestioned, the authorship of 1 and 2 Peter is highly debated. In addition to the standard New Testament introductions, see J. N. D. Kelly, *A Commentary on the Epistles of Peter and of Jude,* HNTC (New York: Harper, 1969); E. G. Selwyn, *The First Epistle of St. Peter,* 2d ed. (London: Macmillan, 1947): J. Ramsey Michaels, *First Peter,* WBC (Waco: Word, 1988); Bo Reicke, *The Epistles of James, Peter and Jude,* AB (Garden City, N.Y: Doubleday, 1964).

ment about the Old Testament can be found in 1 Peter 1:10, a verse that expresses a point of view that is distinctively typological.[75] The usage of the Old Testament by the apostle Peter was in continuity with early Christian interpretation and mirrored a distinctly apostolic treatment. There are a number of parallels between its teaching and those attributed to Peter in the Book of Acts.[76] Peter's typological approach paralleled Paul's, as is evidenced in 1 Peter 3:21.[77] Noah's deliverance through the waters of the flood was seen as a prefiguration and type of the saving event of baptism, which thus became the antitype. The typological material that was appropriate for the purpose of the epistle was not only Christ's life and death, but the church's corporate salvation in relation to the exalted Jesus.

First Peter, broadly speaking, can be considered an exposition of Isaiah 53. The author employed phrases from this prophecy to describe the sufferings of Christ (1 Pet. 2:22–25). The comparison of Jesus with a lamb (1 Pet. 1:19) found its basis in Isaiah 53:7. The price of redemption (1 Pet. 1:18) was grounded in Isaiah 52–53. The epistle presented a typological comparison that communicated that Jesus' death was effective because "when he offered his blood, Jesus acted as a lamb suitable for sacrifice." Even in this brief analysis we can see that Peter interpreted the Old Testament in a truly typological fashion that appears to conflate the patterns of Jesus, the early church in Jerusalem, and a Pauline influence.

Author of Hebrews

The author of Hebrews is unknown to us, but what is known is that the author was thoroughly immersed in the Old Testament, viewing it as a divine oracle from first to last. As Bruce has indicated,

> It is a divine oracle . . . not only passages which in their original setting are the direct utterance of God (such as Psalm 110:4, . . .) but others are treated as spoken by God—like the words of Moses in Deuteronomy 32:43 (Hebrews 1:6) and the words of psalmists concerning the messengers of God (Psalm 104:4, quoted in Hebrews 1:7), addressed to a royal bridegroom (Psalm 45:6f., quoted in Hebrews 1:8f.), or addressed to God (Psalm 102:25–27, quoted in Hebrews 1:10–12). Chapter 3:7 introduces a quotation from Psalm 95:7–11 with the words "even as the Holy Spirit saith"—words which apply not only to the divine utterance quoted in Psalm 95:8ff., but the psalmist's cry

75. Goppelt, *TYPOS,* 152–54. See the brilliant survey by R. Bauckham in *It Is Written: Scripture Citing Scripture. Essays in Honour of Barnabas Lindars,* ed. D. A. Carson and H. G. M. Williamson (Cambridge: Cambridge University Press, 1988).

76. Longenecker, *Biblical Exegesis,* 190–91; Leonhard Goppelt, *Theology of the New Testament,* 2 vols., trans. John Alsup (Grand Rapids: Eerdmans, 1982), 2:186–89.

77. Muller, "Type," 906. This is possibly because Silas served as an amanuensis for Peter's first letter. If so, the Pauline influence in Peter can be attributed to Silas.

> which precedes them: "O that you would hear his voice today!" (Psalm 95:7b). In the details of the Old Testament sanctuary the Holy Spirit signifies spiritual truths for the present time (Hebrews 9:8). The psalmist's words of consecration and obedience in Psalm 40:6–8 are spoken by the Messiah "when he cometh into the world" (Hebrews 10:5–7).[78]

From this brief overview, we can see the dominance of the Old Testament as a foundation for the Epistle to the Hebrews. Yet, the letter cannot be classified as a typical representative of biblical interpretation in the apostolic period.[79] It was generally assumed by many interpreters in the early part of this century that the author of Hebrews was influenced by Philo and the Alexandrian philosophy. With the work of Celaus Spicq, however, this approach has been reversed. The explanations given in the epistle combine elements of pesher interpretation, viewing the Old Testament as a mystery that anticipates explanation,[80] and a form of messianic typology. Spicq observes, "We never find in our author the least trace of that allegorical exegesis which was to remain, alas, the specialty of the Alexandrian school."[81]

The author of Hebrews builds his argument around (1) Psalm 2; 2 Samuel 7; and Deuteronomy 32; (2) Psalm 8:4–6; (3) Psalm 95:7–11; (4) Psalm 110:1–4; (5) Jeremiah 31:31–34. While these verses may have carried some messianic nuances in certain quarters of pre-Christian Judaism, the author seems to have given these passages a new christological meaning that had possibly developed within the church.[82] How he brought these passages together is unknown. He may have adopted some particular collection of messianically relevant texts known to his readers. Or it may have been his own original contribution to the church's Christology. To date there is no consensus on this point in the study of Hebrews, so all we can do is suggest hypotheses.

78. F. F. Bruce, *The Epistle to the Hebrews,* NIC (Grand Rapids: Eerdmans, 1964), xlix–l.

79. See Marcus Barth, "The Old Testament in Hebrews," in *Current Issues in New Testament Interpretation,* ed. W. Klassen and G. F. Snyder (New York: Harper and Row, 1962), 65–67; J. C. McCullough, "The Old Testament Quotations in Hebrews," *NTS* 26 (1980): 363–79; Donald A. Hagner, "Interpreting the Epistle to the Hebrews," in *The Literature and Meaning of Scripture,* ed. Morris A. Inch and C. Hassell Bullock (Grand Rapids: Baker, 1981), 217–42.

80. Bruce, *Biblical Exegesis in the Qumran Texts,* 75–77.

81. Ceslaus Spicq, *L'Epitre aux Hebreux,* 2 vols. (Paris: Gabalda, 1952–53), 1:61. Others have strengthened Spicq's position; see C. K. Barrett, "The Eschatology of the Epistle to the Hebrews," in *The Background of the New Testament and Its Eschatology,* ed. W. D. Davies and David Daube (Cambridge: Cambridge University Press, 1954), 363–93.

82. See the discussion in David M. Hay, *Glory at the Right Hand: Psalm 110 in Early Christianity* (Nashville: Abingdon, 1973), 21–33; also Simon J. Kistemaker, *The Psalm Citations in the Epistle to the Hebrews* (Amsterdam: Van Soest, 1961); Longenecker, *Christology of Early Jewish Christianity,* 75–79.

What can be ascertained is that these Old Testament passages were interpreted to point to the coming of Messiah. They were used to underscore the incompleteness of the old economy under Moses and looked forward to a forthcoming consummation.[83] The author depended upon a typological approach that combined the ideas of the corporate solidarity of the people of God with historical correspondence. This can be summarized in one statement, as Longenecker suggests. The author of Hebrews approaches the Old Testament with a straightforward question, What do the Scriptures mean viewed from a christocentric perspective?[84] While there is originality in his approach, he was still in continuity with the christological hermeneutic that had preceded him.

Conclusion

We have noted the approach that Jesus and the apostles employed when interpreting the Old Testament. We have seen that they were dependent upon hermeneutical practices established in late Judaism, but they adapted the methods to the church with the addition of a christological focus. The early church, probably unconsciously rather than intentionally, practiced the exegetical procedures of later Judaism, but the Jewish context in which the New Testament was born was not the primary paradigm for the formation of Christian hermeneutics. As C. F. D. Moule maintains, "At the heart of their biblical interpretation is a christological and christocentric perspective."[85]

Jesus became the direct and primary source for the church's understanding of the Old Testament. The new paradigm developed because the prior paradigm lacked the christological focus. What was needed was a hermeneutical perspective that could transform the Torah into the messianic Torah.[86] Thus, through the pattern that Jesus had set and his exalted lordship expressed through the Spirit, Jesus served as the ongoing source of the early church's hermeneutical approach to the Scriptures. The christological perspective of the earliest Christians, therefore, enabled them to adopt Jesus' own usage of the Scriptures as normative and to look to him for guidance in their hermeneutical task. We will now move to the second century to see if this pattern continues among the apostolic fathers.

83. Walter C. Kaiser, Jr., "The Old Promise and the New Covenant: Jeremiah 31:31–34," *JETS* 15 (1972): 11–23.

84. Longenecker, *Biblical Exegesis,* 185.

85. Moule, *Birth of the New Testament,* 58.

86. Birger Gerhardsson, *Memory and Manuscript: Oral Tradition and Written Transmission in Rabbinic Judaism and Early Christianity,* trans. E. J. Sharpe (Lund: Gleerup, 1961), 327.

2

The Second Century: From Functional to Authoritative Hermeneutics

While the apostolic fathers were on the whole more wildly fanciful than the New Testament writers, they followed the New Testament exegetical pattern and remained, like the apostles, christocentric in their interpretation. At the close of the apostolic age, some marked changes began to occur; primarily, the New Testament was in the process of being recognized as Scripture. The relation of the New Testament to the Old Testament was the issue raised by the Gnostics and the issue confronting the second-century church. Marcion and the Gnostics abandoned the Old Testament as a Christian book, and recreated New Testament texts to suit themselves. The motivating factor that raised the issue among the orthodox Christians was the Gnostic view that the God of the Old Testament was incompatible with the God revealed in Christ in the New Testament. As texts were challenged, altered, and even abandoned, the church had to demonstrate on biblical grounds that the same God was revealed in both Testaments and that, therefore, the church should not abandon the Old Testament. This chapter will focus on how the apostolic fathers continued the New Testament hermeneutical practices and how they modified those practices so that the emphasis was placed on the moral usage of Scripture. I have chosen to identify this approach as a "functional hermeneutic." By this I mean the readers applied the text to their own context and situation without attention to its original context or situation. Meaning was bound up with Scripture's functional application. Thus, Scripture explained to the church, primarily on the basis of the words of Jesus, what it was to do. Similarly, the Gnostics turned to the words of Jesus for their authority, yet they were considered heretics. The church was faced with new problems. Which approach to the words of Jesus was correct? By what authority could this be known? This chapter addresses these concerns.

Functional Hermeneutics in the Apostolic Fathers

The formation of the New Testament was part of a larger process of the beginnings of Christian literature. The separation of the New Testament from the rest of these writings gradually began to take place as the New Testament canon took shape. The collection, usage, and prestige of the widely accepted apostolic writings boosted them to the position of priority and authority for the ongoing life of the church. Before examining the use of Scripture among the second-century church leaders, it will be useful to note that the church's hermeneutical concerns developed in the church's worship.

The Church's Worship

Biblical interpretation was grounded in the church's exposition, not in the theoretical analysis of the academy. Following the synagogue pattern, the exposition of the Word was of utmost importance in the church's worship. The church's pattern followed that established by Jesus' exposition of Isaiah 61 at the beginning of his ministry, which he interpreted in light of his own messianic mission (cf. Luke 4:16–27), and continually practiced in the early church's worship (cf. Acts 13:14–44; 14:1; 17:1; 19:8).

Justin Martyr, in his *First Apology,* a work written to the emperor Antoninus Pius (ca. A.D. 150), summarized an early church worship service into two basic parts.[1] Such a service was similar to the following outline:

I. The Liturgy of the Word
   a. Lessons from the Old and New Testaments
   b. Sermons
   c. Prayers
   d. Hymns

II. The Liturgy of the Eucharist
   a. Kiss of Peace
   b. Offering of Bread, Wine, and Water

1. Justin Martyr *First Apology* 67.

c. Prayers and Thanksgiving over Bread and Wine
d. The Narrative of the Last Supper and a Command to Continue in It
e. Amen, Said by All the People
f. Communion/Lord's Supper
g. Concern Offered for the Poor and Reserved Portions of the Supper Taken by the Deacons to Those Absent

Our concern is of course with the first half of the service, the Liturgy of the Word.

In 1 Timothy 4:13, the young Timothy was exhorted to devote attention to the public reading of Scripture. The matter of public reading of Scripture, which was given by the inspiration of God, was able to make the hearer wise unto salvation which is in Jesus Christ. For this reason, the place the reading and exposition of Scripture held in the divine ordering was always considered central. The model Christian service, like the worship of Judaism, was a word-of-God service.[2] The reference in 1 Timothy was the first historical allusion to the use of the Scriptures in the church's liturgy. Justin described a second-century service in Rome in chapter 67 of his *First Apology:* "The memoirs of the Apostles and the writings of the Prophets are read as long as time permits. Then, when the reader has finished, the President speaks admonishing and exhorting the people to follow noble teaching and examples."[3] We learn from this that by the time of the apologists, the New Testament had reached a similar canonical status as the Torah and Prophets of the Old Testament.

The New Testament letters were read in the public meeting of the churches (cf. Col. 4:16; Rev. 1:3). Apparently the apostles expected their letters to be accepted as authorities in their own lifetimes (cf. 2 Thess. 2:15; 2 Pet. 3:15–16). The letters were gradually accepted and circulated and read aloud in the public gatherings. In this way they became the object of study and meditation. Polycarp wrote two letters to the Philippians (ca. A.D. 110–117) and said of the Pauline letters, "from the study of which you will be able to be built up into the faith."[4]

The reading of Scripture was accompanied by its exposition. Almost all of the church's interpretation of Scripture and corresponding theologizing developed from the sermon. The real meaning of preaching was set forth by the apostle Paul in 1 Corinthians 1:17–23. He claimed he came to preach the gospel, which he identified as the message of the cross, Christ crucified. This preaching came in demonstration of the Spirit's power so

2. Cf. Walter Bauer, *Der Wortgottesdienst der alesten Christen* (Tübingen, Mohr, 1930).
3. Justin Martyr *First Apology* 67.
4. Polycarp *Two Epistles to the Philippians* 3.2.

that faith would be in demonstration of God's power (cf. 1 Cor. 2:1–6). The apostles' theology of preaching was built around the elements of the *kerygma:* the incarnation, death, burial, resurrection, and ascension of Christ. In this sense preaching in the context of the worshiping community reenacted the event of Christ, the event that provided shape and meaning not only to worship but to the lives of the worshipers.[5]

The church's preaching understood the Old Testament Scripture in terms of Christ's coming. This was evidenced in their attitude toward the Old Testament. They regarded the law and the prophets as well as the events and worship of Israel as part of the Christian tradition because they believed that they testified to Jesus Christ. Paul, for example, in 1 Corinthians 15:3–4, insisted that everything regarding Christ took place "in accordance with the Scriptures." Soon, a typological interpretation of the Old Testament became a standard way of expounding the Scriptures in the church's worship. For example, the *Epistle of Barnabas,* a treatise written around A.D. 135 in Alexandria, claimed that "the prophets having obtained grace from him (Jesus Christ), prophesied concerning him."[6] In Melito's *Paschal Homily,* written around A.D. 170, the paschal lamb in Exodus 12 typologically pointed to Christ, the true paschal lamb. Thus it was through the early church's preaching that the initial typological exegesis was practiced. But this approach was not dominant until the middle of the second century. First, let us look at the functional approach of the apostolic fathers.

The Apostolic Fathers

The title *apostolic fathers* functions as a designation of a group of church leaders and their writings between A.D. 90 and 150. It is possible, though not demonstrable to the point of certainty, that at least two of their writings were at least as old as parts of the New Testament. *First Clement* has been dated shortly after or during the persecution under Domitian (ca. A.D. 96), and the *Didache,* a treatment summarizing the teaching of the New Testament tradition, was probably authored in the early second century and possibly even before the close of the first century.

The interpretation of the Old Testament to show how the life and work of Christ was prefigured by the Old Testament writers is not as prominent in the apostolic fathers as in the New Testament. This should not surprise us when we consider that the Fathers were primarily concerned with moral and ethical instruction, rather than explaining the significance of the life and work of Jesus. This is not to imply the absence of a christological reading of the Old Testament; in the letter of Ignatius to the *Magnesians* (chap. 9), for example, the Old Testament prophets were described

5. Ralph P. Martin, *Worship in the Early Church* (Grand Rapids: Eerdmans, 1964), 68–76.
6. *Epistle of Barnabas* 5.1.

as the disciples of Christ, who waited for Christ as their teacher, and who Christ raised from the dead when he came. In *1 Clement* the author exhorted his readers to a life of humility illustrated not from Christ's earthly life, but from the passion accounts prefigured in Isaiah 53 and Psalm 22.

At one time or another any or all of the following have been included in the collective title of apostolic fathers: Barnabas, *1 Clement, 2 Clement,* the *Didache,* Diognetus, the Doctrinal, Ignatius, the *Martyrdom of Ignatius,* Papias, Polycarp, the Martyrdom of Polycarp, Quadratus, and the *Shepherd of Hermas.* The recognized standard work, *The Apostolic Fathers: A New Translation and Commentary,* edited by Robert M. Grant (1964), includes *1 Clement, 2 Clement,* Barnabas, the *Didache,* Ignatius, Polycarp, Martyrdom of Polycarp, Papias, and the *Shepherd of Hermas.*[7] Grant, commenting on the term, explains: "'Fathers' has come to mean 'significant orthodox writers of the past'; 'apostolic' in the early usage referred to those who were not apostles but were disciples of apostles. The two words combined thus referred to the earliest orthodox writers outside the New Testament."[8] Apart from the *Didache,* which was didactic, and the *Shepherd of Hermas,* which was apocalyptic, the rest of the works were epistolary in style. For our purposes, an examination of Clement and Ignatius will give us an adequate picture of the use of Scripture in the apostolic fathers.[9]

Clement

First Clement, a letter from the church at Rome to the troubled church in Corinth, has been traditionally ascribed to Clement of Rome near the end of the first century (ca. A.D. 90–100). The letter began with a common epistolary salutation, *he ekklesia tou Theou he paroikousa Romen tei ekklesiai Tou Theou tei parakousei korinthon* (The church of God which sojourns in Rome to the Church of God which sojourns in Corinth). Elements in *1 Clement* indicated a use of both Greek and Jewish-Christian sources.[10] Hellenistic influences may be seen in such examples as the stoicism of *1 Clement* 20[11] and the use of some Platonic terms.[12] Further, a Hellenistic style underlies

7. Robert M. Grant, ed., *The Apostolic Fathers: A New Translation and Commentary,* 6 vols. (New York: Thomas Nelson, 1964). See also Michael W. Holmes, ed., *The Apostolic Fathers* (Grand Rapids: Baker, 1989).

8. Grant, *Apostolic Fathers,* 1:v; see also J. Ramsey Michaels. "Apostolic Fathers," *ISBE,* 1:203–13.

9. We are aware that Barnabas is very important for the struggle between Jews and Christians at this time. Polycarp is most influential for early biblical interpretation, but our work, by design, is intentionally selective.

10. Cf. James A. Kliest, trans., *The Epistles of St. Clement of Rome and St. Ignatius of Antioch,* Ancient Christian Writers (New York: Newman, 1946), 3–4.

11. See W. C. van Unnik, "Is *1 Clement* 20 Purely Stoic?" *VC* 4 (1950): 181–89.

12. M. H. Shepherd, Jr., "Clement, Epistles of," *IDB,* 1:467; see Barbara Ellen Bowe, "A Church in Crisis: Ecclesiology and Paranesis in Clement of Rome" (Th.D. diss., Harvard University, 1986).

the letter, suggesting that Clement was evidently trained in the school of Hellenistic rhetoric evidenced by the flowery praises he used to address the Corinthians in the early chapters. Herbert T. Mayer notes, "Perhaps he can be classified as basically a Hellenist exegete who had been trained to study ancient documents primarily to obtain moral examples from them by separating the events from their original historical contexts and demythologizing all possible offensive connotations."[13] Jewish Christian influences may be seen in frequent quotations of and allusions to the Old Testament, intertestamental writings, and the New Testament.

Regarding the use of the Old Testament, *1 Clement* included 166 quotations or allusions.[14] He never quoted the New Testament verbally. Sayings of Christ were given now and then, but not in the words of the Gospels. It cannot be demonstrated, therefore, that Clement knew the synoptic Gospels. He mentioned Paul's First Epistle to the Corinthians, and also appeared to imply knowledge of Second Corinthians. He certainly knew Romans, Titus, and other Pauline letters. He referred to James and 1 Peter, but Hebrews was the most frequently employed of all New Testament books. For Clement, God's revelation can primarily be found in Old Testament Scripture. Clement quoted it over and over with the introductory formulas *gegraptai*[15] (it is written) and *legei he graphe*[16] (the Scripture says), which designated divine authority. Scripture is *ho hagios logos* (the holy word),[17] for it is God who speaks in it.[18] Therefore, nothing which is written in it can be false,[19] and he offered praise because his flock was well versed in Scripture.[20]

Clement interpreted Scripture in a christological fashion, not unlike his predecessors. Yet he did not so much seek to discover the Old Testament's message concerning the work of Christ, but offered the pictures of Christ as basis for moral obedience. In *1 Clement* 16, we find the prophecies of the servant song in Isaiah 53 applied to Jesus. Like the author of Hebrews, he was especially fond of Psalms 2, 22, and 110, as is seen in *1 Clement* 36.

He generally took the biblical texts in their literal sense and, in a characteristic functional way, applied them to the Corinthian situation. At times,

13. Herbert T. Mayer, "Clement of Rome and His Use of Scripture," *CTM* 42 (1971): 537.

14. Cf. Donald A. Hagner, *The Use of the Old and New Testaments in Clement of Rome,* supplement to *Novum Testamentum,* no. 34 (Leiden: Brill, 1973). It must be noted, however, that Clement does not use any single known standardized LXX text; see Kliest, *Epistles of St. Clement of Rome,* 6.

15. E.g., *1 Clement* 4:1; 14:4; 39:3; 50:4.

16. E.g., *1 Clement* 23:2; 34:6; 35:7.

17. *1 Clement* 13:3; 56:3.

18. *1 Clement* 13:1; 45:2.

19. *1 Clement* 45:3.

20. *1 Clement* 45:2; 62:3.

he even used the words of the prophets or the apostles as though they were his own. Only once, in *1 Clement* 12:7–9, did he attempt a spiritual interpretation. He did, however, use the term *gnosis* (knowledge) quite frequently as though he acknowledged some hidden meaning in Scripture.[21]

He held forth Jesus as a model for piety (1:2), for help in suffering (2:1), for humility (16:2), and for self-emptying (7:4; 12:7; 21:6; 49:6). These examples did not come from the Gospels, but apparently from a developing tradition concerning Jesus. In *1 Clement* 19:2, he said, "We, who are partakers of so many great and glorious deeds, let us return quickly to the goal of peace which has been handed down (from 'paradidonai') to us from the beginning." This tradition had not yet developed into any sort of doctrinal creed or rule of faith, though such possibilities were implicitly present.

Ignatius

Seven letters by Ignatius, bishop of Antioch (ca. A.D. 35–107), are generally accepted as authentic: (1) the Ephesians, (2) the Magnesians, (3) the Trallians, (4) the Romans, (5) the Philadelphians, (6) the Smyrnaeans, and (7) Polycarp. These letters, from the beginning of the second century A.D., were apparently written by Ignatius as he traveled on his way to his anticipated martyrdom in Rome. They were written to churches whose messengers Ignatius had met, churches in cities in Asia Minor where he stopped on his journey to Rome, to the church at his intended destination, and to Polycarp, Bishop of Smyrna.[22]

The name of this apostolic father was Roman, or rather ancient Italian, not Greek or Syrian, as we might have expected.[23] The most ancient reference to Ignatius is found in Polycarp, and this reference tells us nothing about the period prior to Ignatius's own writings. It must be remembered that Ignatius's writings were not autobiographical, but pastoral in nature. Thus, "practically nothing is known about his birth, education, background, or employment."[24] L. W. Barnard's summary is appropriate:

21. Cf. Rudolf Bultmann, *"Ginoskö," TDNT,* 1:707.

22. Other writings were attributed to Ignatius. They dealt primarily and graphically with his martyrdom, but are no doubt spurious. Cyril C. Richardson contends that they are "pure romances, resting on no historical foundations." See Cyril C. Richardson, ed., *Early Christian Fathers,* vol. 1 of The Library of Christian Classics (Philadelphia: Westminster, 1953), 74–76; idem, *The Christianity of Ignatius of Antioch* (New York: Columbia University Press, 1935); Milton Perry Brown, *The Authentic Writings of Ignatius* (Durham, N.C.: Duke University Press, 1963).

23. J. B. Lightfoot, ed. and trans., *The Apostolic Fathers,* 5 vols. (London: Macmillan, 1889–90), 1:22–24.

24. A. A. K. Graham, "Their Word to Our Day: IV. Ignatius of Antioch," *ExT* 80 (1969): 100; see also James Moffatt, "An Approach to Ignatius," *HTR* 29 (1936): 1–38.

> Ignatius appeared for only a brief moment, as the author of seven pastoral-type letters, all probably written within a fortnight, then he disappeared from sight leaving behind only scanty personal references and the basis for later embellished legends.[25]

Ignatius was one of the most creative minds of the second century. Let us examine how this creative mind interpreted Scripture.

In comparison with Clement, it is remarkable how little use Ignatius made of the Old Testament. There are only two actual quotations,[26] though there are possibly eight other allusions. Both quotations are introduced by the formula *gegraptai* (it is written). The first of the two passages from Proverbs, "God resists the proud," is shared by Ignatius with New Testament writers (James 4:6; 1 Pet. 5:5); the second, "the righteous one is his own accuser," was not quoted by others, but does indicate Proverbs was a favorite book for Ignatius.[27] Even this scanty evidence indicates the authority the Old Testament Scripture must have had for Ignatius. The allusions suggest Ignatius knew something of the Old Testament, though it cannot be said that his mind was steeped in it.[28]

Ignatius was highly influenced by the Pauline letters and seems to have had 1 Corinthians memorized. There are almost fifty references to this one book alone in his writings. A few illustrations will show the remarkable care with which Ignatius used the apostle's writings. In *Ephesians* 17:2–18:1 Ignatius wrote,

> Why are we foolishly perishing, ignoring the gift which the Lord has truly sent? My spirit is devoted to the cross, which is a stumbling block to the unbelievers but salvation and eternal life to us. Where is the wise man? Where is the debater? Where is the boasting of the so-called intelligent?

Here Ignatius was clearly following 1 Corinthians 1:18–20 with remarkable care. The Pauline passage reads,

> For the message of the cross is foolishness to those who are perishing, but to us who are being saved it is the power of God. . . . Where is the wise man?

25. L. W. Barnard, "The Background of St. Ignatius of Antioch," *VC* 17 (1963): 193.

26. Ephesians 5:3 and Magnesians 12 quoting Proverbs 3:34 and 18:17.

27. Robert M. Grant makes this suggestion in "Scripture and Tradition in St. Ignatius of Antioch," *CBQ* 25 (1963): 322–35.

28. Robert M. Grant, *After the New Testament* (Philadelphia: Fortress, 1967), 38; Othmar Perler, "Das Vierte Makkabaeerbuch, Ignatius von Antiochien und die aeltesten Martyrer berichte," *Rivista di Archeologia Cristiana* 25 (1949): 47–72, notes that 4 Maccabees was especially significant for Ignatius. No doubt this was due to his impending martyrdom, and the Maccabean martyrs exercised considerable influence not only on Ignatius's style but also on his thought.

> Where is the scholar? Where is the philosopher of this age? Has not God made foolish the wisdom of the world?

He also used isolated phrases from Paul's first letter to the Corinthians in Trallians 12:3 and in Romans 5:1:

> I need your love, so that I may be judged worthy of the lot which I am set to obtain, "lest I be found a castaway" (cf. 1 Cor. 9:27).

> I became more of a disciple because of their wrong doing, "but not by this am I justified" (cf. 1 Cor. 4:4).

These three texts illustrate the functional hermeneutic employed by Ignatius. He could take Pauline expressions from their contexts and use them in his own context. This functional usage hardly surprises us. In fact, Ignatius could not have used Pauline expressions in Pauline contexts. This indicates that exegesis was not yet the art form it would become with the Alexandrian, not a science as it would become with the Antioch school.

It should also be observed that Ignatius felt unrestrained to paraphrase Paul's words in various contexts. In 1 Corinthians 6:9–10, Paul wrote,

> Do you not know that the wicked will not inherit the kingdom of God? Do not be deceived . . .

He continued by defining certain types of unrighteous practices. Ignatius used these verses in several ways. He paraphrased them in Ephesians 16:1:

> Do not be deceived, my brothers; those who corrupt families will not inherit the kingdom of God.

Another matter was emphasized as he used the passage in Philadelphians 3:3:

> Do not be deceived, my brothers; whoever follows a schismatic will not inherit the kingdom of God.

What we see in these examples is that Ignatius uses Pauline words and even synthesizes them with other New Testament thoughts without attempting an exacting exegesis of what Paul said. Ignatius also uses the apostle's words as his own in the form of an allusive quotation (cf. Eph. 21:2; Magnesians 14; and Trallians 13:1 using Pauline phrases from 1 Cor. 15:8). All three of these forms of quotations or allusions underscore Ignatius's functional hermeneutical method. As Grant has concluded, "Any idea of exactness in analyzing his usage must be read in by the analyst. It does not exist in Ignatius' own writings."[29]

Ignatius served as a transitional figure. As has generally been the case in theology, a paradigm shift brings something new while maintaining much of what has preceded it. With Ignatius, who was perhaps fifteen years later than Clement, we have an initial movement toward an authoritative or apologetical hermeneutic. By this I mean Scripture could be used to show the false beliefs of the heretics. This was done by establishing the correct theological meaning of Scripture, with the guidance of the bishop. He warned the congregations against heretics and urged them to close unity in submission to the hierarchy, especially the bishop. As the church faced conflicts, the rise of heretics, docetics, and Judaizers, Ignatius appealed to the authority of the bishop as the exemplar of orthodoxy.[30] Thus it was the need to address the rise of heresy and the equal need for church unity that initially pushed the church in the direction of authoritative hermeneutics.

It has been widely assumed that the early Christian communities were governed by colleges of elders, as Jewish synagogues were, and that in the course of time a monarchial episcopate or single bishop developed. Disagreement about when and how this happened is also widely known. The need to have a liturgical president, not unlike the ruler of the synagogue, may have enhanced the process. But by the time of Ignatius of Antioch it was possible to claim that the bishop or his representative was essential for the meeting of the church.[31] Ignatius underlined the importance of the bishop in the church.[32] Nothing was to be done in the church without the bishop (Magnesians 7:1; Polycarp 4:1). This new emphasis in church government and policy paved the way for the development of an authoritative exegesis in the latter part of the second century. Ignatius apparently knew at least the Gospels of Matthew and John and Paul's letters to the Corinthians. His marvelous memory and creative skill enabled him to use and interpret these works in a functional manner for the church of his day.[33] We have observed the beginning of a paradigm shift or devel-

29. Grant, *Apostolic Fathers,* 1:58–59.

30. Justo L. Gonzalez, *A History of Christian Thought,* 3 vols. (Nashville: Abingdon, 1970), 1:70–80, 123–259; cf. Jules Lebreton, S. J., and Jacques Zeiller, *Heresy and Orthodoxy* (New York: Collier, 1962), which traces the rise of heresy and challenges to orthodoxy primarily in the early third century, but also interacts with matters of the second century. See also Harold O. J. Brown, *Heresies* (Garden City, N.Y: Doubleday, 1984), 38–94; Walter Bauer, *Orthodoxy and Heresy in Earliest Christianity,* ed. Robert Kraft and Gerhard Krodel (Philadelphia: Fortress, 1971), 61–194.

31. P. Hinchliff, "Bishop," *NDLW,* 92–93.

32. Ignatius refers to the "bishop" in all his letters except *The Epistle to the Romans.*

33. H. Riesenfeld, "Reflections on the Style and the Theology of St. Ignatius of Antioch," *Texte und Untersuchungen* 79 (1961): 312–22.

opment toward an authoritative exegesis. We must now examine the events that brought about such a movement.

Heresy, Orthodoxy, and Hermeneutical Confusion

In a very basic way, the hermeneutical task facing the second-century church was to show the continuity of the Old Testament with the New or, put another way, how the Old Testament could remain the church's Bible. Galatians, Colossians, John, 1 John, and 1 Peter especially evidence the struggles of the early Christians. During the second century, and especially in the latter half of that century, the rise of heresies became so widespread that they provoked in the church at large a reaction that was to be of enormous significance for the history of Christian thought and Christian hermeneutics.

Judaizing Christianity

The initial challenge to the young church was that of its relationship to Judaism and especially to groups of Jewish Christians known as Judaizers. The first church council was called to wrestle with this issue (cf. Acts 15). The issue was larger than whether Christianity was a sect of Judaism or an autonomous movement. Rather, it had to do with how Christians, and especially Gentile Christians, were to relate to the laws and rituals of Judaism.

The relationship of Christian believers to the law of the Old Testament brought at least four different responses. First, there were some moderate Judaizers who themselves obeyed the law but did not seek to compel others to do so. Second, a more extreme group not only followed the law but felt that all true Christians should do the same.[34] A third response, however, affirmed that all must obey the law of the Old Testament; thus, Paul's teachings about the law were apostate and all who followed Paul were likewise apostate.[35] Coupled with this affirmation was an adoptionist Christology which maintained that Christ was not divine from the beginning, but had been adopted as Son of God because he so capably and excellently fulfilled the law.[36] Finally, at another level there were debates

34. These two distinctive approaches can be found in Justin Martyr's *Dialogue with Trypho* 47.

35. Cf. Gonzalez, *History of Christian Thought,* 1:125.

36. These adoptionist groups are called Ebionites. The term *Ebionite* first appears in Irenaeus *Against Heresies* 1.26.2. Cf. Walt W. Wessel, "Ebionites," *ISBE,* 2:9–10. Our knowledge of Ebionite theology and hermeneutics is primarily dependent upon the antiheretical writers such as Justin and Irenaeus. A body of literature developed that expressed Ebionite teaching under the heading "The Preaching of Peter" and is therefore a witness to the doctrines of this group.

over the relationship between Christianity and Judaism that attempted to reinterpret not only Christianity itself, but Judaism as well. This type of Judaizing Christianity was also influenced by Gnosticism.[37] It maintained that all should keep the law of the Old Testament, as well as rituals like circumcision, and that Jesus was only a prophet. It also expounded certain Gnostic teachings related to dualism, numerology, and astrological speculation.[38] The challenge for the early church was to demonstrate how the Old Testament was to be interpreted, clearly showing the superiority of the New Covenant to the Old in a way that the church could still call the Old Testament its Scriptures without being bound to the law of the Old Testament. Two answers were proposed: (1) the typological approach of Justin Martyr, in chapter 40 in his *Dialogue with Trypho*, and (2) the imaginative allegorical approach advanced by Origen and the Alexandrians.

Gnosticism

Gnosticism was such a broad movement that a nearly all-encompassing description is needed to define it. The breadth of the Gnostic orientations has been confirmed by the discovery of a Gnostic library at Nag Hammadi in Egypt. Fifty-two tractates, six of which are duplicates, are included in the thirteen ancient codices. A large number clearly present a Christian Gnostic perspective, the most familiar being the Valentinian gospels: the Gospel of Thomas (composed of brief sayings of Jesus); the Gospel of Philip (a collection of sayings and esoteric arguments); and the Gospel of Truth (a discourse on deity and unity reflecting language of the canonical fourth Gospel). Also included among the Christian Gnostic tractates are the Apocryphon of James, the Acts of Peter and the Twelve Apostles, the Treatise on the Resurrection, the long collection known as the Tripartite Tractate, and three editions of the Apocryphon of John.

Before the Nag Hammadi discoveries, our understanding of Gnosticism was almost totally dependent upon the second-century apologists, who have been referred to as heresiologists. The heresiologists regarded Gnosticism as the product of the combination of Greek philosophy and Christianity. Tertullian, a late second-century apologist, for example, after

37. Cf. Jean Danielou, *The Theology of Jewish Christianity* (London: Darton, Longman and Todd, 1964), 56–67.

38. Cf. Hans Joachim Schoeps, *Theologie und Geschichte des Judenchristentums* (Tübingen: Mohr, 1949), 325–34. The main exponent of this type of Judaizing Christianity seems to have been Elxai (also spelled Elkesai, Elcesai, or Elchasai). His teaching is heavily influenced by Ebionism and Gnosticism. It is based on a revelation that Elxai claimed he had received from an angel who was ninety-six miles tall. This angel was the Son of God. Next to him was another gigantic angel, although feminine, who was the Holy Spirit. Cf. Ethel Stefana Drower, "Adam and the Elkasaites," *StPat* 4 (1961): 406–10.

describing the Gnostic heretics, declared, "What indeed has Athens to do with Jerusalem? What Concord is there between the Academy and the Church? What between heretics and Christians? . . . Away with all attempts to produce a mottled Christianity of Stoic, Platonic, and dialectic composition."[39]

This view was accepted and articulated by historical theologians before the Nag Hammadi findings. An understanding of Gnosticism as an acutely secularized or philosophically tainted Christianity has been challenged in recent times by some who have contended that Gnostic thought was more narrowly conceived, grounded in Jewish apocalyptic.[40] Yet, the broader concept of Hans Jonas seems more encompassing and accurate. Jonas suggests that Gnosticism was a general religious phenomenon of the Hellenistic world and was the product of the fusion of Greek culture and Oriental religion. The Greek conceptualization of Eastern religious traditions—that is, Jewish monotheism, Babylonian astrology, and a philosophical dualism—formed the basis of Gnosticism.[41]

When Gnosticism is defined so broadly, we hardly know where the challenge was specifically effected. When the general Gnostic view was conjoined with Christian teaching, Christians felt that their faith was threatened on three basic points: (1) the doctrine of creation and of the divine rule over the world; (2) the doctrine of salvation; and (3) Christology.

Gnosticism was opposed to the traditional Christian doctrine of creation because it saw the material world as the result of an error committed by an inferior and evil being, not the work of the eternal God. According to Gnosticism, the things of this world are not merely worthless, but evil. In this, Gnostics were diametrically opposed to the Judeo-Christian doctrine of creation, which maintained that all things were created good by a good God, who still acts in the history of the world.

Similarly, the doctrine of salvation among Gnostics was at odds with mainstream Christian thought. In Gnosticism, salvation consisted in the liberation of the divine and immortal spirit that was imprisoned within the human body. The role of the human body in the plan of salvation was

39. Tertullian *On Prescription Against Heretics* 7.1.

40. Cf. Robert M. Grant, *Gnosticism and Early Christianity* (New York: Oxford University Press, 1960); Gershom Gerhard Scholem, *Jewish Gnosticism, Merkabah Mysticism and Talmudic Tradition* (New York: Jewish Theological Seminary, 1960); R. McL. Wilson, *The Gnostic Problem and Gnosis and the New Testament* (London: Mowbray, 1958).

41. Hans Jonas, *The Gnostic Religion: The Message of the Alien God and the Beginning of Christianity* (Boston: Beacon, 1958); cf. Gerald L. Borchert, "Insights into the Gnostic Threat to Christianity as Gained Through the Gospel of Philip," in *New Directions in New Testament Study*, ed. Richard N. Longenecker and Merrill C. Tenney (Grand Rapids: Zondervan, 1975), 79–96; Edwin M. Yamauchi, *Pre-Christian Gnosticism: A Survey of the Proposed Evidences* (London: Tyndale, 1973).

merely negative. Contrary to this Gnostic aberration, traditional Christianity affirmed that salvation included the human body, and that the final fulfillment of God's plan for the salvation of humankind would not take place without the resurrection of the body.[42]

This Gnostic dualism had definite consequences when applied to Christology. When matter was not considered the product of the divine will, and especially the matter that formed the human body, but rather the product of some other principle that was opposed to that will, it therefore followed that matter and the human body could not serve as a vehicle for the revelation of the supreme God. The results of this approach to Jesus produced at least two forms of Gnosticism. One class of early Gnostics separated the spiritual being Christ from the man Jesus. They supposed that the Christ entered Jesus at the time of his baptism, and left him at the moment of his crucifixion. Thus the Christ was neither born a man nor suffered as a man. In this way they obviated the difficulty, inseparable to the Gnostic mind, of conceiving the connection between the highest spiritual agency and gross corporeal matter. This was involved in the church's doctrine of the incarnation and passion. The other class of Gnostics assumed that the human body of Jesus was only a phantom body, and not real flesh and blood.[43] Thus his sufferings and his death could not have been real, for it was inconceivable that the supreme God would thus give himself up to the evil and destructive power of matter. This was why orthodox Christians saw Gnosticism, not as a different version of their own faith, but as heresy, an attempt to deprive that faith of the very heart of its message.[44] Gnosticism shared these common beliefs among its specific forms articulated by Marcion, Valentinus, Ptolemy, and Basilides among others.[45] One common thread among the forms of Gnosticism was its functional hermeneutic. Of particular interest to Gnostic interpreters were the stories of Genesis, the Gospel of John, and the Pauline Epistles. In fact, Gnostics such as Heracleon and Ptolemaeus were the first commentators on the fourth Gospel. They tended to use biblical texts for their own purposes. The Christian apologists were scathing in their denunciations of the Gnostics, who were perceived as leading Christians astray by the manipulation of words and the twisting of scriptural meanings. Irenaeus likened such interpretations to someone who has taken apart a beautiful picture of a king and reassembled it into a picture of a fox.[46] Let us now see how

42. Edwin M. Yamauchi, "Gnosticism," *NIDCC*, 416–18.

43. A. M. Renwick, "Gnosticism," *ISBE*, 2:487–91.

44. Gonzalez, *History of Christian Thought*, 1:132–33.

45. Cf. Robert M. Grant, ed., *Gnosticism: A Source Book of Heretical Writings from the Early Christian Period* (New York: Harper and Row, 1961); idem, "The Earliest Christian Gnosticism," *CH* 22 (1953): 81–98; Robert Haardt, *Gnosis: Character and Testimony* (Leiden: Brill, 1971).

46. Irenaeus *Against Heresies* 1.8.1.

the Gnostics applied their functional hermeneutical method to their philosophical and theological presuppositions.

Marcion

Marcion was a native of Pontus, where he was a prosperous shipmaster. He taught in Rome (ca. A.D. 140–155). He made an absolute distinction between the God of the Old Testament, who was perceived as harsh and rigorous, and the good God of the New Testament, who was completely love. He also affirmed the common Gnostic dualism and docetism.

At the time of Marcion, during the early and middle decades of the second century, the interpretation of the Jewish Scriptures remained the central hermeneutical task. This held true even in the case of Marcion, whose polemically-reduced Christian canon was probably the signal leading to the formation of an authoritative collection of apostolic writings among other Christians of the second century.[47] He reached the conclusion that he had to reject the Jewish Scriptures as the work of a wrathful, vicious, evil God who was opposed to the God of love proclaimed by Jesus and revealed to Paul. Suspicious of the harmonizing tendency of allegorical and typological exegesis, he declared that only the Epistles of Paul, the true apostle,[48] and portions of Luke's Gospel, purged of Jewish contamination, were acceptable for Christian use.

Marcion believed that the Scriptures should be taken literally and authoritatively, but his presuppositions forced him to eliminate most of what was recognized as Scripture by the professing church. He thus arrived at a truncated canon. Marcion's approach was condemned and the Jewish Scriptures in their Christian understanding were retained as the inspired prophetic witness of the truth of the Christian faith.[49] It has been suggested that Marcion was perhaps a greater danger to the church than any of the other early heretics. In many ways, answering Marcion's challenge created for the church a different set of problems of similar magnitude. As Karlfried Froehlich has noted, the Jewish Scriptures in their Christian understanding

> had proved to be a most effective apologetic and missionary tool. At the end of the controversy stood a normative Christian canon in two parts. But the decision against Marcion also had a disturbing consequence. By making the Jewish Scriptures resolutely a Christian book the Old Testament, which had

47. Karlfried Froehlich, *Biblical Interpretation in the Early Church* (Philadelphia: Fortress, 1984), 10–11.

48. Cf. John James Clabeaux, "The Pauline Corpus Which Marcion Used" (Ph.D. diss., Harvard University, 1983); Elaine H. Pagels, *The Gnostic Paul: Gnostic Exegesis of the Pauline Letters* (Philadelphia: Fortress, 1975).

49. Cf. R. Joseph Hoffmann, *Marcion: On the Restitution of Christianity* (Chico, Calif.: Scholars, 1980).

> only one legitimate continuation: the New Testament, the emerging Christian movement defined itself once more in sharpest antithesis to the Jewish community. In fact, the tighter the grip of Christians on the Jewish Scriptures, the deeper the estrangement from the community of living Jews.[50]

The church was now faced with challenges from two quite different perspectives. It was the task of the apologists to demonstrate the continuity of the two Testaments to the Gnostics and the discontinuity of the same Testaments to the Judaizers. The challenge rested with the "right" understanding of John and Paul.[51]

Valentinus

Valentinus was born on the Egyptian coast soon after A.D. 100 and received a thorough Hellenistic education in Alexandria. When he was introduced to Christianity is unknown, but tradition maintains that he had very close relations with the church in Rome. It has been suggested that his character and power were so clearly recognized in the church that he was on the verge of becoming a bishop when his heresy disqualified him. He has long been regarded as the greatest of the Gnostics, an acute thinker with a touch of mysticism and a philosopher's delight in contemplating things *sub specie aeternitatis.*[52]

The Valentinians seem to have been the first group in Christendom to have produced commentaries on early Christian writings, especially the Gospel of John and the Pauline corpus. Elaine H. Pagels has summarized the purpose of Valentinian exegesis as the coordination of Gnostic cosmology and soteriology with a hermeneutical grid extracted from the Pauline epistles.[53] His hermeneutical approach was more sophisticated than Marcion's, beginning with a simple literal interpretation of the biblical passages and moving to a more esoteric instruction on ethical and spiritual truth.[54]

50. Froehlich, *Biblical Interpretation in the Early Church,* 11.

51. For works that seek to show Marcion rightly understood Paul, see Adolf von Harnack, *History of Dogma,* trans. Neil Buchanan, 3d ed., 7 vols. (New York: Russell and Russell, 1958), 1:88ff., and Paul Tillich, *A History of Christian Thought: From Its Judaic and Hellenistic Origins to Existentialism,* ed. Carl E. Braaten (New York: Touchstone, 1967), 34–44. Examples of recent treatments that indicate a greater continuity between Paul and the Old Testament, in contrast to Marcion, are James D. G. Dunn, "The New Perspective on Paul," *BJRL* 65 (1982–83): 95–122; Morna D. Hooker and S. G. Wilson, eds., *Paul and Paulinism* (London: SPCK, 1982); E. P. Sanders, *Paul, the Law, and the Jewish People* (Philadelphia: Fortress, 1983); David L. Balas, "Marcion Revisited: A Post-Harnack Perspective," in *Texts and Testaments,* ed. E. March (San Antonio: Trinity University Press, 1980), 95–108.

52. Grant, *Gnosticism,* 143–61; Tertullian, *On Prescription Against Heretics,* comments that Valentinus was an able man in both talent and eloquence.

53. Pagels, *The Gnostic Paul.*

54. Cf. chapter 5 of Grant, *Gnosticism and Early Christianity.*

Other Gnostics

Ptolemy, Basilides, and Saturninas continued the Gnostic influence into the third century. The functional hermeneutic of Gnosticism was exercised through their philosophical, cosmological, and theological grid. All the Gnostics regarded the Old Testament and the New Testament as revelations of two different deities. They looked upon the God of the Jews as far inferior to the Supreme Being, called by them the Abyss. The God of the Old Testament, often referred to as the demiurge, was the creator of the evil world. Some Gnostic groups considered the demiurge completely separated from and opposed to the true God. The rise of Gnosticism compelled Christians in the second and third centuries to think through the limitations of their functional hermeneutic. This led to the rise of anti-Gnostic works, an authoritative hermeneutic, and the rule of faith. Gnosticism also provided a powerful impetus to the formation of the New Testament canon of Scripture, for the Gnostics claimed to have the authoritative Gospels and Epistles, though they did not usually agree among themselves. It thus became imperative for the church to distinguish between spurious and genuine scriptures to establish the normative New Testament canon.[55] Before viewing the church's response to the Gnostic challenge, we must briefly look at one more group that claimed authoritative revelation competing with the beliefs of the early church.

Montanus/Montanism

Montanus, a Phrygian Christian, began to prophesy in the small village of Ardabar in Phrygian Mysia about A.D. 170. Two women, Priscilla and Maximilla, who also prophesied, became his devoted followers and were influential in the dissemination of his teachings.[56] The followers of Montanus and the prophetesses were usually referred to as Cataphrygians by the Fathers, the title indicating the Phrygian provenance of the movement. They preferred the term *the new prophecy* when referring to themselves. They were later called Montanists after their founder.

The Fathers indicated that the Montanists produced numerous treatises. Apart from the treatises written by Tertullian after he had adopted Montanism, all other treatises perished. Our understanding of Montanism depends primarily, therefore, on those few Montanist fragments preserved in the Fathers.

The Montanists' hermeneutical method was strongly related to their name, "the new prophecy." "The new prophecy" was a summons to pre-

55. See Johannes Quasten, *Patrology,* 4 vols. (reprint; Westminster, Md.: Christian Classics, 1984), 1:256–77.

56. Timothy David Barnes, "The Chronology of Montanism," *JTS* n.s. 21 (1970): 403–8.

pare for the return of Christ by heeding the voice of the Paraclete speaking, often in the first person, through his prophetic mouthpieces. The manner of their prophecies, which included ecstatic utterances, were perceived to run counter to the tradition of orthodox Christian prophecy. Nothing strictly heretical could be charged against Montanists. Yet the prophets' extravagant pretensions, while not intended to displace the emergent New Testament, were felt to threaten the authority of both Scripture and the bishop. Recognition of the Paraclete in the new prophecy was their touchstone of authenticity.[57]

Montanists developed a "Spirit-led" illumination (cf. John 14–16) that added a new prophetic dimension to the prevailing functional exegesis. As it had with Gnosticism, the response by the apologists and heresiologists focused on the authority of the bishop and the primacy of the rule of faith. Whether Montanism arose because of the church's trend to ground its authority in the bishop, canon, and creed as an attempt to revive a more primitive form of the church, or whether its appearance was simply coincidental to this trend has not been conclusively determined by church historians and is beyond the scope of this work. It was, nevertheless, the issue of authority that was problematic for the church and brought the response of an authoritative hermeneutic.

The Hermeneutical Responses to the Challenge of Heresy

In the latter part of the second century the church had to demonstrate that the God of Israel was also the God of the church. The challenge involved confirming for the Gnostics the continuity between the Testaments; and demonstrating to the Montanists the development, as well as the cessation, of revelation; and convincing the Judaizers within Christianity as well as Judaism in general of the discontinuity of the two Testaments. Two responses arose: (1) the typological hermeneutics of Justin Martyr, and (2) the authoritative approach of Irenaeus and Tertullian.

Justin Martyr

His Background

The scant knowledge of Justin's life (ca. A.D. 100–165) is based largely on his own words supplemented by references from his pupil Tatian, brief oblique references in Irenaeus, Tertullian, and Epiphanius, and the witness

57. David F. Wright, "Why Were the Montanists Condemned?" *Themelios* 2:1 (1977): 15–22; see also William Tabbernee, "Early Montanism and Voluntary Martyrdom," *Colloquium* 17 (1985): 33–43; Frederick C. Klawiter, "The New Prophecy in Early Christianity: The Origin, Nature, and Development of Montanism, A.D. 165–220" (Ph.D. diss., The University of Chicago, 1975).

in Eusebius. In the opening words of the *First Apology* he identified himself as "Justin, the son of Priscus and the grandson of Bachius native of Flavia Neapolis in Palestine."[58] In his *Dialogue with Trypho* he described himself as a Samaritan, although in a fashion that distanced him from their influence: "For I gave no thought to any of my people, that is, the Samaritans, when I had a communication in writing with Caesar."[59] He appears to have been a representative of the Graeco-Roman urban middle class, "loyal, detached from ancient tradition, and cosmopolitan in outlook, intellectually active and interested, honest of mind, and economically independent."[60]

Justin described his philosophical quest in *Dialogue with Trypho* 2. He first attached himself to a Stoic, then he studied with a shrewd Peripatetic, later followed a celebrated Pythagorean, and finally became a Platonist.[61] While some historians offer the possibility that Justin's philosophical journey was only a stereotyped formula, Barnard insists Justin actually followed a fourfold philosophical odyssey.[62] It should be noted that Justin did not consider Christianity the next step on his quest, or a better version of Greek philosophy. He believed his turn to Christianity was a genuine conversion from his past and, as David F. Wright observes, "Only insofar as the Greek sages are in accord with Christian doctrine does Justin acknowledge them as teachers of truth."[63] Or, as Henry Chadwick contends, "Justin does not merely use Greek philosophy; he passes judgment on it."[64]

Of the surviving works of Justin, only three are considered to be genuine: The First and Second *Apologies* and *The Dialogue with Trypho.* The *Apologies* preceded the *Dialogue,* but the latter work was the locus of Justin's hermeneutic. Through the use of typological exegesis, Justin attempted to persuade Trypho, probably an imaginary dialogue partner, that Judaism was solely a preparation for Christianity and that the latter is certainly superior. Jon Nilson considers the actual audience of the *Dialogue* to be non-Christians at Rome who were favorably disposed toward both Chris-

58. Justin Martyr *First Apology* 1.1.

59. Justin Martyr *Dialogue with Trypho* 120.

60. Hans von Campenhausen, *The Fathers of the Greek Church,* trans. Stanley Godman (New York: Pantheon, 1959), 13.

61. Robert M. Grant, "Aristotle and the Conversion of Justin," *JTS* 7 (1956): 246–48.

62. L. W. Barnard, "Justin Martyr in Recent Study," *SJT* 22 (1969): 154. He argues the fact that Justin's preconversion experiences may have been shaped by culture, but this does not deny their historicity; see also Oscar Skarsaune, "The Conversion of Justin Martyr," *ST* 30 (1976): 53–74, who provides a rigorous defense for the authenticity of the account.

63. David F. Wright, "Christian Faith in the Greek World: Justin Martyr's Testimony," *EQ* 54 (1982): 81; see also Robert L. Wilken, "Toward a Social Interpretation of Early Christian Apologetics," *CH* 39 (1970): 437–58.

64. Henry Chadwick, *Early Christian Thought and the Classical Tradition* (Oxford: Clarendon, 1966), 20.

tianity and Judaism, but unable to distinguish between the two.[65] Trypho, ignorant of Hebrew and interested in philosophy, represented the kind of Jew that Justin sought to persuade. He served as a good sparring partner for Justin to prove the superiority of Christianity.[66] A. J. B. Higgins cautions, however, that even if the *Dialogue* actually took place, there is no reason to accept that Trypho gives an accurate report of contemporary Jewish beliefs: "The fact is that Justin has overplayed his role of Christian apologist."[67] Trypho must be taken as representative of Judaism only insofar as he represented the larger known consensus. While paying careful attention to these cautions and concerns, our purpose is to see how Justin interpreted Scripture, even if he overstepped the boundaries in his apologetics.

His Hermeneutical Approach

For Justin both general and special revelation were the outgrowth of the Logos.[68] Pagan philosophers possessed the Logos, Jesus was and is the Logos, and the Bible contains the written residue of the Logos. His view of biblical revelation allowed little room for development of the message from the Old Testament period to the New. This formed the basis of his views concerning the authority of biblical inspiration resulting in a noncontradicting Bible.[69] He seemingly had little concern for Scripture's original context or the meaning of Scripture for its original readers. His typological exegesis was characteristically christocentric; the Old Testament in its entirety pointed to Jesus.[70] In demonstrating the christocentric nature of Scripture, Justin used terms such as "mystery, announcement, signs, parable, symbol and type."[71] All six of these terms were essentially synonymous, indicating a representative or inner meaning of an act or a person representative of a later act or incident. At times it is difficult to distinguish between an allegorical interpretation and a typological one because Justin seemed to delight in finding esoteric meaning in cryptic passages.[72]

65. Jon Nilson,"To Whom Is Justin's *Dialogue with Trypho* Addressed?" *TS* 38 (1977): 538–46.

66. Cf. Ben Z. Bokser, "Justin Martyr and the Jews," *JQR* 64 (1973): 97–122; idem, "Justin Martyr and the Jews," *JQR* 64 (1974): 204–11; Clark M. Williamson, "The *Adversus Judaeos* Tradition in Christian Theology," *Encounter* 39 (1978): 273–96.

67. A. J. B. Higgins, "Jewish Messianic Belief in Justin Martyr's *Dialogue with Trypho*," *NovT* 9 (1967): 305; yet Schneider is probably correct in commenting that most, if not all, are agreed that the setting of the *Dialogue* cannot be taken literally. Cf. H. P. Schneider, "Some Reflections on the *Dialogue with Trypho* in Justin Martyr," *SJT* 15 (1962): 164–75.

68. Cf. Justin Martyr *First Apology* 46.

69. Willis A. Shotwell, *The Biblical Exegesis of Justin Martyr* (London: SPCK, 1965), 2–5.

70. Justin Martyr *Dialogue* 40–46.

71. Shotwell, *Biblical Exegesis of Justin Martyr*, 8.

72. Cf. Joel C. Gregory, "The Chiliastic Hermeneutic of Papias of Hierapolis and Justin Martyr Compared with Later Patristic Chiliasts" (Ph.D. diss., Baylor University, 1983).

Any person or event in the Old Testament that foreshadows an episode in either the life or work of Christ was gladly employed.[73]

Willis A. Shotwell has analyzed and compared the hermeneutical approach of Justin with that of Jesus, Paul, and other New Testament writers. Justin shared a christocentric use of the Old Testament with Jesus and the apostles. He, like the New Testament writers, used midrashic methods to argue for the relationship of Judaism with Christianity while contending for the superiority of the latter. Justin argued from minor to major, from general to particular, and from analogy in the New Testament. It has been pointed out that there were at least forty Justinian parallels with rabbinic exegesis.[74]

Justin used rabbinic methods to his advantage so that his arguments and counter arguments could spring from this approach. Trypho used the *Haggada,* but Justin also employed haggadic material to further his apology. Upon examination there appears substantial agreement between the hermeneutical principles of Justin and those of Hillel regarding some of his basic principles in the exegesis of Scripture.[75]

In following the christocentric hermeneutics of the New Testament writers and employing the principles from Hillel, Justin linked the Old Testament to the New, the very antithesis of both Judaism and Marcionite Gnosticism. Marcion's total rejection of the Old Testament was the exact opposite of Justin's typological viewpoint. Drawing on real or supposed messianic prophecies from the Jewish tradition, he argued that Jesus clearly was the expected Messiah who fulfilled all of the Old Testament Scriptures literally or typically. Thus Justin established his apologetic method on proof from prophecy. His writings, primarily the *Dialogue,* served as a gold mine of information on second-century Christian typology. In line with the developing Christian creed, the rule of faith, Justin found all the major features of the creed prefigured in the message of the Old Testament text, as summarized by Froehlich:

> Christ's virgin birth; his healing ministry, suffering, death and resurrection; Christian baptism; the church. Types of the cross were of particular interest: Justin found them not only in the figure of Moses praying in the battle against Amalek (Exod. 17:10–11) or in the horns of the wild ox (Deut. 33:17) but in every stick, wood, tree mentioned in the Bible.[76]

73. Justin Martyr *Dialogue* 33, 53; Shotwell, *Biblical Exegesis of Justin Martyr,* 31–33.

74. Shotwell, *Biblical Exegesis of Justin Martyr,* 48–64, 88–93.

75. Ibid., 93.

76. Froehlich, *Biblical Exegesis in the Early Church,* 13; cf. *Dialogue* 86–91; cf. also Cullen I. K. Story, *Nature of Truth in "The Gospel" and in the Writings of Justin Martyr: A Study of the Pattern of Orthodoxy in the Middle of the Second Century* (Leiden: Brill, 1970); Oskar Skarsaune, *Proof from Prophecy: A Study in Justin Martyr's Proof-Text Tradition* (Leiden: Brill, 1987).

The immense range of types illustrates Justin's christocentric-typological exegetical method. The usage of the creed paved the way for the forthcoming authoritative exegesis used to respond to the challenges of the heretics.

Irenaeus and Tertullian

The church's estimate of its theological norms underwent certain adjustments in the final decades of the second century. While the Old Testament was being challenged by the Gnostics, the established church was simultaneously promoting the apostolic Scripture to a position of supreme authority. This developing perspective was assisted and indeed made possible by the recognition of the New Testament as fully canonical and entitled to equal status alongside the Old as God-inspired Scripture.

Equally important historically and more significant hermeneutically, the distinction between Scripture and the church's living tradition, as coordinate instruments in conveying the apostolic testimony, became more clearly appreciated, and a growing importance, if not a primacy, began to be attached to the latter.[77] This development resulted from the great struggle between orthodoxy and the Gnostic heretics previously described. Irenaeus claimed that not only did the Gnostics exploit Scripture to their own ends, but one of their successful techniques was to appeal, in support of their positions, to an alleged secret apostolic tradition (the *gnosis*) for which they alone claimed to have access.[78]

This developing, more mature position is exemplified, with minor differences, in the writings of Irenaeus and Tertullian. J. N. D. Kelly comments, "For both of them Christ Himself was the ultimate source of Christian doctrine, being the truth, the Word by Whom the Father had been revealed; but He had entrusted this revelation to His apostles, and it was through them alone that knowledge of it could be obtained."[79]

Their Background

It will be helpful to glance briefly at the background of these two giants of the second-century church. Irenaeus (ca. A.D. 130–200) in his youth was influenced by Polycarp (ca. A.D. 70–160), bishop of Smyrna and probable disciple of the apostle John. Irenaeus, bishop of Lyons in Gaul, in seeking to be faithful to the meaning of his name ("peaceful"), sought to mediate between the churches of Asia Minor and Rome in the Montanist and the Quartodiciman disputes.

77. J. N. D. Kelly, *Early Christian Doctrines*, 4th rev. ed. (San Francisco: Harper and Row, 1978), 35–41.

78. Irenaeus *Against Heresies* 3.2.1.

79. Kelly, *Early Christian Doctrines*, 36; cf. Robert M. Grant, *Greek Apologists of the Second Century* (Philadelphia: Westminster, 1988).

Irenaeus's two major treatises survive: (1) *The Proof of the Apostolic Preaching*, and (2) *Against Heresies: Refutation and Overthrow of the Gnosis Falsely So Called*. The first was believed to have been written for an apologetic or a catechetical purpose. It presented Christ and Christianity as the fulfillment of the Old Testament by means of a christological-typological reading of the text. Salvation history was structured according to the various covenants of God with man. The second was a polemical work opposing Gnosticism. Against the Gnostics' mythological interpretation of Scripture, association of matter with evil, and spiritualizing eschatology, Irenaeus proposed an interpretation of Scripture according to a summary of the apostolic preaching, called the *regula fidei* (rule of faith). Irenaeus was the earliest author whose works survive to argue from Scripture as a whole, New Testament as well as Old Testament, and a range of New Testament writings similar to the present canon.[80]

Tertullian (ca. A.D. 155–255), whose full name was Quintus Septimius Florens Tertullianus, was born in Carthage, near modern Tunis in North Africa, sometime after A.D. 150. He probably came from a middle-class family and received a sound literary, legal, and philosophical education that included a good knowledge of Greek. Very little, or nothing at all, is known of his private life or occupation, apart from the fact that he was married, though it is probable that his wife died young.[81]

A number of puzzling features about his writings defy solution in our present state of knowledge. For example, it is unknown how he was able to write so freely at a time when the church was suffering persecution, nor is it at all certain exactly how he related to the church at Carthage. According to church tradition, he became a presbyter in the Carthaginian church, a conclusion that appears accurate, although Tertullian never referred to himself as an officeholder in the church. Like Clement of Alexandria and Origen, he never rose above the rank of presbyter. In Tertullian's case, it was probably because of his later Montanist association. One of the more puzzling things about Tertullian, a man who devoted so much of his time to both apologetical[82] and polemical[83] works, was his pilgrimage into Montanism in his latter years.[84]

80. Quasten, *Patrology*, 1:287–313.

81. Cf. Timothy David Barnes, *Tertullian: A Historical and Literary Study* (Oxford: Clarendon, 1971); also James Morgan, *The Importance of Tertullian in the Development of Christian Dogma* (London: Kegan Paul, Trench, Trubner and Co., 1928).

82. His apologetical works include *To the Heathen, Apology, Testimony of the Soul, To Scapula,* and *Against the Jews.*

83. His polemical works were *Prescription Against Heretics, Against Marcion, Against Hermogenes, Against the Valentinians, On Baptism, Scorpiace, On the Flesh of Christ,* and *The Resurrection of the Flesh.*

84. Two important works written after his involvement with Montanism were *On the Soul* and *Against Praxeas.* These were in addition to numerous practical and devotional writings.

The Montanists "new prophecy" had predicted the end of the world would occur in A.D. 177. Tertullian was drawn to Montanist teachings about thirty years afterwards, when the falsity of the "new prophecy" would have been obvious to everyone. Yet, it may not have been the prophetic element that was attractive to him, for he was noticeably selective in his use of their writings, saying nothing about the end of the world, but concentrating almost entirely on their holiness teachings. It seems plausible, therefore, that Tertullian saw Montanism as a movement that advocated some of his own teachings. Nothing is know for certain about his death, though tradition maintains that he died at Carthage sometime after 212.[85]

Their Hermeneutical Approach

The task faced by these two important thinkers was to demonstrate the unity of the Testaments and the validity of the complete New Testament in light of the challenges from Marcion and other Gnostics. The rise of a specifically Christian literature solved some problems, for the main outlines of the gospel were now fairly well fixed, not to say preserved, but the diversity within the New Testament raised new issues.[86] As we have noted earlier, Marcion solved the problem rather neatly, by merely rejecting much of the Christian tradition and what was to be the Christian Scripture. According to Irenaeus, it was characteristic of heretics that they took only a part of the evidence: "The Ebionites or Jewish Christians used only Matthew; Marcion took Luke; Docetists who separated 'Christ' from Jesus, used only Mark; Valentinian theosophists liked John."[87] Also, the followers of Marcion claimed that Paul alone knew the truth of revelation.[88] What was to be done under such circumstances? Obviously the former functional usage of Scripture was in need of an expanded paradigm.

Irenaeus presented the view accepted by most. He maintained that the true interpretation of the Scriptures was to be found among those who had received the apostolic tradition along with the apostolic succession, and who possessed the charismatic gift of truth.[89] Irenaeus contended:

> True "gnosis" is the teaching of the apostles, and the ancient structure of the church throughout the world, and the form of the body of Christ in accordance with the successions of bishops to whom the apostles delivered the church which is in each place; this teaching has come down to us, preserved without any use of forged writings, by being handled in its complete

85. Barnes, "The Chronology of Montanism."

86. Robert M. Grant, "From Tradition to Scripture and Back," in *Scripture and Tradition*, ed. Joseph F. Kelly (Notre Dame, Ind.: Fides, 1976), 20–21.

87. Irenaeus *Against Heresies* 3.11.7.

88. Ibid., 3.13.1.

89. Cf. R. P. C. Hanson, *Tradition in the Early Church* (London: SCM, 1962), 95–96; also Robert M. Grant, *The Formation of the New Testament* (London: SCM, 1965), 135–37.

fullness, neither receiving addition nor suffering curtailment; and reading without falsification, and honest and steady exposition of the scriptures without either danger or blasphemy; and the special gift of love . . . [90]

As can be observed, Irenaeus's rule of faith[91] was not exactly a law, and yet by this time it had become an external authority that would permanently fix the meaning of Scripture. This produced a hermeneutical method in which church tradition determined the meaning of Scripture. By this, a hermeneutical circle was enacted: church tradition was created by the interpretation of Scripture and the interpretation of Scripture was then governed by the church's tradition in the rule of faith.

Because Irenaeus's writings were primarily polemical, his arguments tended to reduce themselves to the claim that there is but one God, the Creator, who is the God of Jesus Christ and the God of both the Hebrew Scriptures and the New Testament. If we look beyond the polemical nature of the work, however, we can see that his understanding of Christianity focuses upon Jesus Christ as Savior, adopting and expanding the christological hermeneutic present in the church from Jesus to Justin Martyr.

We can summarize Irenaeus's hermeneutical practice in the following way. His conviction concerning Scripture, both in theory and in practice, was that the Old Testament and New Testament represented a unity. The prophets were fulfilled in Christ.[92] The apostles, meaning the entire New Testament (the apostolic preaching), in turn preached the same God the Father, the Son, and Spirit and the same economy of salvation. The heretics, on the contrary, according to Irenaeus, chose from the whole of the Scriptures what seemed to them to support their particular doctrines.[93] But, as Irenaeus showed again and again, because of the unity of the underlying message, their errors could be refuted even from their own restricted scriptures themselves.

The rule of faith preserved the apostolic tradition in the church and functioned as the normative guide for interpretation. In this connection, we can better understand the meaning and function of the rule of faith. While defined in several ways, the rule of faith could be best expressed as the church's belief "in one God, the Father Almighty, Maker of heaven and

90. Irenaeus *Against Heresies* 5.20.1; cf. P. Hefner, "Theological Methodology in St. Irenaeus," *JR* 44 (1964): 294–309.

91. The terms *rule of faith* and *rule of truth* are used interchangeably for *regula fidei* (or *regula veritatis*). While not specifically defined from the apostolic fathers through the third century, it was particularly prominent in Irenaeus, Tertullian, Clement of Alexandria, and Origen. Each of these theologians used the term as the creedal expansion of the baptismal formula to define the apostolic tradition of faith against Gnostics and other heretics.

92. Irenaeus *Against Heresies* 4.33.10–15.

93. Ibid., 3.1.1.

earth, and the sea, and all things that are in them; and in one Christ Jesus, the Son of God, who became incarnate for our salvation; and in the Holy Spirit."[94] This contained, in summary form, the fundamentals of the apostolic preaching which were preserved, one and the same, by the succession of bishops in the whole church. It did not add to the content of Scriptures, since the same teaching was found in both; actually it could be unfolded in detail.[95] It could and did function, however, as a criterion against the misinterpretations of the Scriptures by the heretics.[96] While we have mentioned Irenaeus's classic illustration, it is worth noting again. The heretics were like those who take apart an artful mosaic of precious stones representing the image of the king and compose with the same pieces an inferior picture of a fox.[97] Extending this comparison beyond its explicit use by Irenaeus, it can be said that the rule of faith provided the essential Christian message transmitted by the apostolic preaching and writings, enabling the church to recognize any heretical distortion for what it was.[98]

In dealing with the heretics who were using the Bible to defend their position, Tertullian forced them to take their stand on two questions: (1) Whose are the Scriptures? (2) How should they be understood? The Scriptures belonged to the church, not the heretics; the heretics could not use them. He commented, "Only the churches which stand in the succession of the apostles possess the teaching of Christ."[99]

Tertullian was not as consistent as Irenaeus. As Grant notes, Tertullian "in exegesis shows his characteristic mixture of good sense with occasional perverseness."[100] Sometimes he was literal, sometimes wildly fanciful. The authoritative exegesis of this time made available an allegorical interpretation within certain limits.[101] The first use by Tertullian of the term *rule of faith* occurred in *Against Marcion* 4.2.5. For Tertullian, this passage used the synonyms: "the Gospel," "the Faith," "the *Kerygma*," "the Apostles," and "the authority of Christ."[102]

94. Ibid., 1.10, 22; 2.25; 3.4.2.

95. Ibid., 3–5.

96. Cf. Rowan A. Greer, "The Dog and the Mushrooms: Irenaeus' View of the Valentinians Assessed," in *The Rediscovery of Gnosticism*, vol. 1, *The School of Valentine*, ed. Bentley Layton (Leiden: Brill, 1980), 146–75.

97. Irenaeus *Against Heresies* 1.8.1; 1.9.4.

98. Irenaeus could interpret the prophetic and apostolic texts in light of other texts taken from the whole of Scripture. Like Justin, he did not seem interested in the original literary or cultural context.

99. Tertullian *On Prescription Against Heretics* 20.1.

100. Robert M. Grant with David Tracy, *A Short History of the Interpretation of the Bible*, rev. ed. (Philadelphia: Fortress, 1984), 66.

101. Cf. T. P. O'Malley, *Tertullian and the Bible: Language—Imagery—Exegesis* (Utrecht: Dekker and Van de Vegt N.V. Nijmegen, 1967).

102. Cf. Tertullian *Against Marcion* 4.1.2.–4.2.5.

Certainly Irenaeus was the father of authoritative exegesis, but as can be seen from Tertullian's *Against Marcion* and *On Prescription Against Heretics,* Tertullian shifted the issue from a right understanding of Scripture to the more sharply stated issue of whether the Gnostics could even use Scripture. According to Tertullian, arguing with Gnostics about scriptural interpretation was useless. He reached this conclusion after realizing that functional exegesis produced ambiguity at best and opened the door for heretical interpretations to dictate the theological agenda. He moved the issue away from interpretation to question the heretics' very right to use Scripture at all.[103] Apostolic Scriptures, he argued, belong to the apostolic church, as did the apostolic tradition contained in the rule of faith.[104] The Gnostic heretics, in Tertullian's approach, had no right to use apostolic Scripture because only the public succession of teaching passed down in the churches could measure apostolicity and correct interpretation. "Apostolicity" and "correctness" were grounded in the rule of faith.[105] In contrast, the Gnostics who championed Matthew 7:7 ("Seek and you will find") as their warrant continually searched for the secret knowledge (*gnosis*) to read Scripture. Tertullian countered with Pauline warnings from 2 Timothy 3:7, that the Gnostics were "always learning but never able to acknowledge the truth." For true believers, the search had ended. The true faith, understood through the rule of faith, had been found and now must only be defended against its erosion by ideal and unfounded curiosity. As Froehlich summarized, "For both Irenaeus and Tertullian, illicit curiosity is the true danger of a Gnostic hermeneutics of inquiry."[106]

Conclusion

In the second century, the apostolic fathers, apologists, and heresiologists found the true understanding of the Bible in the teaching of the apostles. But the rise of Gnosticism and other challenges to accepted orthodoxy caused the functional exegesis of the apostolic fathers to receive further

103. Cf. Froehlich, *Biblical Interpretation in the Early Church,* 13–15; also R. D. Sider, "Approaches to Tertullian: A Study of Recent Scholarship," *SC* 2 (1982): 228–60.

104. Tertullian, *On Prescription Against Heretics* 20; see also Jean Daniélou, *The Origins of Latin Christianity* (Philadelphia: Westminster, 1977), 139–60, 209–14, 261–328. Whereas Justin before Tertullian, and Origen after him, attempted to synthesize Christianity with philosophy, particularly with forms of Platonism, Tertullian's reactionary and separatistic approach is evident in his dealings with philosophy in general and with heretical uses of Scripture. Just as heretics had no right to interpret Scripture, so Christianity had nothing to do with philosophy, or in his famous words, "What has Jerusalem to do with Athens?"

105. Tertullian *On Prescription Against Heretics* 14.1–2.

106. Froehlich, *Biblical Interpretation in the Early Church,* 15.

hermeneutical development. For if a functional exegesis resulted in the possibility of hermeneutical confusion and ambiguity, as well as bringing about questions regarding the unity of Scripture and its message, then an authoritative answer must be found to handle such matters.

The second century saw the rise of a normative canon, an authoritative bishop, and an accepted rule of faith. Beginning with Ignatius and progressing with Justin, Irenaeus, and Tertullian, there developed the contention that if anyone wished to know the true meaning of Scripture, he or she must interpret the texts under the guided authorities of the rule of faith and the bishops or presbyters of the church. All other interpretations were viewed as alienated from the truth and unacceptable in the church.[107]

Rowan A. Greer incisively and a helpfully summarizes this period:

> 1. A Christian Bible is the product of the formative period of early Christianity (30–180 C.E.). Before Irenaeus, we find the church struggling to define its Scriptures and to come to terms with their interpretation, but it is only by the end of the second century that the diversity of earliest Christianity has yielded to an ecumenical unity. The emergence of a Christian Bible is a central feature of that unity.
> 2. Basic to the task of the formative period is the transformation of the Hebrew Scriptures so that they may become a witness to Christ.
> 3. With Irenaeus we find the first clear evidence of a Christian Bible and also a framework of interpretation in the church's rule of faith. The rule of faith, as a kind of creed, outlines the theological story that finds its focus in the incarnate Lord.[108]

Reading the Scripture through this theological grid at times forced the biblical text into a preconceived set of theological convictions. Usually the text was interpreted without regard to its literary or historical context. But in light of the challenges faced by the church, this hermeneutical approach appeared to be the proper response. Included in the second-century hermeneutical approach was a continuity with the typological-christological methods of Jesus and the apostles. The addition of the rule of faith expanded the hermeneutical paradigm by providing the presuppositions through which Scripture should be read. This resulted in a hermeneutical circle that safeguarded the church's message but reduced the possibility of creativity among individual interpreters. The authority of the

107. Irenaeus *Against Heresies* 4.32.1.

108. Greer, "The Rise of a Christian Bible," in *Early Biblical Interpretation* (Philadelphia: Westminster, 1986), 111–12.

church, the canon, and the church's faith had been exalted, but the liberty of the human spirit tended to vanish. This tension had to be faced with the creative genius of the Alexandrians, Clement, and Origen. We must now see if the work of the Alexandrians supplemented or supplanted the conclusions of the second-century church.

3

The Alexandrian School: Allegorical Hermeneutics

While several Christian writers of the second and third centuries engaged in biblical interpretation, the first important scholarly commentator was Origen of Alexandria. He brought the touch of a master to what had "been nothing much more than the exercise of amateurs."[1] He was the greatest of the interpreters associated with the Alexandrian school of interpretation, those Christian scholars who understood biblical inspiration in the Platonic sense of utterance in a state of ecstatic possession. Therefore it was appropriate that the words imparted in this way should be interpreted mystically if their inner significance was to be known.[2] In this chapter we shall examine the background of allegorical hermeneutics, its application and usage at Alexandria, two representative practitioners, and responses from later theologians.

The Background of Allegorical Hermeneutics

Contemporary scholarship has questioned whether we can properly speak of a "hermeneutical school" of Alexandria.[3] Yet, we shall, following tradition, refer to the Alexandrian school without implying a fully-orbed

1. R. P. C. Hanson, *Allegory and Event: A Study of the Sources and Significance of Origen's Interpretation of Scripture* (Richmond: John Knox, 1959), 360.

2. F. F. Bruce, "The History of New Testament Study," in *New Testament Interpretation*, ed. I. Howard Marshall (Grand Rapids: Eerdmans, 1975), 26.

3. Robert M. Grant with David Tracy, *A Short History of the Interpretation of the Bible*, rev. ed. (Philadelphia: Fortress, 1984), 52–53.

school. Philo, a contemporary of Jesus and the apostles, seems to have been largely without influence in his own Jewish community as the articulator of allegorical hermeneutics in Alexandria and forerunner of the hermeneutics of Clement and Origen. It will be helpful to observe the beginnings of allegorical interpretation and its influence on Philonic exegesis.

We know the first allegorists, like the earliest Greek philosophers, only through the fragments of their work preserved by later authors.[4] Most ancient witnesses as well as the majority of modern scholars regard Theagenes of Rhegium as the founder of the practice of allegorical interpretation, though some suggest Pheresydes of Syros[5] (early sixth century B.C.), based on a quotation from Celsus's *True Word* found in Origen's refutation:

> Celsus says that the words of Zeus to Hera are the words of God to matter, and that the words to matter vaguely hint that at the beginning God divided it in certain proportions, bound it together, and ordered it and that he cast out all the demons round it which were arrogant, inflicting on them the punishment of being sent down here to earth. He maintains that Pherecydes understood these words of Homer in this way, when he said: "Beneath that land is the land of the Tartarus, and it is guarded by the daughters of Boreas, the Harpies and Thyella; there Zeus casts out any of the gods if ever one becomes arrogant."[6]

Regardless, the allegorical tradition began in the pre-Socratic period of classical Greece, which eventually influenced much of pagan, Jewish, and Christian philosophical and religious expression. Several major works have traced this history of allegorical interpretation.[7] The seedbed of allegory is found in the primitive philosophers' practice of expressing philosophical ideas with mythological imagery. The technique was especially popular with the Sophists, less prominent with Plato, and all but ignored in Aristotle. E. Zeller's treatment of Stoic allegorism is set in the context of the relation of Stoicism to popular religion. While perfectly capable of criticizing the superstitious excesses of the popular cult and mythology, the

4. Cf. H. Diels and W. Kranz, eds., *Die Fragmente der Vorsokratiker* (Berlin: Weidmann, 1960).

5. Cf. J. Tate, "The Beginnings of Greek Allegory," *CR* 41 (1927): 214–15; idem, "On the History of Allegorism," *CQ* 28 (1934): 105–14; idem, "Plato and Allegorical Interpretation, 1," *CQ* 23 (1929): 142–54; idem, "Plato and Allegorical Interpretation, 2," *CQ* 24 (1930): 1–10.

6. Origen *Contra Celsum* 6.42.

7. E. Zeller, *A History of Greek Philosophy from the Earliest Period to the Time of Socrates*, trans. S. F. Alleyne, 2 vols. (London: Longmans and Green, 1881); J. Pepin, *Mythe et allegorie: Les origines grecques et les contestations judeo-chretiennes*, new and rev. ed. (Paris: Etudes Augustiniennes, 1976); Burton L. Mack, "Exegetical Traditions in Alexandrian Judaism: A Program for the Analysis of the Philonic Corpus," *StPhil* 3 (1974–75): 71–112.

Stoics nevertheless sought to discover, in the inappropriate form, an essentially true content. This attempt led to allegorical interpretation that served to bring the old myths, taken mainly from Homer and Hesiod, into relation with the philosophy of the interpreters. Etymology was the principal instrument for this activity.[8]

The next major instance, taken in historical order, that so influenced the Alexandrians was that of heterodox Judaism. While other groups and individuals practiced allegorical interpretation, Philo Judaeus of Alexandria dominated. Philo regarded the Jewish Scriptures as the divinely inspired, infallible, and all-sufficient Word of God which required an unconditional submission by the interpreter. The Alexandrian Jews were more cosmopolitan than many of their Palestinian relatives, especially the lower classes of Palestinian Judaism that tended to be reactionary as a result of their disenfranchisement. Furthermore, the Alexandrian Jews were more directly exposed to Greek culture and philosophy. It is not surprising, therefore, that a Jew such as Philo, antecedently committed to the Bible as the Word of God on account of his Jewish background yet also anxious to be a modern person of his time and a philosophically sophisticated man, would adopt a method to bring these commitments together. As Samuel Sandmel has emphasized, Philo wished to maintain Jewish conformity to the laws in a literal sense, yet he seemed to regard that literal observance as rather secondary.[9] The significant thing for Philo was the philosophical meaning contained in the Bible discoverable by allegorical interpretation. For Philo, this philosophical meaning was the practice of religion, culminating in the mystic vision or holy communion with God. His eclectic appropriation of Greek philosophy was primarily an attempt to communicate the truth of Judaism to his enlightened Hellenistic contemporaries. Donald A. Hagner comments:

> Basic to Philo's entire approach is the fundamental dualism between material and non-material. It is the latter, the intelligible world, which is ultimately all-important to Philo, who by his allegorical exegesis presses consistently beyond the material, whether in matters of understanding or conduct, to Plato's transcendent realm of Ideas. Philo borrows the Stoic concept of the Logos as the mediating factor between the transcendent God and the material world.[10]

8. Zeller, *History of Greek Philosophy,* 1:55–58; cf. Walter Otto, *The Homeric Gods: The Spiritual Significance of Greek Religion* (London: Thames & Hudson, 1954).

9. Cf. Samuel Sandmel, *Philo of Alexandria* (New York: Oxford University Press, 1979), 20–36; see also R. Scott Birdsall, "The Naasene Sermon and the Allegorical Tradition: Allegorical Interpretation, Syncretism, and Textual Authority" (Ph.D. diss., Claremont Graduate School, 1984), 21–41.

10. Donald A. Hagner, "Philo," *NDT,* 509–10.

Philo interpreted Genesis 1:1 as the forming of an incorporeal pattern, like a Platonic Idea. In connection with the six days of creation, his discussion of the qualities of the number six showed Pythagorean influence. He offered a meaning for the four rivers of Paradise (Gen. 2:10–14) as prudence, self-mastery, courage, and justice, the cardinal Platonic virtues. It has been suggested that there are parallels in method and wording between Philo and John (John 1:3), where the Logos, the Word, is the agent in creation; and between Philo and Hebrews (Heb. 8–10), where the earthly tabernacle is the copy of the heavenly.

In general, Philo regarded the biblical text as having a multiplicity of meanings. Because of his view of inspired Scripture, every expression, every word, and even every letter contained a meaning. Etymology was an important way to discover the hidden meaning of words, and numbers were also a fruitful source for allegorical exegesis.

Philo's purpose was apologetic in the sense of wedding together Judaism and Greek philosophy.[11] In his mind, Judaism, properly understood, differed little from the highest insights of Greek revelation. God revealed himself to the people of Israel, God's chosen nation, but this revelation was not radically different from his revelation to the Greeks. The point of tension arose for Philo with Israel's understanding of their election and special place in God's redemptive plan and with the theological distinction between revelation in Scripture and revelation in nature. Robert M. Grant notes that Philo attempted to deal with this problem by trying to explain away Israel's election and the apparent anthropomorphisms of God used in Scripture in favor of a philosopher's God and a Hellenistic internationalism. For the Philonic and Platonic tradition the allegorical hermeneutics of the Christian school at Alexandria, called *Didaskaleion,* developed[12] and produced some of the greatest scholars of the early church, particularly Clement and Origen.[13] They had to face challenges to Chris-

11. Cf. R. McL. Wilson, "Philo and the Fourth Gospel," *ExT* 65 (1953): 47–49. For his influence on Origen, see H. J. Mumm, "Origen as an Exegete of the Fourth Gospel" (Ph.D. diss., Hartford Seminary Foundation, 1952); Donald K. McKim, "The Doctrine of Scripture in Origen and Its Use in the *Commentary on John*" (master's thesis, Pittsburgh Theological Seminary, 1972). On the relationship between Philo and the Epistle to the Hebrews, see R. Williamson, *Philo and the Epistle to the Hebrews* (Leiden: Brill, 1970).

12. Joseph Wilson Trigg, *Origen: The Bible and Philosophy in the Third-Century Church* (Atlanta: John Knox, 1983), 31–75.

13. Eusebius *Ecclesiastical History* 5.10, 6.1–4. We have noted earlier that some scholars question the nature of the "school" at Alexandria. Our usage of the term is not a contradiction or a challenge to that observation, but a continuation of the traditional usage of the term *Alexandrian school* (like the "Antiochene school"; see chap. 4). It is very difficult to reconstruct the historical development of the "school" at Alexandria. Some have considered that there existed a formal institution that has been called the Catechetical School of Alexandria. Others have thought it better to think of the school of Alexandria not as an institu-

tianity from many sources, including Greek philosophy,[14] Graeco-Roman and Egyptian religions,[15] and Gnosticism.[16] At the end of the second century and the beginning of the third, Alexandria was one of the primary cities of the Roman Empire. By the time of Clement and Origen, the city had become a rich center of knowledge and wisdom. Justo L. Gonzalez notes that the city

> was like a pot boiling with diverse teachings, all eclectic in nature: the Gnosticism held by Basilides, the Neoplatonism of Ammonius Saccas and Plotinus, the Hellenistic Judaism that followed in the tradition of Philo, and the esoteric and Platonist Christianity of Clement and Origen.[17]

It was this setting and background coupled with these challenges that caused the paradigm of authoritative hermeneutics of the second century to be expanded by the Alexandrians' allegorical approach.

The Development Beyond Authority at Alexandria

The approach of the late-second-century fathers, however, could not stem the challenge of the times. A more mature and scientific hermeneutical methodology was the direction for the future. The movement and maturation came from the famous teachers at Alexandria: Pantaenus (late second century), and of course Clement and Origen. The primary challenge facing the church of the third century paralleled that of the previous century.

The church recognized that many Gnostic teachings were inconsistent with the rule of faith advanced by Irenaeus and Tertullian. The rule excluded the Gnostics by insisting on the identity of Jesus' Father with

---

tion, but as a theological center or tendency toward a particular approach to biblical and theological studies. Regardless, this school was involved in the basic instruction of converts, preparing them for baptism. For a splendid discussion of the educational practices of this time, see H. I. Marrou, *A History of Education in Antiquity*, trans. George Lamb (New York: Sheed and Ward, 1956).

14. Cf. Marrou's introduction in *A History of Education in Antiquity;* R. C. Lilla, *Clement of Alexandria: A Study of Christian Platonism and Gnosticism* (London: Oxford University Press, 1971).

15. Cf. Harold Idris Bell, *Cults and Creeds in Graeco-Roman Egypt* (Liverpool: At the University Press, 1954); Hans Lewy, *Chaldean Oracles and Theurgy: Mysticism, Magic, and Platonism in the Later Roman Empire*, ed. and rev. Michel Tardieu (Paris: Etudes Augustiniennes, 1978).

16. See the section on Gnosticism in chapter 2. Many contend that in the process of combating Gnosticism, Origen adopted too many of the opposition's ideas. For example, see Joseph McLelland, *God the Anonymous: A Study in Alexandrian Philosophical Theology* (Cambridge, Mass.: Philadelphia Patristic Foundation, 1976), 114–20.

17. Justo L. Gonzalez, *History of Christian Thought*, 3 vols. (Nashville: Abingdon, 1970), 1:191.

the God of the Old Testament, the applicability of Old Testament messianic passages to Jesus, and the genuineness of the humanity of Jesus. This nascent form of orthodoxy did not lack capable defenders, and Origen possibly knew the articulate anti-Gnostic work by Irenaeus.[18] When the second-century heresiologists had no further answers to the Gnostics' questions about the character and work of God, after exposing the principal inconsistencies and absurdities of the heretical system, the Fathers resorted to denying the Gnostics their right to use Scripture, extolling the virtues of simple faith. Both Irenaeus and Tertullian contended that there were many questions that really should not be raised. If Irenaeus, the finest defender of orthodoxy in the second century and the able articulator of the hermeneutical framework, the rule of faith, found himself reduced to such a position, we can imagine that others in the church retreated even more quickly. This approach was not satisfactory for the Alexandrians, particularly Origen. The Alexandrians did not think it was sufficient to expose the flaws of Marcion, Valentinus, and other Gnostics, if perhaps the faith professed and taught was similarly untenable. The answer was found in a comprehensive hermeneutical system. This system attempted to retain the rule of faith as well as both Testaments of the biblical canon while simultaneously seeking to meet the challenges raised by the Gnostics.[19]

The Alexandrians were exposed to Christianity, Hellenistic philosophy, and Gnosticism, seemingly conflicting systems. Like Philo and Judaism, so with the Christian church at Alexandria: there was a strong commitment to the reliability of Scripture. Also, in line with Christian tradition, the Alexandrians maintained the primacy of the rule of faith.[20] But as far as Hellenistic thought was concerned, the Christian rule of faith was just one more barbarian superstition.[21] The Bible, measured by Greek aesthetic standards, was not worthy of serious study because none of its books conformed to accepted genres or acceptable literary Greek. Gnosticism not only raised questions, but provided answers for matters that the rule of faith did not even envision, thus either dismissing or transforming accepted biblical interpretation. The Alexandrians' intellectual commitments

18. Allain Le Boullvec suggests Origen knew Irenaeus's work. See "Ya-t-il des traces de la polemigue antignostigue d' Irenee dans le *Peri Archon* d'Origene?" in *Gnosis and Gnosticism*, ed. Martin Krause (Leiden: Brill, 1977), 138–47.

19. Cf. Hanson, *Allegory and Event*, 237–38; J. N. D. Kelly, *Early Christian Doctrines*, 4th rev. ed. (San Francisco: Harper and Row, 1978), 73.

20. Michael W. Holmes, "Origen and the Inerrancy of Scripture," *JETS* 24 (1981): 221–32. A study that disputes that Origen had any intention of maintaining an ecclesiastical norm in his teaching is Franz Heinrich Kettler, *Der ursprungliche Sinn der Dogmatik des Origenes*, *BZNW* 31 (Berlin: Topelmann, 1966).

21. Trigg, *Origen*, 52.

demanded that they attempt to deal with these issues in a manner superior to the approach of Irenaeus. Just as Philo had sought to reconcile Judaism with Hellenism, particularly Platonism, so Clement and Origen turned to Platonic philosophy and allegorical hermeneutics to handle the pressing objections to the rule of faith and the Bible.[22]

The Art and Science of Allegorical Hermeneutics

The methods of exegesis adopted in the preceding periods were primarily of two types: (1) the literal and (2) the typological, with a christological emphasis. By literal interpretation, we are referring to the communicative value that belongs to a statement in its own sociocultural context, whether regarded as the "author's intention" or the "original hearers' understanding."[23] The literal meaning was primarily employed in passages dealing with moral issues, while typological hermeneutics worked along very different lines. Following the example of Jesus and the apostles, the church fathers practiced a hermeneutical technique for bringing out the correspondence between the two Testaments and took as its guiding principle the idea that the events and personages of the Old Testament prefigured and anticipated the events and personages of the New. The typologist took history seriously; it was the scene of the progressive unfolding of God's consistent redemptive purpose. It was assumed that the same redemptive plan could be discerned in the sacred history from creation to judgment, the former stages serving as shadows of the latter. Christ was the ultimate climax; because God in his dealings with humankind was leading to this point, it seemed appropriate to find typological pictures or pointers in the experiences and events of the chosen nation.[24]

There was, however, an approach separate and distinct from either the literal or typological that had been practiced in an infant manner: allegorical interpretation. Already in the Epistle of Barnabas, a century prior to

22. Cf. G. W. H. Lampe, "Christian Theology in the Patristic Period," in *A History of Christian Doctrine*, ed. Hubert Cunliffe-Jones with Benjamin Drewery (Philadelphia: Fortress, 1978), 64–84.

23. We are dependent upon the discussion in Dan E. McCartney, "Literal and Allegorical Interpretation in Origen's *Contra Celsum*," *WTJ* 48 (1986): 281–301, especially n. 17. By the definition offered in the text, an allegorical meaning could also be the literal meaning if the text in its original setting indicated that it was of an allegorical genre. The degree to which it is possible to recover the literal meaning, and the degree of certainty one may have regarding this recovery, are additional questions beyond our concerns. For an excellent overview of Origen's excessive allegorical interpretations, see Charles J. Scalise, "Allegorical Flights of Fancy: The Problem of Origen's Exegesis," *GOTR* 32 (1987): 69–88.

24. Kelly, *Early Christian Doctrines*, 70–71.

Origen, an Alexandrian type of allegorical exegesis had been practiced. Dan E. McCartney has also discovered what he believes to be an allegorical approach in Justin Martyr's hermeneutic of apologetics,[25] but probably it is best understood as an excess of the typological method when synthesized with his philosophical theology.[26] By the third century, the Alexandrian church was probably caught between a desire to maintain the historical reality of the gospel events and the need to contextualize the gospel or to experience it in a modern way. The Alexandrian fathers, Clement and Origen, obviously felt this tension, as is evidenced by Origen's attempt to defend the literal interpretation in *De Principiis (On First Principles)*. They also advocated the validity of allegorical hermeneutics, unlike those who decried such a practice because it was a method completely accepted by the Valentinians. We shall now see how the Alexandrians wrestled with these tensions while shifting the hermeneutical paradigm beyond the authoritative framework of Irenaeus.

Clement of Alexandria

His Background

Titus Flavius Clement (ca. A.D. 150–215), considered by many to be the first Christian scholar, became the leader of the Alexandrian school in A.D. 190, a position he held until after the turn of the century. His principal literary works produced during this time were the trilogy of *Protrepticus (Exhortations to Conversion)*, the *Paidagogus (The Tutor)* and *Stromateis (Miscellanies)*. The Logos, according to Clement, first of all converts us, then disciplines us, and finally instructs us.[27]

25. McCartney, "Literal and Allegorical Interpretation," 285.

26. Cf. Oskar Skarsaune, *Proof from Prophecy: A Study in Justin Martyr's Proof-Text Tradition* (Leiden: Brill, 1987).

27. Cf. R. Seeburg, *Textbook of the History of Doctrines*, trans. C. E. Hay, 2 vols. (Grand Rapids: Baker, 1977), 1:142; Jean Daniélou, "Typologie et allegorie chez Clement d'Alexandrie," *StPat* 4 (1959): 50–57. For centuries, scholars have generally assumed that Clement wrote these texts in some kind of literary relationship to each other. They assumed that the purpose of the "trilogy" was to provide the reader with a complete profile of instruction leading to the higher theology which Clement understood as Christian knowledge. No scholar or commentator, however, has actually ever been successful in attempting to prove by means of internal evidence that these compositions were originally intended to be linked together as a trilogy. In recent years, Clementine research has begun to question whether it might be the case that the *Protrepticus*, the *Paidagogus*, and the *Stromateis* in fact were written independently. These questions are beyond the scope of this chapter. For an examination of the evidence, see John K. Brackett, "An Analysis of the Literary Structure and Forms in the Protrepticus and Paidagogus of Clement of Alexandria" (Ph.D. diss., Emory University, 1986); Walter Wagner, "Another Look at the Literary Problem in Clement of Alexandria's Major Writings," *CH* 37 (1968): 251–62.

His Hermeneutical Approach

Clement, Origen's predecessor at Alexandria, found a solution to the tension faced by the church by seeing the literal meaning as a "starting point," suitable for the mass of Christians, and as something that piques the curiosity of the more spiritually advanced. He suggested that "finding the deeper meaning is thus the process by which God gradually, by means of parable and metaphor, leads those to whom God would reveal himself from the sensible to the intelligible world."[28] It is clear that the Alexandrians lived in a complex hermeneutical environment. Out of this environment Clement began to forge a hermeneutical methodology. He believed that in every text there was always one or more additional or deeper meanings beyond and above its primary or immediate sense. These deeper meanings were to be uncovered through allegorical interpretation. This method insisted that the literal sense, particularly of historical passages, did not exhaust the divinely purposed meaning of such passages, but that they also included a deeper, higher, spiritual, and mystical sense. The literal sense indicated what was said or done, while the allegorical showed what should be believed. The allegorical approach, then, was adopted for apologetical and theological purposes.

Clement believed that this method should be used because God's bountifulness was such that it would be folly to believe that there could only be one teaching in a particular text.[29] He maintained that God is so loving and merciful that in the same text he can reveal himself from the wise to the ignorant, speaking to them at whatever level of perception each group of believers possessed. The first of his hermeneutical principles, then, included two levels: first, the literal sense must be observed, and then, the allegorical sense must be discovered. Yet, this allegorical interpretation must not discard the primary meaning of the text unless such meaning violated what was previously known of God's character and dignity. Neither was this first principle one which was a boundless allegorism, for the rule of faith still provided a framework for interpretation.[30] In fact, there were many cases where the levels of interpretation were blended so that the resulting exegesis was typological rather than allegorical.

Clement occasionally echoed the ideas of Tertullian, making the rule of faith the norm for the interpretation of Scripture, and maintained that since the Logos himself has descended from heaven there was no need to run to Athens in pursuit of human wisdom.[31] Yet Clement's approach to

28. Clement *Miscellanies* 6.15.126.

29. Cf. Danielou, "Typologie et allegorie," 51–53.

30. Cf. Rowan A. Greer, "A Framework for Interpreting a Christian Bible," in *Early Biblical Interpretation,* 155–76; idem, "Applying the Framework," *Early Biblical Interpretation,* 177–99.

31. Clement *Miscellanies* 7.16.94.

the question of authority in religion was generally quite different from Tertullian's. He concerned himself very little with the hierarchically organized church and its successions of accredited teachers passing on the apostolic doctrine in the apostolic sees. Likewise, in contrast to Tertullian, he welcomed the insights of Platonic philosophy as a propaedeutic by which minds can be trained to receive the full truth revealed by Christ.[32]

Clement contended that Platonism was given to the Greeks as preparation for the coming of Christ and the calling of the Christian community, just as the Mosaic law was given to the Jews for the same purpose.[33] The knowledge of truth gained by the philosophers was incomplete and partial.[34] Yet, even if Platonism did not grasp the truth, and failed to supply strength to obey the Lord's commands, it did nevertheless prepare the way for the supremely royal teaching.[35] From this expansion of the rule of faith by the use of Platonism, Clement expanded the hermeneutical insights of the early church.

Clement's second principle was that each text should be interpreted in the light of the rest of Scripture. This step involved understanding a text in its immediate context and beyond, seeing how similar ideas, words, things, names, and numbers are understood and then transposing that sense to the text currently under consideration. It was at this point that Clement's exegesis often resulted in its most extravagant interpretations, following Philo, using etymology and numerology to discover or create meanings.[36]

Like his predecessors, Clement aimed to show how Christ was the supreme source and content of knowledge in its most profound sense. In using the Old Testament, his approach was that Christ has spoken in the Old Testament, and that what he said there was both anterior to, and the source for, all that was best in Greek philosophy.

Clement's *Paidagogus* presented the divine Word as the teacher and trainer of humankind from the beginning. He acknowledged, "Our Instructor is the holy God Jesus, the Word, who is the guide of all humanity. The living God himself is our Instructor."[37] The Alexandrian theologian contended that the divine Word was the Instructor of Abraham, Jacob, and Moses, and he emphasized that according to John 1:17, the law was given

32. Ibid., 1.19.92.
33. Ibid., 6.18.159.
34. Ibid., 6.18.160.
35. Ibid., 1.16.80.
36. John Rogerson, Christopher Rowland, and Barnabas Lindars, *The Study and Use of the Bible*, vol. 2 of *The History of Christian Theology*, ed. Paul Avis, 3 vols. (Grand Rapids: Eerdmans, 1988), 28–29. See also Edwin Hatch, *The Influence of Greek Ideas and Usages on Christianity* (New York: Harper, 1957).
37. Clement *The Tutor* 1.7.

through Moses, not *by* Moses.[38] Thus, Clement affirmed the highest possible view of the Mosaic law because it was the teaching of the divine Word, the Logos, himself. The law is not the cause of sin but a revealer of sin when the law is disobeyed.[39] It is not contrary to the gospel but in harmony with it, and therefore binding upon all. Thus, according to Clement, the Mosaic law was the source of the laws formulated by Plato.[40]

Not every part of the Mosaic law, however, was to be interpreted in the same way. Clement, therefore, divided the Mosaic writings into four aspects:

> the historic, and that which is specially called the legislative, which two properly belong to an ethical treatise; and the third, that which relates to sacrifice, which belongs to a physical science; and the fourth, above all, the department of theology, the vision.[41]

Usually, the historic part of the Pentateuch was interpreted literally and the other parts were assigned a spiritual or an allegorical meaning. Yet, examples of allegorical interpretation of historical narratives can certainly be found.[42] In many cases, Clement applied the spirit of the law to form the basis for Christian and spiritual obedience.[43] For instance, in dealing with the clean and unclean beasts he said, "The Instructor, by Moses, deprived them [the Jews] of the use of innumerable things, adding reasons—the spiritual ones hidden; the carnal ones apparent, to which indeed they have trusted."[44] The hidden meaning of the division between clean and unclean creatures, discovered by his allegorical interpretation, was interpreted to be the distinction between the church and heretics.

Clement, in interpreting the story of Abraham, Sarah, and Hagar (Gen. 16), understood Abraham's choice for Hagar as an example of choosing only what was profitable from Platonic philosophy, and when Abraham said to Sarah, "Your servant is in your hands" (Gen. 16:6), it meant that Abraham embraced secular culture as a handmaid, but God's knowledge he honored and reverenced as a true wife.[45]

38. Ibid.
39. Clement *Miscellanies* 2.7.
40. Ibid., 1.25.
41. Ibid., 1.28.
42. Ibid., 1.21.
43. Ibid., 2.18, 23; *The Tutor* 2.10.
44. Clement *The Tutor* 2.1.
45. For Clement as well as Origen, allegorical hermeneutics were more commonly employed in the Old Testament than the New. His reading of Paul, for example, was more consistently literal, or in line with the historical meaning.

With Clement, a point of unifying harmony was reached between the Testaments through his implementation of Platonic thought and allegorical exegesis. The tension between law and gospel was eliminated because the same Instructor gave both, not merely to Israel and the church, but to all men and women.[46]

The goal of interpretation was to obtain "true gnosis," including both intellectual as well as ethical qualities, in contrast to the "false gnosis" of the Gnostic heretics. Allegorical interpretation along with Platonic dialectics and personal inspiration were the means by which true gnosis was achieved.[47] His methods and aims, allowing for the distinction between Christian and Jew, were Philo's: (1) apologetic in the face of pagan philosophical polemics in Alexandria, with which the old christocentric typology could not cope; and (2) an allegorical interpretation that went beyond, and sometimes evidenced complete disregard for, the literal-historic sense. Thanks to allegorical hermeneutics, Clement was able to accept the Scripture without surrendering his broad and universalistic outlook. Grant has analyzed five ways that Clement interpreted Scripture: (1) historically, (2) doctrinally, (3) prophetically, (4) philosophically, and (5) mystically.[48] Of these, the historical and doctrinal were fairly literal, the prophetic was typological in the tradition of the apostles and the Fathers, and the philosophical and mystical were allegorical after the manner of the Stoics and Philo. In Clement's exegesis the allegorical was certainly uppermost.[49]

Clement's hermeneutical approach has been evaluated differently by scholars of various traditions. For some, he was a praiseworthy pioneer breaking free from a hampering authoritative traditionalism, boldly putting the meaning of Scripture in contemporary forms and making significant breakthroughs into educational circles. For others, he was a man of compromise, wedding Scripture with forms of Platonic philosophy and Gnosticism. A better evaluation is that Clement's approach had ultimately a strategic rather than a material character. It is important to see how Origen implemented this strategy to raise allegorical interpretation to new heights.

46. Clement *Miscellanies* 1.21.

47. Cf. Walter Wagner, "The Paideia Motif in the Theology of Clement of Alexandria" (Ph.D. diss., Drew University, 1968).

48. Grant with Tracy, *Short History of the Interpretation of the Bible,* 64.

49. We have noted that Clement did employ the literal sense, so by claiming that the allegorical was uppermost, it is not a disavowal of the literal sense. Rather amusingly, in *Miscellanies* 12.16 Clement attacks the heretics for their misuses of Scripture, accusing them of "not looking to the sense but making use of the mere diction" and of altering the "natural" meaning of texts. These sound all too much like Clement's own practices. Perhaps it indicates that Irenaeus was right. An authoritative interpretation is needed that goes beyond hermeneutical guidelines. A creedal statement of faith in Christ, in his person and work, is the sufficient key to Scripture. Cf. the discussion in Gerhard Delling, *"Stoicheo," TDNT,* 7:666–69.

Origen

His Background

Origen (ca. A.D. 185–254) was undoubtedly the prince of Christian allegorical interpreters, its most extensive practitioner and its most adequate exponent. Most of the information about the life of Origen can be located in the sixth book of Eusebius's *Ecclesiastical History*. Origen, born in Egypt, studied under Clement in the school of Alexandria. He followed Clement as the leader and primary teacher in this school, a position he held for twenty-eight years while pursuing an ascetic and extremely pious life. In his early manhood, he sought literally to obey the teachings of Matthew 19:12: "For some are eunuchs because they were born that way; others were made that way by men; and others have made themselves eunuchs because of the kingdom of heaven. The one who can accept this should accept it." In order to obey this teaching, he castrated himself, probably so that he could instruct his female students without fear of scandal. Thousands came to hear him. According to tradition, a wealthy convert hired secretaries to write down his lectures and then published them. This accounts for his prolific literary accomplishments (more than two thousand different works). Having studied with the father of neo-Platonic thought, Ammonius Saccus, his work was greatly influenced by this approach.[50]

His Hermeneutical Approach

Origen's linguistic and textual equipment was unrivaled; his mastery of the whole realm of contemporary learning was unsurpassed. Yet, because of his neo-Platonic bias, even when he brought the whole weight of his scholarly gifts to the biblical text, he often failed to appreciate the biblical writer's sense of history.

Although Origen was far from being literalistic in his interpretation of the sacred text, he strongly affirmed the literal inspiration of every word of Scripture.[51] The most obviously determinative, explicit assumption Origen made regarding the biblical text was that it is of divine origin. In *Against Celsus*, Origen maintained, "For it was fitting that the creator of the whole world should have appointed laws for the whole world and given a power to the words that was able to overcome men everywhere."[52] And in another passage he said, "The Logos of God arranged the scriptures and spoke them."[53] R. P. C. Hanson cites A. Zollig: "For Origen, holy scripture has a divine nature, and this not simply because it contains divine ideas,

50. Walter Bauer, *Orthodoxy and Heresy in Earliest Christianity*, ed. Robert Kraft and Gerhard Krodel (Philadelphia: Fortress, 1971), 59. Many of his writings were lost due to a later condemnation by the emperor Justinian I in 543.

51. Hanson, *Allegory and Event*, 187.

52. Origen *Against Celsus* 1.18.

53. Ibid., 4.71.

nor because the breath of the divine Spirit breathes in its lines . . . but because it has God as its author."[54] For this reason Origen took the task of restoring the original biblical text and interpreting it as so important.[55]

The literal sense of Scripture, however, was not necessarily the primary sense. Like Clement, Origen thought it absurd that a God-inspired Scripture should not be interpreted in a spiritual manner, which meant finding the deeper meaning in the text. From this supposition Origen developed a threefold hermeneutical approach. He thought that Scripture had three different, yet complementary, meanings; (1) a literal or physical sense, (2) a moral or psychical sense, and (3) an allegorical or intellectual sense. The threefold sense was based upon his belief in a corresponding threefold division of humankind: (1) the physical, (2) the emotional or psychical, and (3) the spiritual or intellectual.[56] In classifying the different senses, he followed Clement and Philo, though he adopted three senses instead of the prior two. Yet in his spiritualization of Scripture, he often "out Philos Philo."[57] Rarely did he develop his exegesis in a systematic manner based upon the threefold meaning of the text. Generally, he worked with just two meanings: the literal and the spiritual. Moreover, there are places where he found numerous spiritual meanings in a single text, thus creating an entire scale of allegorical interpretations.[58]

54. Hanson, *Allegory and Event,* 187–88, citing and translating A. Zollig, *Die Inspirationslehre des Origenes* (Freiburg: Strassburger Theologische Studien, 1902), 13–15.

55. Cf. Rogerson, *The Study and Use of the Bible,* 34–35, where he discusses Origen as text-critic. He says, "The early fathers read the Old Testament not in Hebrew, but in the Greek translation that derived from the work of Jewish scholars in Alexandria, which was known as the Septuagint (LXX). Origen appears to have learned sufficient Hebrew to enable him to appreciate the considerable differences that existed at some points between the Hebrew Bible and the Septuagint that conformed as closely as possible to the Hebrew, but without undermining the authority that the Septuagint had come to have for the church. Origen, while at Caesarea, compiled his *Hexapla.* This massive work, estimated to be 6,500 pages long, set out in six parallel columns the Hebrew, a transliteration of the Hebrew into Greek, and the translation of Aquila and Symmachus, the Septuagint, and the translation of Theodotion. In some sections the number of columns was reduced to five, in others it was enlarged to seven or eight, and in the case of the enlargement Origen utilized translations that he had discovered in his travels, including one discovered near Jericho, and possibly concealed in a wine jar. A work called the *Tetrapla,* containing the four columns of the four principal Greek versions was compiled either before or after the *Hexapla.* Where the Septuagint contained material not in the Hebrew, or lacked what was in the Hebrew, the fifth column was marked with text-critical signs derived from Alexandrian practice."

56. Origen *First Principles* 4.2.4–17; cf. Kelly, *Early Christian Doctrines,* 70–75; cf. Robert M. Grant, *The Letter and the Spirit* (New York: Macmillan, 1957). Origen based this upon his translation of Proverbs 22:20, "write them in a threefold way."

57. Hanson, *Allegory and Event,* 237.

58. R. J. Daly, "The Hermeneutics of Origen: Existential Interpretation of the Third Century," in *The Word in the World* (Cambridge: Weston College Press, 1973), 135–44.

It is extremely problematic to enumerate the principles behind Origen's hermeneutical procedure. Gonzalez has perceptively enumerated the foundations of this procedure. First, every text is pregnant with profound mysteries and should be discovered through allegory. Second, nothing should be said of God which is unworthy of him. Third, each text was to be interpreted in the light of the rest of Scripture. Finally, nothing contrary to the rule of faith was to be affirmed.[59] While some in the history of the church have regarded Origen's approach as heretical,[60] his brilliance and groundbreaking work cannot be ignored. It should also be noted that Origen affirmed the primary doctrines of the Christian tradition[61] and felt no freedom to deny the essence of the rule of faith.[62] Therefore, as we shall see, the rule of faith served to keep his interpretation—at least in part—within the sphere of the traditional doctrine of the church. Because of Origen's prominence and importance, it will be necessary to analyze his hermeneutical approach more extensively than that of any other individual in this work. Having summarized his foundational principles, we can now look more carefully at his method and purpose.

An Analysis of His Hermeneutical Method

Karen Jo Torjesen has identified a pattern present in Origen's exegetical method, regardless of the genre of Scripture being interpreted. These steps can be distinguished and identified in terms of the question which is posed to derive each step. In the initial step Origen queried, What is the grammatical or literal sense of the text? Included in this step was the question, What is the historical reality to which the grammatical sense refers? Second, he asked, What is the allegorical sense of the passage, which he understood as the intention of the Holy Spirit, in Scripture? Third, Origen questioned, What is the role of church tradition or other Scripture in understanding a text?[63] We shall now look at Origen's approach to these three questions.

59. Gonzalez, *History of Christian Thought,* 1:220; cf. Lampe, "Christian Theology in the Patristic Period," 69–73.

60. See the different evaluations in Jean Daniélou, *Origen,* trans. Walter Mitchell (New York: Sheed and Ward, 1955); Hanson, *Allegory and Event;* Maurice F. Wiles, "Origen as Biblical Scholar," *CHB,* 1:454–88; and the initial chapter in Karen Jo Torjesen, "Hermeneutical Procedure and Theological Structure in Origen's Exegesis" (Ph.D. diss., Claremont Graduate School, 1982). See also Gary W. Barkley, "Origen's Homilies on Leviticus: An Annotated Translation" (Ph.D. diss., The Southern Baptist Theological Seminary, 1984).

61. For more on this matter, see R. P. C. Hanson, *Origen's Doctrine of Tradition* (London: SPCK, 1954).

62. Albert C. Outler, "Origen and the *Regula Fidei,*" *CH* 8 (1939): 212–21.

63. Torjesen, "Hermeneutical Procedure and Theological Structure in Origen's Exegesis," 255–56. I have adopted and modified Torjesen's questions based upon my own reading of Origen.

Literal Sense. With very few exceptions, Origen's interpretation began with the citation of the text. The grammatical sense of the text functioned as the foundation stone of the interpretation. Origen distinguished between the text as a written document, the letter, and the history or event that stood behind the text. The words of the text had a special meaning for Origen, for their origin rested in a historical spiritual process in the historical moment of inspiration. The words were chosen both by the human writer and by the Holy Spirit for one and the same purpose, which is to teach the mysteries of the Logos to the following generations. It was the very literalness of Scripture that demanded a referential meaning.[64] The referential meaning points to the reality to which the grammatical sense referred. These two aspects taken together constitute what Origen understood as the literal sense.

Perhaps the literal sense is one of the more neglected areas in the study of Origen. In his words, "The passages that are true in their historical meaning are much more numerous than those which are interspersed with a purely spiritual signification."[65] He certainly did not hesitate to regard much of the history recorded in the Old Testament as authentic, and he certainly accepted the moral teaching of Mosaic law, such as "honor your father and your mother" (Exod. 20:12), in its literal and grammatical sense.[66]

In *Contra Celsum (Against Celsus),* Origen identified three positive values for the literal meaning: (1) the Bible contains true and important history;[67] (2) the literal meaning has an edifying value for the simple;[68] and (3) the literal has an apologetic value in attracting people to study the Bible.[69] It should be noted that this set him apart from Philo. It seems that Philo, in spite of his attempt to preserve the literal meaning of the moral portions of Scripture, had virtually no sense of history.[70] For all Origen's desire to find deeper meanings, he was sensitive enough to the New Testament and its message that he recognized its historical foundations, though he did not hesitate to spiritualize its eschatology. Also, one of the functions of the literal sense, according to Origen, was to attract people to a study of the Bible so that they may proceed to the allegorical meaning of texts.[71]

64. Hanson, *Allegory and Event,* 187–89.
65. Origen *First Principles* 4.1; 3.4.
66. Ibid., 4.1.
67. Origen *Against Celsus* 3.43.
68. Ibid., 1.17; 18; 27.
69. Ibid., 7.60.
70. Hanson, *Allegory and Event,* 52.
71. Cf. McCartney, "Literal and Allegorical Interpretation," 287–89. My understanding of Origen on this point has been greatly enhanced by McCartney's work.

Spiritual Sense. The movement to the spiritual meaning of the text involved a shift to another plan that included both moral and allegorical interpretations. Origen assumed that generally there must be some correspondence between the literal and spiritual meanings of Scripture.[72] For the allegorical to be true, the literal should also be true. At this step of interpretation, there was a concern for the realm of spiritual and eternal realities. Torjesen has described the two techniques Origen followed in moving from the level of the literal to the spiritual.[73] The first can be observed if it can be remembered that the literal sense was representative of the spiritual realities; then the allegorical functioned as a natural step to discovering the level of the spiritual and eternal.

In his interpretation of Jeremiah 1:10, Origen commented that Jeremiah "received the word of God in order to tear down and destroy nations and kingdoms."[74] The text in Jeremiah reads:

> See, today I appoint you over nations and kingdoms to uproot and tear down, to destroy and overthrow, to build and to plant.

Origen noted, "The nations and kingdoms should not be thought of as physical (*somatikos*), but rather allegorically (*Tropologein*) as the kingdom and nations of sin."[75] In this case the terms *kingdom* and *nations* have a historical reference on the level of the literal-grammatical sense and have an allegorical meaning on the level of the spiritual sense. That a single term contained the potential of a double reference made the allegorical transposition possible.

The second way in which Origen made the progression from the literal to the spiritual can also be illustrated from his *Homily on Jeremiah.*[76] The first three verses of Jeremiah 1 describe the time during which Jeremiah prophesied, from the reign of Josiah to the reign of Zedekiah up until the time of the captivity of Jerusalem. Origen interpreted the literal sense by showing what historical questions should be answered (*historia*). Following this, he sought to discover the spiritual (*To Boulema*). He noted,

> God had judged Jerusalem on account of her sins and sentenced her to be delivered into captivity, and when it was impending God in his love for men as before, sent this prophet in the third reign before the captivity, so that

72. Ibid., 289–90.

73. Torjesen, "Hermeneutical Procedure and Theological Structure in Origen's Exegesis," 263–66.

74. Origen *Homily on Jeremiah* 1.7.

75. Ibid.

76. Ibid., 1.1.

> those willing to reconsider might repent through the ministry of the prophetic word.[77]

The second approach was not an allegorical transposition, but rather was accomplished simply by historical generalization. There was no double meaning of the terms in this example, but an attempt to see what the historical revealed about the nature of God and the form of his dealings with humanity.

For Origen, like the Hellenistic world at large, all divine texts were regarded as bearing an allegorical meaning. Not only was this true, but for a text to be divine, it must bear an allegorical meaning. If a text cannot be interpreted allegorically, it must then be relegated to a state of unimportance.[78] Therefore, if a text is divine, it must be interpreted allegorically.

In Origen's polemic against Celsus, the arguments were concerned with these matters. Celsus found fault with Christians for interpreting the Old Testament allegorically.[79] Origen brilliantly responded that Celsus had not played fairly by saying that "the Bible cannot be inspired because it cannot be interpreted allegorically and it cannot be interpreted allegorically because it is not inspired."[80] This was likened by Origen to Trasymachus' restrictions on Socrates which made the true answer an impossibility to provide. Of course, Origen was also guilty of circular reasoning by affirming Scripture's inspiration by the fact that it contained a hidden sense and that he knew that it had a hidden sense because it was inspired.[81]

Origen shared Clement's view that the deeper meanings derived from allegorical interpretation were for the spiritually mature.[82] Origen's hermeneutical procedure, as we have noted, was built upon the concept of a double meaning of texts. Many have two meanings: one for the weak and one for the intelligent; and often in the same text both were present for those who knew how to hear it.[83] For Origen, the ability to interpret allegorically was a mark of intelligence and spirituality.[84]

This double meaning of Scripture indicated that often things were communicated to the immature which may not be actually true but nevertheless are designed for their good.[85] At the point where Scripture's descrip-

77. Ibid.
78. Origen *Against Celsus* 4.49.
79. Ibid., 1.17.
80. Ibid.
81. Ibid., 1.17; 26.
82. Cf. Clement *Miscellanies* 6.15; cf. Origen *First Principles* 4.2.
83. Origen *Against Celsus* 4.71.
84. Ibid., 1.27.
85. Ibid., 4.71.

tion of God appeared contrary to Origen's presuppositions, he was forced to shift from the text's literal sense to the spiritual. He thought, for example, that descriptions of God's wrath were designed for immature believers.[86] At this point the literal meaning was forced to give way to the allegorical because when the literal sense does not conform to preconceived proper expectations, the literal was understood as being a form of accommodation to the weak, and was thus rather facilely abandoned. Origen explained,

> These truths were proclaimed still under the form of a story because they were children . . . but now to those who seek for the meaning and wish to advance in it, what hither to were myths, if I may use the word, have been transformed into the inner truth which had been hidden from them.[87]

This easily made it possible to eliminate difficulties raised by those who challenged orthodoxy, but it certainly created the possibility for Origen to be charged with what he wished to avoid, namely, that Christians were quick to flee to allegorical interpretation.[88] But Origen defended his usage because he believed it was used by the ancients, Jesus, and the apostles.[89] The allegorical approach was an extension of the church's christological interpretation, for the deeper meaning that Origen sought was christocentric. For Origen, Christ was the center of history and the key to under-

86. Ibid., 5.16; cf. Gillian R. Evans, "Patristic and Medieval Theology," in *The Science of Theology*, by Gillian R. Evans, Alister E. McGrath, and Allan D. Galloway, vol. 1 of *The History of Christian Theology*, ed. Paul Avis, 3 vols. (Grand Rapids: Eerdmans, 1986), 32–38.

87. Origen *Against Celsus* 5.42.

88. Origen would later be criticized by Methodius (d. A.D. 311) and others, especially the Reformers in the sixteenth century. Cf. R. F. Surburg, "The Significance of Luther's Hermeneutics for the Protestant Reformation," *CTM* 24 (1954): 241–61; J. W. Aldridge, *The Hermeneutics of Erasmus* (Richmond: John Knox, 1966); A. Skevington Wood, *Luther's Principles of Biblical Interpretation* (London: Tyndale, 1960).

89. A common charge against Christianity was that it was a recent innovation, and Origen defended Christianity and his allegorical interpretation simultaneously in *Against Celsus* 4.21. Here he appealed to Moses' antiquity (that he was older than Homer or Socrates) and also to the Psalms ("I will open my mouth in parables," Ps. 78:2) as an indication that the prophets spoke allegorically (*Against Celsus* 4.49). He appealed to another psalm, "Open my eyes that I might behold wondrous things out of your law" (Ps. 119:18), as proof that the ancient prophets regarded the Torah as containing hidden truth (*Against Celsus* 2.6; 3:45). He appealed to Paul's usage of *allegoreō* in Galatians 4 (*Against Celsus* 4.44), and finally, Origen appealed to Jesus himself since he spoke in parables (allegories) and showed the disciples the hidden meaning of God's redemptive program in Luke 24 (*Against Celsus* 4.42). I have discussed the distinction between allegory and allegorical interpretation in chapter 1, a distinction blurred by Origen and others as well (James Barr, *Old and New in Interpretation: A Study of the Two Testaments* [London: SCM, 1966], 103–48). The distinction between *theoria* as typological or allegorical will be discussed in chapter 4.

standing the Old Testament. Christ had superseded the laws and ceremonies of the Old Testament, and the literal approach to its meaning had to be changed. Old Testament events, people, and rules were really images or reflections of Christ or the body of Christ, and the allegorical method revealed this truth. The spiritual meaning of Scripture in turn provided the principles and methods that should govern the believers between Christ's appearance in the New Testament and his second coming. Origen's allegorical interpretation was generally limited only by his imagination. There were, however, other parameters or safeguards that he established for himself: (1) the Scripture itself and (2) the church's rule of faith.

Scripture and Tradition. While Augustine of Hippo is generally credited with the phrase *scriptura scripturam interpretatur*, the idea was implicit in Origen. He indicated that one must interpret obscure passages on the basis of more clear texts, comparing text with text. He insisted that Scripture be taken not piecemeal but as a whole, commenting, "Every interpretation which is outside scripture is not holy. . . . No one can bring his own interpretations unless he shall have shown them to be holy, from that which is contained in the divine scriptures."[90] Included then in Origen's hermeneutical method was the concept that the guardian of scriptural interpretation is the Scripture itself.

The church's faith, contained in the rule of faith, served as the ultimate framework for Origen. While not abandoning intellectual rigor and calling upon a new tool, allegorical hermeneutics, Origen, like Irenaeus and Tertullian, had to struggle with the theological system of Gnosticism. Origen, as a champion of traditional orthodoxy, maintained that allegorical interpretation must be according to the rule of faith, which probably included the following items:

1. *A doctrine of God.* There is one God the Father, who created the universe and governs it by providence. Worship is due to God alone, who gave the law to the Jews and sent his son Jesus Christ to redeem the world.
2. *A doctrine of Christ.* Jesus Christ, the Messiah whom the Old Testament foretold, was a man born of Mary, who as a virgin miraculously conceived him. In Palestine he taught and performed miracles, was crucified under Pontius Pilate, died, and was buried. He descended into hell to liberate the righteous dead. He rose from the dead, appeared to his disciples, and ascended into heaven, where he reigns with God the Father. Christ will return to judge the

90. Origen *Commentary on Matthew* 2.18; cf. Wiles, "Origen as Biblical Scholar," *CHB*, 1:485–89; and Karen Jo Torjesen, "Origen's Interpretation of the Psalms," *StPat* 18 (1982): 144–58.

living and the newly resurrected dead. Jesus Christ is divine and hence worthy of worship but not identical with God the Father.
3. *A doctrine of the Spirit.* God's Spirit inspired the prophets and apostles who wrote the Bible and continues to animate believers.
4. *A doctrine of spiritual beings.* There are rational beings not confined, as we are, to earthly bodies. Some are angels who worship God and carry out God's commands. Others are demons—probably fallen angels—who follow the commands of Satan, their prince. The demons disguise themselves as gods, thereby deceiving the pagans into sustaining them with sacrifices, and they seek to entice believers into heresy and sin.
5. *A doctrine of last things.* At the end of time, God will destroy the world he made. When this happens, all the dead will resume their bodies, and Christ will then welcome the righteous into everlasting happiness and condemn the wicked, along with Satan and the demons, to everlasting torment.
6. *A doctrine of sacraments.* Baptism, a ritual washing with water, obtains forgiveness of all sins committed prior to it. The eucharist, a ritual meal celebrated with bread and wine, is a communion in the body and blood of Christ that obtains immortality for all who partake of it worthily.[91]

As can be seen, Origen provided the fullest systematic version of the *regula fidei.* The church's response to Marcion and the Gnostics in the latter half of the second century and the early third century accounts for this important development in the *regula fidei* itself and in biblical interpretation in general. Contrary to Adolf von Harnack's contention that Origen recast the rule of faith, it is best to see, following Albert C. Outler, that he attempted deliberately to sum up all doctrinal points on which there was general agreement in the church.[92] It is very important to observe in *De Principiis* (preface 4 and 5) that Origen clearly distinguished between what he designated as "necessary" doctrines, which the apostles "delivered" in plainest terms to all believers, and other doctrines. The necessary doctrines concerned God the Father, Jesus Christ, and the Holy Spirit. This threefold structure of necessary doctrines corresponded to the threefold baptismal formula of Matthew 28. Within Origen's discussion of these doctrines can be found all that is essential to the rule of faith as defined by

91. Trigg, *Origen,* 13–14.
92. Outler, "Origen and the *Regula Fidei,*" 220; cf. P. M. O'Cleirigh, "The Meaning of Dogma in Origen," in *Jewish and Christian Self-Definition, I: The Shaping of Christianity in the Second and Third Centuries,* ed. J. Sanders (Philadelphia: Fortress, 1980), 201–16.

the usage of Irenaeus, Tertullian, and Clement of Alexandria, and which even had traces in *1 Clement.*

In *1 Clement,* however, the essentials of the *regula* were certainly not so systematized as in Origen's preface to *First Principles.* There was obvious development between *1 Clement* and Origen. The emergence of Marcion and succeeding Gnostics can account for this development as the church responded more vigorously with each generation to the challenges to orthodoxy.

The Purpose of Origen's Hermeneutical Method

The ultimate purpose in Origen's biblical interpretation was his love for and nurture of the individual Christians under his care. He was deeply concerned with the formation of spiritual life. Origen maintained that each individual possesses a soul, which accounts for the multiple dimensions of the human personality and gives life to individuals. As such, the soul wills, feels, moves, and desires union. Origen considered the soul imperfect and thus inferior to mind or spirit, which allows for the human person to have a relationship with the creator God. The soul is, however, superior to the body that it inhabits. Since the soul is imperfect, being plagued by ignorance and inexperience, it needs to be trained to discern what can restore it to the original purpose of contemplating God. This training will enable it to perceive less through the bodily senses and more through the spiritual senses.[93]

Origen believed the source of spiritual training is the Bible, for in it God is at work revealing the path for the soul to return to God. Since Scripture is inspired, every word is carefully designed for the soul's progress. Moreover, as we have seen, because Scripture is inspired it has a deeper meaning than that which appeared on the surface. Thus he believed that Scripture contained a literal and a spiritual meaning. The literal sense attracted believers initially by its teachings on morals and behavior. Yet, as one advanced in virtuous living, one developed in ways that allowed the believer to understand the deeper or hidden truths within a text. At the spiritual level, the soul was trained to see that Scripture described the situation of souls in various degrees of spiritual maturation and that it imparted the truth necessary for such souls to attain maturity or perfection. Thus the soul was to begin and proceed on its journey for union with God through the interpretation of Scripture.[94]

93. See the creative work of Randy Lee Akers, "The Perfected Soul as an Exegetical Goal in Origen's Writings on the Song of Songs" (Ph.D. diss., Northwestern University, 1984), 130–33.

94. Ibid., 132; see also Torjesen, "Hermeneutical Procedure and Theological Structure in Origen's Exegesis," 266–74.

Two other purposes need to be mentioned briefly. One is that allegorical interpretation served as a source for inspired illustrations of doctrine.[95] The second purpose was to explain difficulties in Scripture or the doctrine of God. Above all, biblical interpretation was to show that all Scripture, even the seemingly irrelevant parts, communicated a contemporary sense and had something to teach the church.[96] Allegorical hermeneutics was ultimately an effective way to interpret ancient writings to communicate their contemporary relevance.

We have seen that Origen was ultimately a churchman and that, while he advanced over the authoritative exegesis of the second century with his creative hermeneutical procedure, there was some degree of tension between Origen's allegorical interpretation and the priority of the rule of faith. With Origen's followers, Athanasius, the Cappadocian fathers, and later with Augustine, there was a removal of the tension as a moderating theological exegesis began to dominate. Let us now briefly turn our attention to Athanasius, the Cappadocians, and Cyril of Alexandria to see the growing subordination of exegesis to creedal statement and ecclesiastical tradition.

Initial Response to Allegorical Hermeneutics: Toward a Theological Interpretation

We have observed that second- and third-century church fathers were guided in their hermeneutical practices by their loyalty to the rule of faith, which was crystallized in the creeds of the fourth and fifth centuries. But whereas Irenaeus and Tertullian were cautious in their speculation regarding the philosophical basis of faith, Origen was brilliant. His hermeneutical approach yielded both constructive solutions to the theological challenges, yet at points his work tended to undermine orthodoxy.

The theological problems of the latter third and fourth centuries sought a solid solution that Origen's creativity could not satisfy. Because the Gnostic systems made Christ an intermediary, rather than creator, thus something less than God and still different from humanity, the implications for the rule of faith had to be expounded more clearly. The issues came to a point of needing definition and clarification at the end of the third century. At this time Lucian of Antioch (ca. A.D. 240–312) founded the School of Antioch in conscious opposition to the excesses of Origenism.[97] The biblical realism of this school tended to accentuate the historical and human

95. Origen *Against Celsus* 4.13; 6.16.

96. Ibid., 6.4; 6.58.

97. Aloys Grillmeier, *Christ in Christian Tradition, vol. 1, From the Apostolic Age to Chalcedon (451)*, trans. John Bowden, 2d ed. (Atlanta: John Knox, 1974), 167–80.

aspects of Jesus, though his heavenly origin was not denied.[98] At this time Arius (d. A.D. 336), who may have been a pupil of Lucian, attempted to maintain monotheism by asserting that Jesus, as God's Son, was lower than God the Father, and indeed owed his existence to the Father's decision to produce the created order. This led to the Arian controversy, in which John 14:28, "The Father is greater than I," became a battleground text.[99]

The point at issue was hermeneutical: How should John 14:28 and similar texts be understood? The Arian view of Jesus was founded upon a literal interpretation of these passages. On the other hand Athanasius (ca. A.D. 296–373), the leading opponent of Arius, argued that theological talk about the nature of God could proceed only by way of analogy, so that it was not possible to construct theology by interpreting all of Scripture literally. The crux of the debate focused around the description of Jesus as *homoousios* (= of one nature, substance), which allowed a proper differentiation between Jesus and the Father, without necessitating an Arian subordinationism. The Arians suggested *homoiousios* (= of a similar nature, substance). Many disapproved of both terms on the grounds that they were unscriptural, tainted by previous use in some of the Gnostic systems and capable of doing injustice to both the equality and distinctions between the Father, Son, and Holy Spirit in the Godhead.[100]

Arianism was considered heretical and Athansius defended his orthodox view by appealing to the meaning of Scripture. He supported the idea of "one substance" (*homoousios*) as conveyed in Scripture in John 1:18; 6:46; 8:42; 10:30; and 14:10, even though the specific word, *homoousios,* was not found in Scripture.[101] Often Athanasius, by way of analogy, found his theological interpretations where the biblical text did not specifically address those matters.[102] Upon reflection, twentieth-century interpreters may have difficulty with Athanasius's struggle with the Arians over texts

98. R. V. Sellers, *Two Ancient Christologies: A Study in the Christological Thought of the Schools of Alexandria and Antioch in the Early History of Christian Doctrine* (London: SPCK, 1954), 202, notes that the two schools could not see they were contending for the same theological principles. What divided them was their philosophical and ecclesiastical differences.

99. Arianism was condemned at the Council of Nicea (A.D. 325), but the controversy continued throughout the century until the Council of Constantinople (A.D. 381). See the lucid discussion in Gerald L. Bray, *Creeds, Councils and Christ* (Downers Grove, Ill.: InterVarsity, 1984), 92–118, 145–71.

100. Karl Bihlmeyer, *Church History,* rev. H. Tuchle, trans. V. E. Mills, 3 vols. (Westminster, Md.: Newman, 1968), 1:246–55.

101. David F. Wells, *The Person of Christ* (Westchester, Ill.: Crossway, 1984), 98–109. The finest work to date on Athanasius's thought and method is Craig A. Blaising, *Athanasius* (Lanham, Md.: University Press, 1992).

102. C. Kannengiesser, "Athanasius of Alexandria and the Foundation of Traditional Christology," *TS* 34 (1973): 103–13; Jerry McCoy, "Philosophical Influences on the Doctrines of the Incarnation in Athanasius and Cyril of Alexandria," *Encounter* 38 (1977): 362–91.

which appear useless to prove the truth of either case, but as Hanson has concluded, "It is hard to deny that the doctrine of Athanasius was more faithful to the New Testament account of the significance of Jesus Christ than that of the Arians, whose fundamental trouble, one suspects, was that they could not believe that God really has communicated himself in Christ."[103] What Athanasius and his followers really did was to interpret the whole Bible by the New Testament and to interpret the New Testament by the Gospel of John.

Athanasius was not an original thinker like Origen, though his writings have come to be regarded as the essential statement of the Alexandrian position on the key christological controversies of the time. He was deeply indebted to Origen for his allegorical hermeneutics, but both his analogical and allegorical readings of Scripture were shaped more by the developing rule of faith[104] than his own creativity or imagination. His expansion of the rule of faith, through which he interpreted Scripture, is worth noting:

> Whoever wishes to be saved
> before all things it is necessary that he hold the catholic faith, which faith, if anyone does not keep it whole and unharmed,
> without doubt he will perish everlastingly.
> Now, the catholic faith is this,
> that we worship one God in Trinity, and Trinity in Unity,
> neither confusing the Persons
> nor dividing the divine Being.
> For there is one Person of the Father, another of the Son, and another of the Holy Spirit
> but the Godhead of the Father, the Son and Holy Spirit is all one, their glory equal, their majesty co-eternal.
> Such as the Father is, such is the Son and such is the Holy Spirit:
> the Father uncreated, the Son uncreated and the Holy Spirit uncreated,
> the Father infinite, the Son infinite and the Holy Spirit infinite,
> the Father eternal, the Son eternal and the Holy Spirit eternal;
> and yet there are not three Eternals but one Eternal,
> just as they are not three Uncreateds, nor three Infinites, but one Uncreated and one Infinite.
> In the same way, the Father is almighty, the Son almighty and the Holy Spirit almighty,
> and yet they are not three Almighties but one Almighty.

103. R. P. C. Hanson, "Biblical Exegesis in the Early Church," *CHB,* 1:453; cf. Johannes Quasten, *Patrology,* 4 vols. (reprint; Westminster, Md.: Christian Classics, 1984), 3:37–39.

104. Cf. the "Athanasian Creed" in J. N. D. Kelly, ed., *Early Christian Creeds* (London: Black, 1972); Henry Bettenson, ed., *Documents of the Christian Church* (Oxford: Oxford University Press, 1963); Roger Beckwith, *Confessing the Faith in the Church of England Today,* Latimer Studies 9 (Oxford: Oxford University Press, 1981).

Thus, the Father is God, the Son is God and the Holy Spirit is God,
and yet there are not three Gods but one God.
Thus the Father is the Lord, the Son is the Lord
and the Holy Spirit is the Lord,
and yet not three Lords but one Lord.

Because, just as we are compelled by Christian truth to confess each Person singly to be both God and Lord,

So we are forbidden by the catholic religion to say, There are three Gods, or three Lords.

The Father is from none, not made nor created nor begotten;
the Son is from the Father alone, not made nor created, but begotten;
the Holy Spirit is from the Father and the Son, not made nor created nor begotten, but proceeding.
So there is one Father, not three Fathers; one Son, not three Sons; one Holy Spirit, not three Holy Spirits.
And there in this Trinity there is no before or after, no greater or less, but all three persons are co-eternal with each other and co-equal.
So that in all things, as has already been said,
the Trinity in Unity, and Unity in Trinity, is to be worshiped.
He therefore who wishes to be saved let him think thus of the Trinity.

Furthermore, it is necessary to everlasting salvation that he should faithfully believe the incarnation of our Lord Jesus Christ.
Now, the right faith is that we should believe and confess that our Lord Jesus Christ, the Son of God, is both God and man equally.
He is God from the Being of the Father, begotten before the worlds, and he is man from the being of his mother, born in the world;
perfect God and perfect man, having both man's rational soul and human flesh; equal to the Father as regards his divinity and inferior to the Father as regards his humanity;
who, although he is God and man, yet he is not two, but one Christ;
one, however, not by the conversion of the Godhead into flesh but by taking up of the humanity into God; utterly one, not by confusion of human and divine being but by unity of Christ's one Person.
For just as the rational soul and the flesh are one man, so God and man are one Christ;
who suffered for our salvation, descended to Sheol, rose from the dead, ascended to heaven, sat down at the right hand of the Father,
from where he will come to judge the living and the dead;
at whose coming all men will rise again with their bodies and will give an account for their own actions,
and those who have done good will go in to live everlasting and those who have done evil in to everlasting fire.

> This is the catholic faith which, if anyone does not believe it faithfully and firmly, he cannot be saved.[105]

Athanasius read Scripture through his theology to such an extent that he obviously received the Bible as a "Bible with notes," not to be interpreted in a vacuum.[106] This methodology greatly influenced the three great Cappadocian fathers: Basil of Caesarea (ca. A.D. 329–379), his friend Gregory of Nazianzus (ca. A.D. 330–389), and his brother Gregory of Nyssa (ca. A.D. 330–395). In this splendid trio the hermeneutical and theological work found its continuation and orthodoxy reached its climax. While Basil was more pastoral and the two Gregorys were more theoretical, they followed Athanasius's allegorical, yet theological, approach to biblical interpretation.[107]

To some extent, the allegorical hermeneutics of Clement and Origen was checked by the theological concerns of Athanasius, the Cappadocians, and Cyril of Alexandria (d. ca. A.D. 444). Though the allegorical method continued to be used for the interpretation of the Old Testament, its value was seen to be in the prefiguring of truths of the New Testament. There is a greater development in this matter with Cyril of Alexandria as pointed out by Barnabas Lindars:

> Cyril . . . in his commentary on John paid special attention to the ways in which it supports the orthodox faith. In his doctrinal work he broke new ground by placing the concensus of patristic teaching alongside scripture as the test of theological orthodoxy. Thus scripture and tradition support each other, and the weakness of exclusive reliance on scripture, which can be made to mean anything, is overcome.[108]

While Cyril continued the practice of Alexandrian allegorical interpretation, with the developments of Athanasius and especially Cyril, the Alexandrian creativity began to give way to a full-orbed canonical and catholic interpretation which became so dominant with Jerome and Augustine.

Conclusion

With the rise of the Alexandrian school, scriptural exegesis reached new levels. Adapting the allegorical interpretation of Philo and the philo-

105. From the translation by Beckwith, *Confessing the Faith in the Church of England Today*. A short commentary is provided by Bray, *Creeds, Councils and Christ*, 207–11.

106. Hanson, *"Biblical Exegesis in the Early Church," CHB*, 1:453; cf. Klaas Runia, *The Present-Day Christological Debate* (Downers Grove, Ill.: InterVarsity, 1984), 11–15.

107. Quasten, *Patrology*, 3:203–4, 263–69; cf. C. W. Macleod, "Allegory and Mysticism in Origen and Gregory of Nyssa," *JTS* n.s. 22 (1971): 362–79.

108. Rogerson, Rowland, Lindars, *The Study and Use of the Bible*, 267.

sophical framework of Platonism, biblical exegesis in Clement and Origen moved beyond the defensive posture of Irenaeus and Tertullian.

Clement's work initiated the allegorical method, but Origen was indeed the premier exegete of this period. Origen, following the threefold makeup of humans, created a three-step hermeneutical methodology. Yet, primarily he practiced a two-step approach: the literal and the spiritual senses. The spiritual sense served an apologetic purpose against the Gnostics and other challengers to the orthodox mainstream, but primarily it served a pastoral purpose to mature the soul. Origen's genius occasionally led him down wrongheaded paths. But the church's tradition or rule of faith had a sobering effect on his exegesis. The allegorical method, at a critical moment in Christian history, made it possible to uphold the rationality of the Christian faith. Yet it was Origen's total worldview, a blend of scriptural ideas, church tradition, and Platonism, that brought the Alexandrian hermeneutics to its new heights, not only in its methodology, but in its spirit.

Because of the christological debates in the fourth and fifth centuries, the followers of Origen became more theologically oriented in their exegesis. The consistent articulation of the church's orthodox faith, coupled with pastoral concerns for the edification of the faithful, provided parameters and norms for the implementation of allegorical exegesis. Allegorical hermeneutics tended to give way to analogical hermeneutics. Their purpose in exegesis was primarily practical and their exegesis cannot be understood until this is realized. The successors of Origen were challenged by the school of Antioch with its emphasis on a literal interpretation. The Antiochenes were reacting to the fanciful hermeneutics of the Alexandrians. New issues were raised which we must examine closely in the following chapter.

4

The Antiochene School: Literal-Historical and Typological Hermeneutics

In order to describe the exegetical school of Antioch, we will return briefly to the second century, a time that predates the apologist Irenaeus and Tertullian, to examine the primary representative of the first Antiochene school, Theophilus of Antioch, who became bishop of Antioch about A.D. 169. We shall next see how the Antiochene school and its tradition reacted to the Alexandrian allegorists. Although Diodore of Tarsus, the initial representative of the "later" Antiochene school, will not be neglected, this chapter will concentrate on John Chrysostom and Theodore of Mopsuestia, particularly the influence of Aristotelian thought and the place of typological exegesis in their overall hermeneutical scheme.

Early Antiochene Exegesis: The Beginning of Historical Interpretation

The distinctive feature of the Antiochenes was their conviction that the primary sense of interpretation was the historical. Wherever possible, the Antiochenes adopted an historical interpretation.[1] The most widely-known representative of the early Antiochene school was Theophilus of Antioch. His main work, *To Autolycus*, predates the works of Irenaeus and Tertullian discussed in chapter 2. Besides the letters *To Autolycus*, none of his

1. John Rogerson, Christopher Rowland, and Barnabas Lindars, *The Study and Use of the Bible*, vol. 2 of *The History of Christian Theology*, ed. Paul Avis, 3 vols. (Grand Rapids: Eerdmans, 1988), 35–36.

work has survived.[2] While *To Autolycus* was written more as an apologetical work than an exegetical one, the second letter gives us some indication of the nature of his hermeneutics. In section 2 of this letter, he described the narrative of the initial chapters of Genesis, and it is obvious that he did not believe these chapters should be interpreted allegorically. Illustrative of this observation is his comment on Genesis 3:8, which reads, "Then the man and his wife heard the sound of the LORD God as he was walking in the garden in the cool of the day, and they hid from the LORD God among the trees of the garden."

> You will say, then, to me: "You have said that God ought not to be contained in a place, and how do you now say that he walked in paradise?" Hear what I say. The God and Father, indeed, of all cannot be contained, and is not found in a place, for there is no place of his rest; but his word, through whom he made all things, being his power and his wisdom, assuming the person of the Father and Lord of all, went to the garden in the person of God, and conversed with Adam.[3]

When Theophilus was confronted with an anthropomorphism that appeared to contradict the omnipresence of God, he did not shift to allegorical exegesis to handle the enigma, but instead viewed the passage literally and historically as a theophany of the second person of the Godhead.[4] Theophilus placed great stress on the Old Testament as a historical book containing the authentic history of God's dealings with his people. Theophilus went so far as to establish a biblical chronology from the creation to his own day.[5] Involved in this historical emphasis was his view of the Bible's inspiration. He maintained that the Old Testament reveals to humankind that the God to whom it bears witness is the creator of the universe. This is possible because the human writers were inspired and instructed by God, and therefore able to write about those things that happened before or after their own times.[6]

John Rogerson has observed, "Genesis 1 is defended as an authentic account of how the world was created, the account being inspired by the Logos of God. However, the difficulty that light is created before the sun is tacitly acknowledged. The light created on the first day comes from the

2. G. L. Carey, "Theophilus," *NIDCC*, 967. *To Autolycus* was divided into three parts and sought to show the superiority of the Christian revelation over pagan mythology. Although called "elementary" by Eusebius, the work was a worthwhile contribution and an advancement over that of his predecessors.

3. Theophilus of Antioch *To Autolycus* 2:22.

4. Cf. Duane A. Garrett, *Chrysostom's "Interpretatio in Isaiam": an English Translation with an Analysis of Its Hermeneutics* (Lewiston, N.Y.: Edwin Mellen, 1992), 19–20.

5. Theophilus of Antioch *To Autolycus* 2.14.

6. Ibid.

Logos."[7] We can see that though Theophilus emphasized the historical meaning of the biblical text, the Old Testament was also given a Christian interpretation, not unlike the interpretations of Jesus and the apostles; that is, God generated the Logos and through the Logos he made all things (John 1:3). The Logos also spoke through Moses and the prophets. As would be expected, Theophilus emphasized the literal meaning of the moral exhortations in Scripture. He likewise attempted to show the harmony between the laws of the Old Testament and the New.[8] Thus, the exhortation in Jesus' Sermon on the Mount to love one's enemies (Matt. 5:44) reflects Isaiah 66:5: "Say to those who hate you . . . you are our brothers."[9]

This is a brief picture of the early Antiochene school. More than one hundred years separated Theophilus's tenure as bishop of Antioch from the later Antiochene school beginning with Lucian and advancing with Diodore, Chrysostom, and Theodore.

Later Antiochene Exegesis: Rejection of Alexandrian Allegorical Interpretation

The Alexandrian allegorical method encountered considerable opposition within the larger church. Robert M. Grant has chronicled this opposition.[10] He noted that early in the third century an Egyptian bishop named Nepos wrote a *Refutation of the Allegorists*.[11] As will be seen in our next chapter, Jerome, under the influence of his Jewish mentors, turned from allegorical hermeneutics to an increasing respect for the literal meaning of Scripture. It is likely that wherever the synagogue's influence was felt, the church's interpretation of Scripture had a tendency toward literalism. Certainly this was the case at Antioch.[12] The artificiality of much allegorical interpretation, however, could not fail to cause a negative response, and the outright rejection of allegorical exegesis was centered in Antioch.

Antioch, the birthplace of Gentile Christianity (cf. Acts 13) and a great city of the eastern empire, had a long tradition of theological learning. The earlier tradition of the Antioch school centered around the practices of Theophilus and was passed on to Lucian, Diodore, and the later Antioch-

7. Rogerson, Rowland, and Lindars, *The Study and Use of the Bible*, 37.

8. Theophilus of Antioch *To Autolycus* 2.14.

9. Ibid.

10. Robert M. Grant with David Tracy, *A Short History of the Interpretation of the Bible*, rev. ed. (Philadelphia: Fortress, 1984), 63–72.

11. Ibid., 63.

12. Rowan A. Greer, *Theodore of Mopsuestia: Exegete and Theologian* (London: Faith, 1961), 86–88.

enes, who were also influenced by the Jewish teachers of Antioch.[13] Within this development, the rejection of allegorization increased. "Theory" or "theoria" was the key to understanding the true meaning of the text. Diodore of Tarsus composed *What Is the Difference Between Theory and Allegory?* Theodore of Mopsuestia wrote *Concerning Allegory and History Against Origen.* Grant has concluded, "The differences between the schools of Antioch and Alexandria were not slight, and the Antiochenes were vigorous defenders of their own view."[14]

Lucian of Antioch

Lucian was born at Samosata (ca. A.D. 240) and completed his education at Antioch. For a time, Lucian was under the censure of the church because of questionable theological views, but he eventually recanted and his influence continued. He is best remembered for his revision of the Septuagint (LXX) and is generally regarded as the founder of the later exegetical school of Antioch. In addition to his study at Antioch, he attended school at Caesarea, where he became acquainted with the allegorical method, as well as methods of text-critical studies. His reputation suggests that he was a fine classical scholar and preacher, and supposedly was well versed in Hebrew. His association with Paul of Samosata and later with his pupil Arius kept him under suspicion for his adoptionist Christology.[15] Recently, however, most scholars have argued that Lucian himself was not a heretic.[16]

Lucian emphasized careful textual criticism, and philological and historical studies. Following the paths of the pagan schools in the city, Lucian and the Antiochenes applied classical learning of rhetoric and philosophy. The result was a sober-minded hermeneutic emphasizing the literal sense of the biblical text. They took the historical sense seriously, but also developed a typological exegetical approach very similar to early Christian typology.[17]

13. C. H. Kraeling, "The Jewish Community of Antioch," *JBL* 51 (1932): 130–41; Eusebius *Ecclesiastical History* 7.32.2.

14. Grant with Tracy, *Short History of the Interpretation of the Bible,* 64; cf. Jean Daniélou with A. H. Couratin and John Kent, *Historical Theology,* vol. 2 of *The Pelican Guide to Modern Theology,* ed. R. P. C. Hanson, 3 vols. (Middlesex, England: Penguin, 1969), 106–8.

15. Lucian accepted the preexistence of Christ, but insisted that this had not been from all eternity. Many of his students, who included Arius and Eusebius of Nicomedia, came to occupy the most important sees in the East, and as fellow disciples of Lucian were sympathetic to Arius. Lucian is often called the father of Arianism. Cf. D. S. Wallace-Hadrill, *Christian Antioch* (Cambridge: Cambridge University Press, 1982).

16. Berthold Altaner, *Patrology,* trans, Hilda C. Graef, 2d ed. (New York: Herder and Herder, 1961), 242. Sidney Jellicoe, *The Septuagint and Modern Study* (Oxford: Clarendon, 1968), 157–59.

17. See Bruce M. Metzger, "Lucian and the Lucianic Recension of the Greek Bible," *NTS* 8 (1962): 194–96; also Richard M. Davidson, *Typology in Scripture: A Study of Hermeneutical*

Diodore of Tarsus

After his studies in Athens, Diodore (d. ca. A.D. 394), a native of Antioch, returned to oversee a monastery there. As head of the Antioch school, he continued the tradition of adhering to the literal and historical exegesis of Scripture. He served as bishop of Tarsus (ca. A.D. 378–390). During this time he wrote many significant exegetical and polemical works, among them an important commentary on the Book of Psalms. Despite some lingering doubts, it seems that some remaining fragments may be confidently assigned to him.[18] In these fragments, the Antiochene polemic against allegorical interpretation was expressed in almost classical formulations. According to Henry B. Swete, "The few fragments which remain exhibit him as a typical Antiochene, clear-sighted, practical, averse to mysticism and allegory."[19]

In the eyes of Diodore, allegorical interpretation was foolishness: it introduced silly fables in the place of the text. He contended that allegorizers abolish history and make one thing mean another.[20] The distinctive feature in the Antiochene hermeneutical method was *theoria*.[21] At this point, Diodore rejected the Alexandrian opinion that the reference of the prophets to the coming of Christ was something added to the original prophecy, that it was an allegorical understanding. By the use of *theoria,* the Antiochenes maintained that the prophet himself foresaw both the immediate event which was to come in the history of ancient Israel and the ultimate coming of Christ.[22] The prophets' predictions were at the same time both historical and christocentric. The Antiochenes argued that the double sense was different and distinct from that which the allegorists superimposed upon an original literal meaning. Diodore argued that the

TYPOS Structures, Andrews University Seminary Doctoral Dissertation Series, 2 (Berrien Springs, Mich.: Andrews University Press, 1981), 23–24.

18. Altaner, *Patrology,* 369. It seems that large portions of Diodore's work are preserved in an eleventh-century manuscript under the name of Anastasius of Nicea. Both the prologue to the Psalter and the preface to Psalm 118 contain important hermeneutical reflections.

19. Henry B. Swete, *Patristic Study* (London: Longmans, Green and Co., 1902), 99.

20. Karlfried Froehlich, *Biblical Interpretation in the Early Church* (Philadelphia: Fortress, 1984), 21.

21. As noted, Diodore wrote *On the Difference Between Theoria and Allegory,* of which only fragments remain. The five volumes of Theodore of Mopsuestia *Concerning Allegory and History Against Origen* were ordered burned at the Second Council of Constantinople in A.D. 553, and are no longer extant. I am most appreciative for Duane Garrett's insights regarding the significance of *theoria* in the Antioch school.

22. Raymond E. Brown, "Hermeneutics," in *Jerome Biblical Commentary,* ed. Raymond E. Brown, Joseph A. Fitzmyer, and Roland E. Murphy (Englewood Cliffs, N.J.: Prentice-Hall, 1968), 612–13.

messianic or prophetic meaning did not depreciate the literal meaning but rather was grounded upon it. This meaning was understood to be real and intelligible to all, not hidden and discernible only to the spiritually mature, as the Alexandrian allegorists maintained.[23]

Diodore insisted upon the factuality of the original setting and explored the text for clues to its historical reconstruction. But in addition to the historical meaning, there was the typological or *theoria* that taught ethics and theology.[24] The content of Scripture was thus lifted to a higher analogy, but the historical meaning did not oppose or contradict the *theoria*.[25]

Diodore's treatment of the Psalms serves as a good illustration of how the Antiochene exegesis was both historical and christological. While Diodore affirmed David as the author of most of the Psalms, he observed that through the gift of prophecy and typological understanding, many of the Psalms which historically refer to the kings and prophets of Israel also refer to the Lord Jesus.[26]

Psalm 2, which reads, "Today I have become your Father. Ask of me, and I will make the nations your inheritance," refers to the honor that was "accorded by the Gentiles to the incarnate Christ." Likewise, Psalm 40:6, which says, "Sacrifice and offering you did not desire, but my ears you have pierced, burnt offerings and sin offerings you did not require," conforms greatly to the things of Christ, according to Diodore. Also, Psalm 45:6 says, "Your throne, O God, will last for ever and ever; a scepter of justice will be the scepter of your kingdom." Diodore thus claimed only Christ could be addressed as God and reign forever. These examples provide insight into the Antiochene typological exegesis that reached full bloom with Diodore's students, John Chrysostom and Theodore of Mopsuestia.

The school of Antioch protested against the allegorical hermeneutics of Alexandria. Generally it can be said that the Antiochene school had a strong historical and philological interest and wanted exact interpretations based upon historical and contextual factors. The school also had a rational

23. This analysis, with which we agree, was offered by Jean Daniélou, *Origen*, trans. Walter Mitchell (New York: Sheed and Ward, 1955), 164–99. He concludes that in both Antioch and Alexandria, true biblical, historical typology was conducted, though in Alexandria the typology became blurred by elements of non-Christian exegesis. Jacques Guillet, "Les exegeses d'Alexandrie et d'Antioche: Conflit ou malentendu?" *Recherches de science religieuse* 34 (1957): 257–302, is correct in suggesting that the Alexandrian exegesis can be classified as symbolic-typological interpretation, and the Antiochene as prophetic-typological interpretation. He is incorrect, however, in concluding that the differences between the two schools were caused only by a fundamental misunderstanding of each other.

24. Froehlich, *Biblical Interpretation in the Early Church*, 22; cf. Rowan A. Greer, *The Captain of Our Salvation: A Study in the Patristic Exegesis of Hebrews* (Tübingen: Mohr, 1973), 155–73.

25. Rogerson, Rowland, and Lindars, *The Study and Use of the Bible*, 37–38.

26. Cf. Rowan A. Greer, "The Antiochene Christology of Diodore of Tarsus," *JTS* 17 (1966): 327–41.

tendency with strong ethical-personalistic interests, in contrast to the mystical-allegorical tendencies of the Alexandrians. As we have previously noted, the two great Antiochene exegetes, Theodore and Chrysostom, belonged to a later period of the Antioch school. Theodore of Mopsuestia, whom later generations venerated as "the interpreter *par excellence*," distinguished between the pure exegete and the preacher: the exegete's task was to communicate the plain teaching of the gospel. If we maintain this distinction, Theodore was the pure exegete while Chrysostom was the expository preacher. Let us now turn our attention to these two giants.

Theodore of Mopsuestia

His Background

Theodore (ca. A.D. 350–428) was born into a wealthy Antiochene family and educated along with John Chrysostom under the outstanding rhetorician and philosopher Libanius. He was ordained presbyter by Flavian in A.D. 383 and made bishop of Mopsuestia about A.D. 393. His prolific literary contributions, keen insight, and erudition are well known. Apart from questions that arose following his death about his influence upon the christological thought of his student Nestorius (d. A.D. 451), his doctrinal integrity is generally unquestioned.[27]

His Hermeneutical Approach

Theodore, the greatest interpreter of the Antiochenes, was also the most individualistic while remaining the most consistent in emphasizing historical exegesis. It is certainly true that all Christian theology during this period was based on Scripture, yet this was especially true for Theodore. That this was the case can be traced to Theodore's hermeneutical method.[28] Theodore, moreover, seems to have employed a more Jewish exegesis than many of his contemporaries. He expressed in a clear fashion the exegetical tradition of the Antiochene school established by Diodore, who said,

> We do not forbid the higher interpretation and *theoria*, for the historical narrative does not exclude it, but is on the contrary the basis and substructure of loftier insights. . . . We must, however, be on our guard against letting the *theoria* do away with the historical basis, for the result would then be, not *theoria*, but allegory.[29]

27. Cf. the biographical discussions in F. A. Sullivan, *The Christology of Theodore of Mopsuestia* (Rome: Gregorian University Press, 1956); and R. A. Norris, *Manhood and Christ: A Study in the Christology of Theodore of Mopsuestia* (Oxford: Clarendon, 1963).

28. Greer, *Theodore of Mopsuestia*, 86.

29. Cited by J. N. D. Kelly, *Early Christian Doctrines*, 4th rev. ed. (San Francisco: Harper and Row, 1978), 76–77.

In order to understand Theodore's method, it is necessary to recognize his distinction between typological, allegorical, and prophetical material. K. J. Woolcombe's useful summary of early church typology follows. While not directly related to the Antiochene school, it is nevertheless extremely helpful:

> Allegorism, typology and the fulfilment of prophecy are consequently to be differentiated. St. Paul's interpretation of the story of Hagar in Gal. 4 is an example not of typological, but of allegorical, exegesis. The account of the Triumphal Entry in Matt. 21 is a record of the fulfillment of Zech. 9:9, and not a piece of typological writing. Admittedly, typological writing and the fulfillment of prophecy overlap each other to a certain extent: in Matt. 21:14 the reference to the blind and the lame has probably been borrowed from the story of David's capture of Jerusalem. There is also a close resemblance between St. Paul's allegorism and his typological exegesis, because his allegorism was of the historical kind. But the similarities between allegorism, typology and the study of the fulfillment of prophecy are not so close as to justify ignoring the differences between them, and using one of the terms to cover them all.[30]

Although this is a useful summary, in reality Theodore did not always clearly make such distinctions. Perhaps, as Rowan A. Greer has suggested, it is better to think of typological exegesis as the normative method of Antiochene exegesis. Allegorical exegesis, if legitimate at all, and distinct from Alexandrian allegorical practices, represented "left wing typology," while fulfillment of prophecy represented "right wing typology."[31]

In his study of the Old Testament, it is clear that Theodore's knowledge of the languages did not carry him too far. Because of his deficiency in Hebrew, Theodore was forced to rely on translations. Following the accepted practice of his day, he accepted the Septuagint as the authorized version, though many, including Origen, considered the version to be divinely inspired. Theodore, however, went further by claiming that the Septuagint followed the Hebrew text more closely than other translations. He rejected Job and the Song of Songs as canonical. Job, according to Theodore, was an Edomite who had heathen associations. The Song was unacceptable because, instead of an allegorical picture of Christ and the church, the book, interpreted literally, was nothing more than an erotic poem.[32]

Theodore carefully distinguished between psalms that are genuinely messianic and those which are entirely historical. Psalms 2, 8, 45, and 110

30. K. J. Woolcombe, "The Biblical Origins and Patristic Development of Typology," in *Essays on Typology,* comp. G. W. H. Lampe and K. J. Woolcombe (London: SCM, 1957), 42.

31. Greer, *Theodore of Mopsuestia,* 94.

32. Ibid., 100–101; 162–63; cf. Dimitri Z. Zuharopoulos, "Theodore of Mopsuestia's Critical Methods in Old Testament Study" (Ph.D. diss., Boston University, 1964), 190–94.

were considered messianic; all others could be understood as pointing to Christ in a typological sense. The books, or chapters within books, that contained no prophetic elements or messianic meanings were considered merely human wisdom, and their canonical status was questionable.[33]

Theodore's work on the New Testament evidenced the expected Antiochene orthodoxy and the Christ of the Gospels is the Christ of Antiochene Christology.[34] Only two New Testament works are extant: his commentary on John and his commentary on the Pauline Letters. In the fourth Gospel he was faced with a writing which had both a strong historical and theological character. Maurice F. Wiles claims that for Theodore, John's Gospel

> had the fullest measure of historical reliability as a firsthand account, with greater attention to chronological exactitude than any of the other gospels. It was also composed with the express purpose of supplementing those other records by bringing out more fully the underlying theological truth, especially of Christ's divinity.[35]

The relation of the christological exegesis of the Gospel to the actual historical circumstances of the life of Jesus did not keep Theodore from offering a full-orbed and wholehearted theological interpretation about the person of Christ. Yet, his concern for the historical all too often kept him from grasping the eternal dimensions of the fourth Gospel. Three brief examples provided by Wiles illustrate this point:

> In 1:51 Jesus promises to Nathaniel a vision of the angels of God ascending and descending on the Son of man; Theodore interprets this as a reference to the literal angelic visitations at the temptation, in Gethsemane, at the time of the resurrection and of the ascension. In 5:25 Jesus declares that "the hour . . . now is when the dead will hear the voice of the Son of God, and those who hear will live"; Theodore refers simply to the widow of Nain's son, to Jairus' daughter and to Lazarus. In 14:18 and 28 Jesus promises to his disciples that he will come to them; Theodore finds the fulfillment of that promise in the historical happenings of the post-resurrection appearances.[36]

It is obvious that Theodore was conscious of chronological development in the theology of the biblical text. His main strength, however, was not his interpretation of John but his exposition of the letters of Paul.[37]

33. Grant with Tracy, *Short History of the Interpretation of the Bible,* 66.

34. Maurice F. Wiles, "Theodore of Mopsuestia as Representative of the Antiochene School," *CHB,* 1:504–5.

35. Ibid.; cf. Greer, *Theodore of Mopsuestia,* 112–50.

36. Wiles, "Theodore of Mopsuestia," 506.

37. Bruce, "The History of New Testament Study," in *New Testament Interpretation,* ed. I. Howard Marshall (Grand Rapids: Eerdmans, 1975), 27; cf. Maurice F. Wiles, *The Divine Apostle: The Interpretation of St. Paul's Epistle in the Early Church* (Cambridge: Cambridge University Press, 1967).

It has sometimes been said that no one can be an equally sympathetic interpreter of Pauline and Johannine theology, that every theologian is born with either a Pauline or a Johannine bias. Certainly Theodore seems far more at home as an interpreter of the Pauline Epistles. One major difficulty for the Antiochene hermeneutical approach was Paul's use of the term *allegoroumena* in Galatians 4:24 in connection with the story of Sarah and Hagar. Theodore argued that by allegory, Paul meant the Antiochene *theoria.* He contended that "Paul knew the Hellenistic term but not the Hellenistic application which would treat the texts like dreams in the night; he gave history priority over all other considerations."[38] Because of the historical considerations, Theodore maintained that Paul was making a comparison (*similitudo*), and the comparison was worthless unless the two things compared really were historical (*rebus stantibus*).[39] The very division of time between the two events, Hagar's story and the Judaizing controversy in Galatia, implied that both really happened. Thus we can see that Theodore rejected allegorical interpretation completely. Yet, Theodore did include metaphorical meaning as part of the literal meaning.[40]

Theodore's exegesis was the purest representation of Antiochene hermeneutics.[41] Theodore was first to treat the Psalms historically and systematically, while treating the Gospel narratives factually, paying attention to the particles of transition and to the minutiae of grammar and punctuation. His approach can be described as "anti-allegorical," rejecting interpretations that denied the historical reality of what the scriptural text affirmed. This was evident in our brief look at his exegesis of Galatians 4. Even where allegorical interpretation could have possibly served to his advantage to bring unity to the overall biblical message, he failed to use it or see its value. For instance, this he could have done with the wisdom literature of the Old Testament, but as we have seen he chose instead to reject Job and the Song from the biblical canon.[42]

The great value of allegorical interpretation for the Alexandrians was that it made possible a theologically unified interpretation of the Bible as

38. Theodore *Epistolas b. Pauli commentarii* 1.73–74; cf. Theodore, "Commentary on Galatians 4:22–31," trans. Froehlich, *Biblical Interpretation in the Early Church,* 95–103.

39. Theodore *Epistolas b. Pauli* 1.76–78. For objections to the distinction between allegorical and typological interpretation, see Paul K. Jewett, "Concerning the Allegorical Interpretation of Scripture," *WTJ* 17 (1954): 1–20; Hans W. Frei, *The Eclipse of Biblical Narrative* (New Haven: Yale University Press, 1974), 82–83; James D. Smart, *The Interpretation of Scripture* (Philadelphia: Westminster, 1961), 93–133.

40. Cf. Greer, *Theodore of Mopsuestia,* 108–9. Cf. Robert J. Kepple, "An Analysis of the Antiochene Exegesis of Galatians 4:24–26," *WTJ* 39 (1976): 239–49.

41. Wiles, "Theodore of Mopsuestia," 489–90, notes that because of this, he was given the title *The Interpreter.*

42. Ibid., 509–10.

a whole. Theodore, attempting to present a unified theological exposition, viewed the Bible as a record of the historical development of the divine redemptive plan. Ultimately, this history must be understood from the perspective of the purposes of God to provide the setting of God's gracious act in Christ Jesus, by which the new age of salvation was realized. The law and the prophets were to be interpreted typologically as types of Christ. Through the hermeneutical tool, *theoria*, the reality of the Old Testament history in its own setting could likewise be maintained. This key plus the stress on historical development was the strength of Theodore's creative interpretation. We must now examine the hermeneutical practices and contributions of Theodore's friend and fellow disciple, John Chrysostom.

John Chrysostom

His Background

Chrysostom (ca. A.D. 354–407), born in Antioch, excelled in rhetorical, philosophical, and legal studies under Libanius.[43] Like Theodore, he studied with Diodore at the Antioch school. He was born into a family of means but not wealth. His father, Secundus, was either of the nobility or possibly a high-ranking member of the civil service. Secundus died while John was still a small child, leaving John to be raised by his widowed Christian mother, Anthusa. G. H. Chase and scholars since him have attributed the tenderness and domestic insight of Chrysostom's sermons to Anthusa's influence.

Abandoning his law career, he devoted himself to Christian asceticism. He was baptized by Bishop Meletius in about A.D. 372, and spent the next decade in theological studies under Diodore. During this time, he developed his friendship with Theodore. His theological education included, in addition to Aristotelian philosophy, the works of the Cappadocian fathers, Josephus, and Holy Scripture.[44]

Chrysostom's ascetical practices were extremely severe. He went for days without food and seriously damaged his health. For the rest of his days he was afflicted by chronic stomach trouble, insomnia, headaches, and colds. It was during this ascetic period, however, that he probably

43. Chrysostomus Baur, *John Chrysostom and His Time*, trans. M. Gonzaga, 2 vols. (Westminster, Md.: Newman, 1959), 1:16–21, identifies Libanius as a leading member of the "second sophistic." Libanius was genuinely concerned for the welfare of his students and was able to get along with those who were Christian. He was the leading teacher of rhetoric of his day. Cf. Thomas E. Amerigen, *The Stylistic Influence of the Second Sophistic on the Panegyrical Sermons of St. John Chrysostom: A Study in Greek Rhetoric* (Washington, D.C.: Catholic University of American Press, 1921).

44. Baur, *John Chrysostom and His Time*, 1:90–98; Jaroslav Pelikan, *The Preaching of Chrysostom: Homilies on the Sermon on the Mount* (Philadelphia: Fortress, 1967), 14–15.

gained the mastery over the content of Scripture that characterized his sermons and commentaries.[45]

In A.D. 381, he was ordained a deacon, and in 386 he was made a preaching elder. In this role he earned the name *golden mouth* (*Chrysostomos*) for his unsurpassed ability as an orator and a biblical expositor. Later generations have continued to affirm his greatness on the basis of his published sermons in which his theology was expressed. Though his theology was neither systematic, precise, nor original, his sermons drew insightful spiritual and moral applications from a grammatical and literal exegesis of Scripture.

Antioch was indeed a difficult place to preach. Nominally, it was overwhelmingly Christian, but it had a reputation for luxury and vice. Indeed, it could be described as a city full of all vices: violence, drunkenness, incontinence, impiety, avarice, and imprudence. It has been said that during this time

> many preachers enjoined not only the general missionary obligation of the laity: they especially stressed the eminent role of exemplary conduct for the recruiting impact of the Christian message on the pagans; Chrysostom was especially insistent and precise in this regard. It distressed him that now, since the great majority had converted to Christianity—he is speaking of Antioch—scarcely any conversions to the pagan minority are to be recorded.[46]

In this situation, Chrysostom, by consensus, became the most popular and unquestionably orthodox of the Antiochene fathers.

Chrysostom's most effective works were from the Gospels of John and Matthew and the Pauline Epistles. His work followed the Antiochene principles of exegesis so carefully exemplified in Theodore's efforts on the same biblical material. The difference between the two men can be observed in style rather than content. Chrysostom's work was expressed in a wordiness that contrasted with Theodore's sparse style. His homilies, for example, were ten times the length of Theodore's. With Theodore and Chrysostom, exegesis had at last come down out of the clouds of the interpreter's imagination and had planted its feet firmly on the earth. While remaining loyal to the principles of the Antiochene school, Chrysostom was not averse on occasion to citing the figurative meaning of a passage, thus demonstrating more flexibility than Theodore.[47] By this time, in the early fifth century,

45. Stephen Neill, *Chrysostom and His Message*, World Christian Books, 44 (New York: Association, 1963), 13.

46. Karl Baus, Hans-Georg Beck, Eugen Ewig, and Herman Josef Vogt, *The Imperial Church-from Constantine to the Early Middle Ages*, trans. Anselm Biggs, in *History of the Church*, ed. Hubert Jedin and Paul Dolan, 10 vols. (New York: Seabury, 1980), 2:214.

47. Kelly, *Early Christian Doctrines*, 78.

ecclesiastical and theological interests had become primary. Like Irenaeus, Clement, Origen, and Athanasius, both Chrysostom and Theodore at times read the rule of faith into both the Old and New Testaments.

His Hermeneutical Approach

Chrysostom gave primary attention to the critical, literal, grammatical, and historical interpretation of Scripture. Like others in the Antiochene tradition, he was influenced by Aristotelian philosophy. Aristotle seemed more down-to-earth compared to Plato's more other-worldly views. Chrysostom, more than his Alexandrian predecessors, was aware of the human factor in Scripture and sought to do justice to the dual authorship of biblical revelation. Yet, he maintained that the Bible spoke with a unified voice.

The Antiochene homilitician insisted that the main reason the Bible existed was for Christians to read it, read it again, meditate over it, and thereby escape the snares of sin. Chrysostom, while a hermit in his ascetic days, memorized the *Testamentum Christi* by heart.[48] His printed treatises and six hundred sermons contain about eighteen thousand Scripture references, about seven thousand from the Old Testament and eleven thousand from the New.[49] His citations often differ from contemporary texts both because of the different textual sources he used and because of his habit of citing from memory, weaving together passages from different sections of Scripture and improvising as his rhetoric moved him along.[50]

The Bible, according to Chrysostom, represented a supreme act of God's accommodation or condescension (*sunkatabasis*) to humankind. The Scriptures were considered to be by Christ and Chrysostom's commentaries were thus not a scientific inquiry but a tool to enable the reader to hear the Scripture more clearly and thereby enable the Bible to do its work more effectively. Regarding the variety in the Gospel accounts, Chrysostom recognized differences in the accounts of the same events. In his *Homily on the Gospel of Matthew,* he writes, "But if there be anything touching times or places, which they have related differently, this in no respect injures the truth of what they have said."[51] He regarded the fact that they agreed in essentials, while evidencing variety in details, as powerful evidence of their veracity. On this issue he says,

> But the contrary, it may be said, hath come to pass, for in many places they are convicted of discordance. Nay, this very thing is a very great evidence of their truth. For if they had agreed in all things exactly even to time, and

48. Jack B. Rogers and Donald K. McKim, *The Authority and Interpretation of the Bible: An Historical Approach* (Grand Rapids: Eerdmans, 1979), 20.
49. Baur, *John Chrysostom and His Time,* 1:315–16.
50. Pelikan, *Preaching of Chrysostom,* 35–36.
51. Chrysostom *Homily on the Gospel of Matthew* 1.6.

> place, and to the very words, none of our enemies would have believed but that they had met together, and had written what they wrote by some human compact; because such entire agreement as this cometh not of simplicity. But now even that discordance which seems to exist in little matters delivers them from all suspicion and speaks clearly in behalf of the character of the writers.[52]

Generally, Jerome D. Quinn has observed, Chrysostom did not involve himself with elaborate, painstaking solutions to discrepancies, and was willing to attribute a discrepancy to the Gospel writer's literary or theological purpose. This was typical of his approach to apparent problems of accuracy in the Bible.[53]

The ultimate issue in biblical interpretation for Chrysostom was whether the Bible, being spiritual in nature, was to be treated as a collection of suprahistorical sayings and ciphers which all, by virtue of Christ's being the center of revelation, spoke of him and his church, or whether it should be interpreted as revelation in history addressed to historical communities, which of course did not exclude Christ from being the center of revelation. As we have seen in the previous chapter, many patristic interpreters, and especially those associated with the Alexandrian school, showed by their allegorization that they preferred the former solution. Chrysostom, however, preferred to interpret the text literally and historically.

Although he recognized metaphors and figures of speech in the Scriptures, Chrysostom generally restrained himself from fanciful interpretation. For example, he interpreted Isaiah's Song of the Vineyard as an extended metaphor about God's faithful but futile attempt to bring the nations of Judah to righteousness and obedience. The passage in Isaiah reads:

> My well-beloved had a vineyard on a fertile hill.
> And he dug it all around, removed its stones,
> And planted it with the choicest vine.
> And he built a tower in the middle of it,
> And hewed out a wine vat in it;
> Then he expected it to produce good grapes,
> But it produced only worthless ones. . . .
> "So now let me tell you what I am going to do to my vineyard:
> I will remove its hedge and it will be consumed;
> I will break down its walls and it will become trampled ground

52. Ibid.

53. Jerome D. Quinn, "St. John Chrysostom on History in the Synoptics," *CBQ* 24 (1962): 142–43; cf. T. V. Philip, "Authority of Scripture in the Patristic Period," *IJT* 23 (1974): 1–8; see also John H. McIndoe, "Chrysostom on St. Matthew: A Study in Antiochene Exegesis" (S.T.M. thesis, Hartford Seminary Foundation, 1972).

> And I will lay it waste;
> It will not be pruned or hoed,
> But briars and thorns will come up.
> I will also charge the clouds to rain no rain on it."
>
> [Isa. 2:5–6 NASB]

In dealing with this passage Chrysostom commented,

> We are not the lords over the rules of interpretation, but must pursue scripture's interpretation of itself and in that way make use of the allegorical method. . . . This is everywhere a rule in scripture: when it wants to allegorize, it tells the interpretation of the allegory, so that the passage will not be interpreted superficially or be met by the undisciplined desire of those who enjoy allegorization to wander about and be carried in every direction.[54]

This comment reveals two hermeneutical principles in Chrysostom's approach: one negative and one positive. First, it is evident how strongly he believed that allegorization is incorrect and misleading. Second, he recognized that Scripture interprets Scripture. In supporting his argument, he referred to Proverbs 5:17–19, Isaiah 8:7–8, and Ezekiel 17. Ezekiel 17 is a particularly good example since the passage is a true allegory with an interpretation provided in its context. The passages from Proverbs and Isaiah are likewise helpful, but are probably best considered as metaphors rather than allegories.

The Antioch preacher's interpretation of the Song of the Vineyard demonstrates his hesitancy to push the details of biblical language for allegorical meaning. Concerning "he built a watchtower" (Isa. 5:2), Chrysostom suggested that it might mean the wall of the city, or the Mosaic law, or God's providence.[55] He argued that the details of the Song have no allegorical significance but were given only to reinforce its main point, primarily that God "has done everything he could and has shown them every consideration."[56] By contrast he noted that Cyril of Alexandria said that the tower was the temple and the wine vat was the altar.[57] Chrysostom, on the other hand, referring to allegorical exegesis, argued, "I disdain this exegesis, and consider the literal to be more accurate."[58]

The crucial proof-text for advocates of allegorical interpretation was, of course, Galatians 4:22–24. Like Theodore, Chrysostom distinguished

54. John Chrysostom *Interpretatio in Isaiam* 5.3. I am deeply dependent on Garrett's work on this point and that which immediately follows.

55. Ibid.

56. Ibid.

57. Ibid.

58. Ibid., 1.7.

between the genre of allegory and allegorical hermeneutics. Concerning Paul's usage of *allegoreo*, Chrysostom explained:

> By a misuse of language he [Paul] called the type allegory. What he means is this: The history itself not only has the apparent meaning but also proclaims other matters; therefore, it is called allegory. But what did it proclaim? Nothing other than everything that now is.[59]

Here Chrysostom reflected the Antiochene concept of *theoria*. Elsewhere he explained the relation of two meanings of Scripture by a parallel from art:

> The type is given the name of the truth until the truth is about to come; but when the truth has come, the name is no longer used. Similarly in painting: an artist sketches a king, but until the colors are applied he is not called a king; and when they are put on the type is hidden by the truth and is not visible; and then we say, "Behold the King."[60]

The outline can be discovered in the historical meaning, but the final form of the portrait was only available in the typological meaning. When the nature of the text required more than a mere historical exposition, Chrysostom preferred a typological methodology that was consistent with the historical event and distinct from allegorization.

Chrysostom rejected out of hand any allegorical interpretation of a passage that failed to agree with Scripture's interpretation of itself. Thus, the rule that Scripture interpreted Scripture took precedence over all others. The details of a passage were not to be separated from the overall context and should not be given allegorical meanings distinct from the text's context. Chrysostom avoided treating Old Testament passages allegorically of Christ and the church; instead he sought typological meanings when the text allowed for it.[61]

G. W. H. Lampe has correctly asserted that some form of typological interpretation of the Old Testament was necessary for Christians who believed that the Bible is controlled by a single series of images, that the Bible's explicit or implicit theme throughout is the people of the covenant, and that Christ is the unifying center point of biblical history. Typology, rightly conceived, asserts that since Christ is the culmination of the line of Abraham and of David and is the fulfillment of the hope of Israel, the Old Testament description of Israel's history, institutions, worship, and prophetic message often anticipate the life and work of Christ.[62] Chrysos-

59. Chrysostom *Commentary on the Epistle to the Galatians* 4.24.

60. Chrysostom *Homily on the Epistle to the Philippians* 10.

61. Rogers and McKim, *Authority and Interpretation of the Bible*, 20–22.

62. G. W. H. Lampe, *"The Reasonableness of Typology,"* in *Essays on Typology*, comp. G. W. H. Lampe and K. J. Woolcombe (London: SCM, 1957), 29.

tom and the Antiochene school distinguished allegorical interpretation from typological in two primary ways. Typological interpretation attempted to seek out patterns in the Old Testament to which Christ corresponded, while allegorical exegesis depended on accidental similarity of language between two passages. Second, typological interpretation depended on a historical interpretation of the text. The passage, according to the Antiochenes, had only one meaning, the literal (extended by *theoria*), and not two as suggested by the allegorists. In the typological approach, the things narrated by the text had to be placed in relationship to things which were not in the text, but which were still to come.

That Chrysostom understood this is plainly evident from his exposition on Psalm 46:

> Some passages must be interpreted literally. Some must be interpreted in a different sense to that which lies on the surface, as with the words, "The wolf shall lie down with the lamb." Yet again others must be taken in a two-fold sense. We must apprehend that which is actual and historical. We must interpret the spiritual meaning, as in the case of the figurative history of Isaac. We know the fact that Abraham's son was offered up, but there is something distinct from this, lament in the conception, which we gather from the words "his son," and this is the cross.[63]

When a historical passage declared not only the obvious fact, but proclaimed some other meaning as well, Chrysostom believed that the other meaning or the typological meaning should be tied firmly to the historical sense of Scripture.

Chrysostom, like Theodore and the other Antiochene representatives, emphasized the literal and historical meaning of the text. While he never articulated his intent, he was attempting to discover the intended meaning of the biblical author. While rejecting fanciful interpretation, he was nevertheless sensitive to figures of speech in Scripture. His sensitivity to bibli-

63. Chrysostom *Expositions on the Psalms* 46.1. Garrett has noted passages in Chrysostom's commentary on Isaiah where he should have, but did not, interpret typologically. Garrett lucidly analyzes such texts, and we can summarize his work:

> Chrysostom's interpretations of other passages, however, reveal that he did not fully comprehend the typological linkage between Christ and Israel. For one thing, it is notable that the significant typological vocabulary is all but absent in the commentary. In addition, there are several passages which he could (and probably should) have interpreted typologically. One important example is his treatment of Isaiah 7:14–16, which he wants to take as a direct prediction of Christ's virgin birth. The meaning of these verses is much debated but probably they should be treated as a prediction of the birth of Maher-shalal-hash-baz, Isaiah's son, and then as a typological prediction of Jesus' virgin birth.

See Garrett, *Chrysostom's "Interpretatio in Isaiam,"* 294; cf. Woolcombe, "The Biblical Origins and Patristic Development of Typology," 73–74.

cal language generally helped him to avoid a wooden literalism. Chrysostom rejected crudely literal interpretations of the Bible from both the Antiochene laity and the criticisms of the Alexandrians. He was cautious that no figurative expression in the Bible be misunderstood either from a too literal or a too fanciful interpretation.

For Chrysostom, theology and hermeneutics were not theoretical exercises, but practical and pastoral. He believed the biblical message made changes in people's lives. He declared that the Scriptures' divine message prepared people for good works. It is generally true that the Alexandrians saw a literal and allegorical meaning in Scripture and the Antiochenes found a historical and typological sense. The Alexandrians looked to the rule of faith, mystical interpretation, and authority as sources of dogma. On the other hand, the Antiochenes looked to reason and historical development of Scripture as the focus of theology. The Antiochenes were more aware of the human factor in Scripture and sought to do justice to the dual authorship of the biblical revelation.

While basic differences existed between an allegorical and a more literal approach to Scripture, the differences were less relevant in the interpretation of Paul's writings than those of the Old Testament or the four Gospels. It is now our purpose to examine how the two schools interpreted the letters of the apostle to the Gentiles.

The Apostle Paul as a Hermeneutical Test Case in the Alexandrian and Antiochene Schools

In the concluding section of this chapter, we shall describe how the two schools viewed Paul's thought, with special reference to the apostle's instruction on soteriology and the spiritual life.[64] Since our purposes remain descriptive, evaluation of the "correctness" of the Fathers' interpretations will be limited. We shall now move to the interpretation of Paul in the expositions of the representative interpreters, particularly Origen and Chrysostom. In summary, we shall address differences in interpretational schemes, including possible reasons for such diversity.

64. Other comparisons, with similar methodologies though different subjects, can be found in Peter Goday, *Principles of Patristic Exegesis: Romans 9–11 in Origen, John Chrysostom, and Augustine* (New York: Edwin Mellen, 1983); Hugh M. Riley, *Christian Initiation: A Comparative Study of the Interpretation of Baptismal Liturgy in the Mystagogical Writings of Cyril of Jerusalem, John Chrysostom, Theodore of Mopsuestia, and Ambrose of Milan* (Washington, D.C.: Catholic University of America Press, 1974); the final section in Greer, *Theodore of Mopsuestia,* comparing Theodore, Irenaeus, and Origen; a comparative study of the role of women in the early church in Elizabeth A. Clark, *Jerome, Chrysostom, and Friends* (New York: Edwin Mellen, 1979); and Charles P. Hammond, "Philocalia IX, Jerome, Epistle 121, and Origen's Exposition of Romans VII," *JTS* n.s. 32 (1981): 50–81.

The New Life of the Individual Believer

Initiation

Origen set the whole concept of grace in a broad cosmic setting. Commenting on Romans 4, he pointed out that in the first place human creation (and particularly creation as rational beings) was a sheer act of divine grace.[65] In what way then did God's grace enter into the human response of faith itself? Origen argued from 1 Corinthians 12:9 and Ephesians 2:8–9 (his method of comparing similar texts) that faith is a gift of the Spirit, also offering Philippians 1:29 and Romans 4:16 as supporting evidence.

By conflating Paul's comments on the Spirit's work (Rom. 12; 1 Cor. 12), he concluded that faith is a gift of God according to the proportion of grace given. There is an initial germ of faith that is believed to be something within the believers' own power (*ek tou eph hemin pistis*), and there is the full faith which can only be achieved with the addition of the God-given grace of faith. For Origen, saving faith itself is not the act of women and men alone, but their acts rewarded and reinforced by the grace of God.[66]

Chrysostom viewed the initiation into grace in a similar manner to Origen, but was more synergistic in his approach. He regarded the desire to respond to God's liberating work as a joint operation of God and humanity. On this subject, he was not as exhaustive as Origen, but his comments on Philippians 2:13 are helpful. He interpreted the words, "it is God who works in you to will and to act according to his good purpose," to mean if humans will on their part, then God gives strength to the willing. Chrysostom could proclaim that the efforts of men and women took the initiative so that grace was a response of God to humanity.[67]

Progress and Development

In a very interesting approach to progress in the Christian life, Origen distinguished three types of people. The first group included those "in the flesh" who war according to the flesh and cannot please God. The second group were those "in the body" who walk by faith and fail to recognize the spiritual meaning of Scripture. A unique explanation was offered for the third group, "the truly spiritual," who walk not by faith but by sight. Faith was characteristic of the weaker, not the more mature, person.[68] It was possible, in Origen's system, to be "partly in the flesh and partly in

65. Origen *Commentary on Romans* 4.1–11.

66. Ibid., 4.16; cf. Rene Cadiou, *Introduction au systeme d'Origene* (Paris: Societe d'edition "Les belles lettres," 1932).

67. Chrysostom *Homilies on Philippians* 2:13; cf. Lampe, "Christian Theology in the Patristic Period," 155–56.

68. Origen *Commentary on Romans* 8.8; cf. 2 Cor. 5:7; also Origen *Fragments on 1 Corinthians* 3.1, where he followed the exegesis of Clement.

the spirit."[69] Being in Christ was something that the believer progressively realized. A person's character could not be changed overnight; the conversion of the will might be immediate, but the development of the habit of consistently good actions was a slow and laborious business. Thus, daily renewal was no mere continuation of the past experience but a developing process of growth.

Chrysostom's approach contrasted with Origen's. Chrysostom's concept of progressive faith was positive and was not viewed in opposition to sight or wisdom. Chrysostom construed faith working with reason. Ratiocination was never able to bring about perfection, but it could explain certain things about the ability to see and hear. It could neither ascertain how the eyes see nor the ears hear; this belongs to the divine realm of faith. Faith was understood as the appropriate means to apprehend true spiritual matters.[70]

Forgiveness and Good Works

Origen often introduced certain restrictions into the range of forgiveness. Origen tended to restrict forgiveness to past sins only.[71] Sins prior to conversion could be forgiven on the basis of repentance, but sins committed after conversion could not be forgiven, though they could be covered by good works. At this point, Origen seemed more like an interpreter of James, rather than an exponent of Paul. Origen was quick to observe that good works must accompany true faith for genuine forgiveness to take place. Works without faith might carry honor, but were unable to bring persons to eternal life. On the other hand, faith without any good works was sufficient to save one from destruction, but could not bring men and women to true glory. This approach was distinctively Origen.[72]

Origen suggested that works could merit the grace of the Holy Spirit. Yet this merit language (*axios*) was probably best understood in an eschatological sense. It is difficult to determine if the merit language was completely, or even primarily, eschatological; if indeed it was, then it was not unique to Origen, but an extension of Paul. Paul's concept of worthiness in the eschaton was that it was a gift received from the merits of Christ.[73]

Theodore, another Antiochian, stressed the concept of forgiveness as a future reality. Ultimate salvation was equated with resurrection.[74] The

69. Origen *Commentary on Romans* 6.11.

70. Chrysostom *Homilies on 1 Corinthians* 4.1.

71. Origen *Commentary on Romans* 3.28; cf. W. J. P. Boyd, "Origen on Pharaoh's Hardened Heart: A Study of Justification and Election in St. Paul and Origen," *StPat* 7 (1966): 434–42.

72. Origen *Commentary on Romans* 2.7–10.

73. Origen *Commentary on Romans* 6.5; 4.7.

74. Theodore on Galatians 1.1, 4; 3.3, 14, 25–26; Ephesians 2.14–16; Philippians 3.10; Colossians 2.14, in Ulrich Wickert, *Studien zu dem Paulus kommentaren Theodors von Mopsuestia als Beitrag zum Verstandnis der antiochenischen Theologie,* Bieheft 27 zur Zeitschrift für die neutestamentliche Wissenschaft und die Kunde der alteren Kirche (Berlin: Topelmann, 1962).

idea of faith and forgiveness had a necessary future reference in Antiochene thought, implying belief in something not yet fully possessed. It was closely associated with themes of promise and hope. While this eschatological emphasis was stressed in Ephesians and Colossians, Theodore stressed that this was the standard teaching in all of Paul's epistles.[75]

The New Life in the Community

Baptism and Union

Origen understood baptism as the act of initiation into the believing community. In Romans 6, Paul described baptism as being buried with Christ, but burial logically presupposed death. Origen maintained that baptism which was not preceded by moral dying with Christ was not really baptism at all. Likewise, he said Christians do not really believe that Christ has been raised from the dead unless he is risen and is living in their hearts as the embodiment of all Christian virtues.[76]

Theodore insisted that baptism represented the moment of the believers' transference to resurrection life.[77] Yet, the transference was not full reality but took place at the level of prefigurative symbol. Baptism imparted the firstfruits of the Spirit, but Theodore insisted that the real evidence to justify Paul's theological assertions could not be found in believers' present experience, but only in the future.[78]

For Chrysostom, the heart of the mystery of union with Christ was found in faith and baptism. At baptism there was not a change of nature, but a ruling purpose in the life of believers. This change did not guarantee a life of virtue, but it did make such a life achievable.[79]

The Dynamics of New Life

As we have seen, Origen's description of the present age as a time of dying with Christ and the future as one of living with him was grounded in its clear emphasis on the superiority of the future. Origen pointed out that Paul regularly spoke of resurrection as a present reality, as well as a more literal future. This tension seemed to puzzle Origen at times. He cited texts that spoke of ordinary Christians as already possessing a wholeness of wisdom. He acknowledged that believers have a fullness of God's gifts. He preferred to stress the incompleteness of the Christian's present position. While believers were to live in the hope of the glory of God, there must still

75. Theodore on Ephesians 1.4, 12; Colossians 1.22, *Studien zu dem Paulus kommentaren Theodors von Mopsuestia.*

76. Origen *Commentary on Romans* 6.3–4.

77. Theodore on Galatians 2.15–16, in *Epistolas b. Pauli commentarii.*

78. Theodore on Ephesians 2.7; on the concept of union and the Lord's Supper, in *Studien zu dem Paulus kommentaren Theodors von Mopsuestia;* cf. Chrysostom *Homilies on 1 Corinthians* 10.16–17.

79. Chrysostom *Homilies on Romans* 6.12.

be an even greater glory that will come in the future.[80] While he did not find it easy to do full justice to those texts which spoke of enjoyment of good gifts in this world, he aimed to take seriously the two sides of Pauline thought. The emphasis in Origen's thought at this point was undoubtedly conditioned by the stress on the transience and the imperfection of this world, characteristic of the neo-Platonist tradition. The focus of Paul's thought, as interpreted by Origen, rested in the future rather than in the past or the present.

In his various writings Chrysostom demonstrated an understanding of Pauline tension. He recognized the tension of Paul's indicatives and imperatives, as well as the tensions created in the call to baptism and faithful discipleship. True believers have put on the new person in their baptism, the Antiochenes maintained, but this still needed to be actualized in life and works. Christians have been buried with Christ, but there was still a need to mortify the sinful members of their bodies while on the earth. Chrysostom interpreted Paul to mean that sin died at the time of the believer's baptism, but it could be brought to life again.

It was Chrysostom's belief that the ultimate outcome of sin after conversion was final,[81] yet the living out of the new life could bring about differing actions and an endless variety of quality among different members in the community. Because their lives prove worthless, some will be saved by fire; this did not mean they will enter into the lower stages of heaven, but will be preserved alive in the eternal torments of fire.[82]

Chrysostom believed that Christians were essentially still in pilgrimage. They had received the earnest of the Spirit on the basis of faith, but the full gift still awaits the completion of a life of good works. Believers do possess some good gifts such as freedom from sin, obedience to righteousness, sanctification, and the attainment of eternal life, but still more awaits the future. He maintained that eschatological gifts, while present hidden truths, could be experienced in this life as a reality, but they could also be lost. The ultimate gifts were considered eternal and irrevocable.[83]

New Life and Freedom

Clement, an Alexandrian, treated much of the law as a tutor to bring people to Christ and as the first stage in confining the reign of sin.[84] Like-

80. Origen *Commentary on Romans* 5.2; 8.19; cf. Paul Lebeau, "L'interprétation origenienne de Rom. 8.19–22," in *Kyriakon: Festschrift Johannes Quasten*, ed. Patrick Granfield and Josef A. Jungman (Munster: Aschendorff, 1970), 336–45.

81. Chrysostom *Homilies on Romans* 6.16.

82. Chrysostom *Homilies on 1 Corinthians* 3.12–15.

83. Chrysostom *Homilies on Romans* 8.18–23.

84. Clement *Stromateis* 2.35.2.

wise, Origen, typical of most early commentators, declared that as Moses gave the first law to those who had come out of Egypt and were beginning their journey to the holy land, so Christ provided a second law for the Christian pilgrimage. Pauline injunctions concerning Christian behavior were often spiritualized by Origen because he believed their literal meaning was platitudinous, absurd, or irrelevant.[85] Where he did keep the straightforward meaning, he often offered Stoic interpretations to the words. The rules and laws were intended to help believers on the spiritual path and were therefore graded for different levels of spirituality. According to Origen, the keeping of certain laws was essential for salvation; others were matters left to the freedom of choice.[86] This pattern of morality was a graded hierarchy adopted to the spiritual capacity of each person. The most spiritual person should seek to be faithful to the law and the gospel's demands of asceticism. The earlier traditions regarding these matters seemed to be very influential for interpreters in the Alexandrian school. Those who exercised their freedom in such matters as marriage or dietary privileges were not the truly spiritual, but yet Clement and Origen conceded such freedom was a choice, though not the best. For example, Origen considered that marriage was the way of the unprofitable servant who only did his duty, but celibacy was the good way that excelled and surpassed duty.[87]

Chrysostom developed this idea further, and two standards of spirituality were established. Those who exercised freedom in certain matters, like marriage, settle to do what suits the weak. On the other hand, those who desire the good and more excellent way, according to Chrysostom, must keep all the rules. If Christians have been freed from the law, it is that they may pass beyond it, not that they may transgress it. Those who are spiritual should move beyond the realm of law keeping to abound more in greater obedience.[88]

The insight of Theodore and Chrysostom is apparent in their understanding of the relation of Paul's moral teaching to the pattern of Paul's thought as a whole. They carefully drew attention to the normal structures of the epistles in which there was a doctrinal section followed by a moral section. Of greater importance than the recognition of structure was the interrelationship between the two aspects of the epistles. Exhortation to moral obedience was built upon doctrinal truth. Theodore observed

85. Cf. Einar Mollard, *The Conception of the Gospel in the Alexandrian Theology* (Oslo: Jacob Dybwad, 1938), 118. For Origen, the Old Testament legal material, indeed the Old Testament itself, was *nomos* (law) insofar as it was obscure and required a spiritual interpretation which pointed to Christ; as *entole* (commandment) it was merely an immediately applicable moral injunction.

86. Origen *Fragments on Ephesians* 4.25–26.

87. Origen *Fragments on 1 Corinthians* 7.25.

88. Chrysostom *Commentary on Galatians* 5.13.

that Paul's teaching on the question of certain foods (Rom. 14) was based not only on creation but also on Christ's sacrificial death.[89] This significant truth distinguished the moral exhortations of Paul from those of the Stoics and other philosophers. Humility was the root of virtue, and humility could be discovered in the extent of Christ's incarnation and salvific work (Phil. 2:5–8). Thus, behind the precepts of regular Christian living lay the matchless wonders of divine grace (Rom. 11:33–12:2).

In this section we have examined the teaching of the Alexandrian and Antiochene fathers regarding the interpretation of Paul's views of the spiritual life. As we stated previously, the distance that separated these two schools in philosophical presuppositions and exegetical method was not as great in the Pauline passages as in other sections of Scripture. Even though the differences between the two ancient schools are not as pronounced, important distinctions remain worthy of observation:

1. The Antiochenes were more concerned with the historical context and the apostle's intent in his letters than were the Alexandrians.
2. Because the Antiochenes were more concerned with the historical context, they were more aware of theological development within the Pauline corpus.
3. In the same vein, the Antiochenes appeared more careful in their explication of the concept of development and progress in sanctification.
4. Because of their concern for the human element in Scripture, the Antiochenes struggled with the concept of divine initiative in the Christian life.
5. On the other hand, the Alexandrians, because of the neo-Platonic influence on their thought, wrestled with the idea of temporal tension in the "already/not yet" aspect of salvation.
6. The Alexandrians were quick to spiritualize the more demanding moral exhortations because of certain Gnostic, neo-Platonic, and Stoic influences upon their interpretation.
7. The Antiochenes carefully and sufficiently grasped the indicative/imperative tension in Paul. It was the emphasis on the human/historical element that allowed room for such tension to exist and be maintained in a balanced way.
8. The neo-Platonic concept of morality may have provided the framework for the Alexandrian elevation of good works and worthiness to a place almost equal to faith in the salvific sphere.

89. Theodore on Romans 14.1–4. in *Epistolas b. Pauli commentarii.*

Conclusion

In this chapter we have described the distinctive approach to hermeneutics of the Antiochene school. We have observed that the Antiochenes rejected allegorical interpretation in reaction to the Alexandrians. Through the development from Theophilus to Chrysostom, their literal and historical exegesis was refined. Like the Alexandrians, the Antiochene fathers brought certain traditions and philosophical presuppositions to the text.[90] Yet this tradition emphasized the literal and historical meaning of the biblical text as opposed to a spiritual or figurative meaning. Likewise, their philosophical foundation was more Aristotelian than Platonic. We have seen that the more mature exegesis of Theodore and Chrysostom, while literal, was not a crude or wooden literalism that failed to recognize figures of speech in the biblical text. Their emphasis on the human element of the text allowed for a critical reading that accounted for doctrinal development within the text itself. This human emphasis scarred the school's reputation. For in the important christological controversies of the day, many thought that the Antiochene hermeneutics gave rise to christological heresy represented by Nestorius, the student of Theodore. The reputation of the Antiochene giants suffered through association with Nestorianism, but there has been a reassessment in modern times, even of the theology of Nestorius himself. This reassessment looks favorably upon two features of Antiochene thought: (1) its stress on the genuine and complete humanity of Christ, who had to advance in moral goodness and achieve a redemptive victory for humankind as a man, and (2) its stress upon literal and historical interpretation of Scripture in reaction against allegorical exegesis. This emphasis upon the literal, historical, and human represented a new advance in patristic exegesis in discontinuity with what had been previously practiced.

Yet, in continuity with earlier practices, the Antiochenes read Scripture christologically. This was accomplished through typological exegesis similar to that of Jesus, the apostles, and Justin. We have noted that their typological usage emphasized the historicity of the parallel event. The term used to describe this twofold aspect of a text, its literal meaning and typological correspondence, was *theoria*. Despite their ingenious effort to dissociate *theoria* from allegorical hermeneutics, the difference was not always as clear as one might wish. But this is not unusual, for practice seldom reaches the consistent level of theory.

We observed that in their exegesis of the Pauline letters, both the Antiochenes and the Alexandrians generally interpreted the apostle literally

90. Cf. Christoph Schaublin, *Untersuchungen zu Methode und Hernkunft des antiochenischen Exegese*, Theophaneia 23 (Cologne-Bonn: Peter Hanstein, 1974).

and contextually, seeking to understand his intended thought. The differences primarily rested in the scope of revelation. The Alexandrian *allegoria* led the soul into a realm of true knowledge where the vision of truth could be discovered. The Antiochene *theoria* led humans into a truly moral life that developed in goodness and maturity that would continue into eternity.

Because of the Nestorian controversy, there developed a greater emphasis upon theological interpretation. With Jerome and Augustine in the West and Theodoret of Cyrus in the East, there developed an eclectic hermeneutical practice that sometimes emphasized the literal and sometimes the allegorical, but always the theological. Nevertheless, the Antiochene tradition never completely died out. As late as the ninth century, Isho'dad, in his *Introduction to the Psalms,* which was based on Theodore's work, railed against allegorism's distortions of the text, appealed for a literalist hermeneutic, and roundly "condemned the impious Origen."[91] The transition to the theological emphases of Jerome, Augustine, and Theodoret will be the concern of our next chapter.

91. Grant with Tracy, *Short History of the Interpretation of the Bible,* 64.

5

Toward Canonical and Catholic Hermeneutics

The emphasis on literal and historical interpretation was important not only for the Antiochenes, but also for the greatest doctors of the church, Jerome and Augustine. Yet, neither was so extreme a literalist as Theodore of Mopsuestia. Instead they stood closer to Chrysostom, who, because of his concern for preaching as opposed to Theodore's pure exegesis, had more spiritualizing tendencies. Jerome and Augustine moved toward a moderate literalism from a different direction. The main lines of their exegesis moved further and further away from the allegorization that they originally admired. Later in the fifth century, the last major representative of the Antiochene school, Theodoret of Cyrus, practiced an eclectic exegesis more open to allegorical hermeneutics than any of his Antiochene predecessors. In this chapter we shall examine the hermeneutical practices of these three significant exegetes—Jerome, Augustine, and Theodoret—to observe the developments toward canonical and Catholic hermeneutics in the late fourth and the fifth centuries.

Jerome

His Background

Jerome (ca. A.D. 341–420) was the most learned person in the Latin-speaking church of the late fourth century. His two major contributions to the religious history of the Christian West were his Latin translation of the Bible, known as the Vulgate, and the promotion of monasticism. There had been Latin translations of the Bible as far back as the second century, but they were poor in style and colloquial in language. Also, the Old Testament was translated from a Greek version and not the Hebrew. Jerome's wide reading and brilliant linguistic gifts enabled him to be one of the greatest biblical scholars of the early church.[1]

Jerome was born at Stridon, a town in northeast Italy. He was sent to Rome to study grammar and rhetoric by his well-to-do parents. During his advanced student days he was baptized, and shortly thereafter he added Christian theological works to his reading. Following a stay in Trier in Germany, Jerome felt a call to the asceticism that was considered by many to be the highest form of Christianity. He joined an ascetic group at Aquileia in Italy, but his lack of tact, sharp tongue, and high-strung temperament made him difficult to get along with for an extended period of time, so he was soon terminated from the group.

In 372, Jerome set out for Palestine but settled instead in Antioch. There he improved his knowledge of Greek but began to struggle with the profound tension between his intellectual interests and his Christian aspirations. In a dream, the Lord asked Jerome who and what he was. Jerome replied, "I am Christian."[2] But the response came: "You lie, you are a follower of Cicero and not of Christ, for where your treasure is, there will your heart be also"[3] (quoting Matt. 6:21). For a decade he resolved not to study pagan literature and retreated into the Syrian desert near Chalcis to become a hermit. Yet worldly desires continued to plague him, and in spite of his severe ascetic disciplines he dreamed about dancing girls in Rome.[4]

With the aid of a Jewish convert, Jerome began the study of Hebrew, and eventually gained a mastery unequalled among the church leaders of his time.[5] Jerome was never well accepted by the ascetics in the Syrian desert, so he returned to Antioch, where he was ordained a presbyter. After spending time in Constantinople, Jerome returned to Rome from 382 to 385. During this time he was commissioned by Damascus, Bishop of Rome, to begin preparing a new Latin translation of the Gospels and the Psalms. Jerome had discovered his life's work, which would be his chief contribution to Western civilization. Working off and on for the next twenty years on the Bible translation, he eventually was to complete the entire Old Testament as well.[6]

While in Rome, Jerome became a spiritual guide and Bible teacher to groups of wealthy, aristocratic widows led by Marcella, Paula, and Paula's

1. Hans von Campenhausen, *Men Who Shaped the Western Church* (New York: Harper, 1964), 129–82.

2. Jerome *Letters* 22.30.

3. Ibid.

4. Ibid., 22.7.

5. James Barr, "St. Jerome's Appreciation of Hebrew," *BJRL* 49 (1966–67): 281–83.

6. Witt Semple, "St. Jerome as Biblical Translator," *BJRL* 48 (1965–66): 228–29.

daughter, Eustochium. The leaders of the Roman church asked Jerome to leave Rome because of his advocacy of asceticism, his influence with prominent women, and his ongoing criticisms of a worldly church.[7]

After visiting the holy places in Jerusalem and throughout Palestine, Jerome and Paula settled in Bethlehem in 386 and established separate monasteries for men and women. A fruitful period of study and writing began. It was, however, frequently interrupted by personal illness and a series of controversies with (1) Jovinian, a Roman monk; (2) Origenism in the West; (3) John of Jerusalem; (4) Rufinus, a close friend of Jerome; (5) Vigilantius; (6) Augustine; and (7) followers of Pelagius. Near the end of his life Jerome finally fashioned a form of ascetic life that combined his ideals of withdrawal with his needs for companionship and intellectual activity.[8]

His Work as Translator and Interpreter

During his years in Bethlehem, Jerome became convinced that translations of the Old Testament must be based on Hebrew and not Greek. He professed to be more literal in theory than he was in practice, opting more for a sense-for-sense rather than a word-for-word translation.[9] In support of his dynamic paraphrase he appealed to the apostles' use of the Old Testament and the Septuagint translation of the Old Testament. His Latin translation, which became known as the Vulgate in the thirteenth century, was completed in 406 and became his crowning contribution to biblical studies. It was not until the ninth century that his work gained full acceptance. The fourteenth-century English translation by John Wycliffe and the sixteenth-century Douai version were based on Jerome's Vulgate.

The adoption of Hebrew as the standard text meant also the recognition of the Hebrew canon of the Old Testament. As a result Jerome refused to accept the apocryphal books that were being circulated at that time in manuscripts of the Greek and Latin versions. Because Jerome was conscious of the difficulty of arguing with Jews on the basis of books they spurned (they regarded only the Hebrew books as authoritative), he was adamant that anything not found in the Hebrew canon was to be classed among the Apocrypha and therefore noncanonical.[10] Later, he grudgingly conceded that the church could read some of these books for edification, but not as support of church doctrine. In spite of his low opinion of the books in the Apocrypha, he eventually translated Tobit, Judith, and the

7. Walter J. Burghardt, S.J., "Saint Jerome," *TNEB* 6 (1985): 535–36.

8. W. H. Fremantle, "Prolegomena to Jerome," *NPNF*, 6:xvi–xxv; see also Y. M. Duval, "Jerome et Origene avant la querrel origeniste," *Aug* 24 (1984): 471–94.

9. Jerome *Letters* 57.5.

10. J. N. D. Kelly, *Early Christian Doctrines*, 4th rev. ed. (San Francisco: Harper and Row, 1978), 55.

additions to Daniel and Esther, but he did so rapidly and without much care. His interest in the Hebrew text and related contact with Jewish hermeneutical practices gave Jerome a sensitivity to the literal and historical sense of Scripture.[11]

As a biblical interpreter, Jerome was strongly influenced by Didymus the Blind (ca. A.D. 313–398), a follower of Origen whom Jerome visited in Alexandria in 385–386 before settling in Bethlehem. From this influence, Jerome developed his early love for the spiritual sense of Scripture.[12] Yet, in his later days he became suspicious of allegorical interpretation. While accepting Origen's three senses of Scripture, he deemed that recourse to the spiritual meaning was made necessary by the anthropomorphisms, inconsistencies, and incongruities that seemingly abounded in the Bible.[13] He therefore attempted to combine attention to the literal sense of Scripture learned from Hebrew scholarship with a christological and spiritual interpretation.[14] For example, John Rogerson observes that Jerome referred many psalms to Christ, as well as David:

> In Psalm 3, the "holy hill" from which God answers the psalmist can refer both to the Son of God and to the church. In Psalm 4, the references can only be to Christ, since the psalmist possesses a righteousness not appropriate even to David. In Psalm 5:2 the phrase "my king and my God" refers to Christ, who is king and God of the church. Again the whole of Psalm 17 pertains to Christ in the person of David.[15]

Jerome's commentaries on Scripture were prepared in great haste. His exposition of Galatians was written at the rate of a thousand lines per day, and his commentary on Matthew was completed within two weeks. His first commentary was almost pure allegorization. At Antioch, however, he came under the influence of the literal-historical method, taught to him by Apollinaris of Laodicea. The influence of the school of Antioch, along with the Jewish influence, caused Jerome to devalue the allegorical

11. H. F. D. Sparks, "Jerome as Biblical Scholar," *CHB,* 1:510–40.

12. John Rogerson, Christopher Rowland, and Barnabas Lindars, *The Study and Use of the Bible,* vol. 2 of *The History of Christian Theology,* ed. Paul Avis, 3 vols. (Grand Rapids: Eerdmans, 1988), 43–44.

13. Kelly, *Early Christian Doctrines,* 75, though he said in *Letters* 27, "I am not so stupid as to think that any of the Lord's words either need correcting or are not divinely inspired; but the Latin manuscripts of the Scriptures are proved faulty by the variations which are found in all of them. My aim had been to restore them to the form of the original, from which my critics do not deny that they have been translated."

14. Cf. P. Jay, "Saint Jerome et le triple sens de l'Ecriture," *REAug* 26 (1980): 214–27; idem, "Allegoriarum nubilum chez St. Jerome," *REAug* 22 (1976): 82–89.

15. Rogerson, Rowland, Lindars, *Study and Use of the Bible,* 44, citing Jerome's *Commentary on Psalms* 177–245.

method, even as presented in its modified form by Gregory of Nazianzus. Robert M. Grant aptly summarizes,

> No matter how ingenious the allegorization, Jerome had to insist upon the reality of the literal meaning. The deeper meaning of scripture was built on the literal, not opposed to it. Everything written in scripture took place and at the same time has a meaning more than historical. This meaning is based on the *Hebraica veritas,* the truth expressed in Hebrew. We must have a *spiritualis intelligenta,* a spiritual understanding of scripture, which goes beyond the *carneus sensus,* the fleshly sense, but will not be opposed to it.[16]

Through Jerome's influence, a modified Antiochene literalism was mediated to the later church.

Jerome's commentary on the Book of Daniel was perhaps his most notable and influential work.[17] His commentary remained strictly within the confines required by the text. He accepted the book as the work of the prophet Daniel, exiled to Babylon in the sixth century B.C. He believed portions of the book to be prophetic by virtue of its inspiration; thus they pointed to events after the time of Daniel, but prior to Jerome's own time. He thought the four empires in Daniel 2 signified by the gold, silver, bronze, and iron mixed with clay were respectively the Babylonians, the Medes and Persians, the empire of Alexander the Great and his successors, and finally, the Roman Empire. The mixture of iron and clay signified the fact that Rome depended upon barbarians to support it. The stone made without hands that smashed the structure composed of all four metals pointed to Jesus, who was to triumph over all empires.[18]

In Daniel 7, Jerome identified the fourth beast which trampled upon the three preceding beasts. The "little horn" of Daniel 7 represented, in Jerome's opinion, a future human ruler who would be used by Satan. The figure of "one like a son of man" was identified as Christ.[19]

Jerome made identifications, when interpreting Daniel 8 and 11, that have had wide-ranging acceptance to the present day. Thus the ram defeated by the male goat in 8:4–7 referred to the defeat by Alexander

16. Robert M. Grant with David Tracy, *A Short History of the Interpretation of the Bible,* rev. ed. (Philadelphia: Fortress, 1984), 69.

17. Cf. Jerome *Commentary on Daniel,* trans. Gleason L. Archer (Grand Rapids: Baker, 1958), 5, where W. M. Smith claims in the introduction, "The most important single work produced by the Church Fathers on any of the prophetic writings of the Old Testament, commenting upon the original Hebrew text, and showing a complete mastery of all the literature of the Church on the subjects touched upon to the time of compensation, is without question St. Jerome's Commentary on the Book of Daniel." Whether or not this extravagant claim is justified, it does point to the influence of this commentary.

18. Ibid., 32.

19. Ibid., 77.

the Great of the Persian empire, and the division of the large horn of the male goat when it died was the division of Alexander's kingdom at his death. In interpreting Daniel 8, Jerome allowed that the "little horn" of 8:9–14 was Antiochus Epiphanes.[20] Jerome suggested that Daniel 11:3, "a mighty king will appear, who will rule with great power and do as he pleases," referred to the events of the struggle for the land of Israel between Antiochus the Great and the Ptolemies at the beginning of the second century B.C. As with all commentators on Daniel, Jerome devoted much space to differing theories about the meaning of the seventy weeks and the sixty-two weeks in Daniel 9.[21]

Generally, Jerome expounded the text in a contextual and historical fashion in line with its dual genre, both historical narrative and prophetic. He was obviously much in sympathy with the ascetically-inclined Daniel and his companions and praised Daniel's apparent refusal of gifts from the king (Dan. 5:17). He recognized in the entire book a picture of God's merciful and bountiful providence. The restoration of Nebuchadnezzar after his madness was a sign of God's sovereign control, a control expected by the three men thrown into the fiery furnace (Dan. 3:18). Unlike the pattern of christological interpretation so common in the early church, Jerome did not identify the fourth person in the furnace as Christ (Dan. 3:18–27), on the grounds that it was unlikely that an ungodly king would be vouchsafed a vision of the Son of God. Instead, he understood Daniel 3:25 to refer to an angel who prefigured Christ.[22]

There are infrequent places of spiritualizing or allegorical interpretation in Jerome's work on Daniel. In his comments on Daniel 5:4, where the gods of gold, silver, bronze, iron, wood, and stone are pictured as heretics and abusers of God, he concluded that the gods of gold rely on human reason, those of silver rely on eloquence and rhetoric, those of bronze and iron refer to fables and divergent ancient traditions, and those of wood rely on absurdities. Yet, in comparison with Origen, Jerome resisted the extreme spiritualizing representative of the Alexandrians.

Jerome's later works of biblical interpretation moved away from an allegorical methodology toward a more historical and philological exegesis. His faults, though few, can probably be traced to working too rapidly and relying too strongly on his memory. Most of his commentaries were written during the midst of controversies and many of his surviving exegetical works are polemical.

20. Ibid., 85.

21. Ibid., 95–110; see Joyce Baldwin's excellent survey of the various views throughout history, *Daniel* (Downers Grove, Ill.: InterVarsity, 1978).

22. Jerome *Commentary on Daniel* 39–40.

An early controversy with Helvidius concerned the perpetual virginity of Mary. It must be admitted that Helvidius had the best of the argument exegetically, yet Jerome's defense of Mary's virginity shaped the Mariology of the Latin church and Western Christian sexual ethics for centuries thereafter.[23] Jerome's attitude so exalted virginity that he considered the benefit of marriage to be that "it brings virgins into the world."[24]

In his work *Against Jovinian,* a former ascetic who had given up extreme practices and had written against the monastic life, Jerome claimed "eating meat, drinking wine, and having a well-fed stomach" formed the "seedbed of lust."[25] In another place, he lauded the ascetic life by replying to the charge that he was against wedlock by saying, "I should like everyone to take a wife who, because of the terrors of the night, is afraid to sleep alone."[26]

Before turning our attention to Augustine, we should briefly note Jerome's clash with Augustine.[27] The dispute concerned the interpretation of Peter's actions, which Paul described in Galatians 2:11–12, when Peter refused to eat with Gentile Christians in Antioch and was rebuked by Paul. Porphyry, exploiting the clash between Peter and Paul, asserted that Peter had only pretended to observe the Jewish law and that Paul had only pretended to rebuke him. Jerome followed this interpretation, but Augustine rejected it on the grounds that this would amount to deliberate dishonesty. Jerome and Augustine agreed that Christians were not bound by Jewish food laws. Yet Augustine, in contrast to Jerome, maintained that Peter's behavior should be accepted and allowed for the privilege of Jewish Christians accepting Jewish ceremonial regulations, provided they did not trust in such observances for salvation.[28]

In conclusion, Jerome was a more able linguist and translator than any of his colleagues in the early church. Yet, his interpretive work lacked originality and at times, while never denouncing orthodoxy, demonstrated a literary artist's distaste for theological concerns. His eclectic methodology combined what was best in both the Alexandrian and Antiochene schools. His mature theory in later years developed some hermeneutical principles in line with the Antiochene school. In practice he was an eclectic interpreter within the Catholic tradition. He insisted that the literal was not contradictory to the allegorical, as was sometimes indicated by the Alexandrians. On the other hand he evaded the wooden literalism of some Jewish scholars with whom he associated.

23. Richard P. McBrien, *Catholicism* (Minneapolis: Winston, 1981), 866–74.

24. Jerome *Letters* 22.20.

25. Jerome *Against Jovinian* 2.7.

26. Jerome *Letters* 50.5.

27. See the description in J. N. D. Kelly, *Jerome: His Life, Writings and Controversies* (London: Duckworth, 1975), 269–73.

28. Ibid., 272.

Without question Jerome ranks as an early biblical interpreter of the first order. His influence as an orthodox theological interpreter and a biblical translator endures.

Augustine

His Background

For Protestants, Augustine (A.D. 354–430) serves as the dominant figure in the history of Christian thought and biblical interpretation between the time of the apostles and the sixteenth-century Reformation. For Roman Catholics, Augustine's influence during this period is rivaled only by that of Thomas Aquinas (A.D. 1225–1274). In the history of philosophy, Augustine is only slightly less important; he was the most influential philosopher between Plotinus, in the third century, and Aquinas.

Augustine's life serves an important key to understanding his thought. Born in what is now Algeria, Augustine's early life was vitally shaped by his Christian mother, Monica. His father, Patricius, was not a Christian and had relatively little influence on him. As described in his *Confessions,*[29] Augustine in his youth seldom lost an opportunity to pursue one sin or another. He took a mistress when he was seventeen and fathered an illegitimate son before he was twenty.[30] About that same time, he began a relationship with a dualistic religious and philosophical system known as Manichaeism, which taught that two principles, Light and Dark, God and Matter, are eternal. Augustine claimed that Manichaeism appealed to him intellectually because it appeared to offer a superior answer to the problem of evil than what he had discovered in his mother's Christianity. Augustine was also drawn to Manichaeism because it made fewer moral demands than Christianity. He could continue to live as he wanted and be faithful to Manichaean principles.[31] Yet he was not a convinced Manichaean, but remained a convinced anti-Catholic. When he gradually realized through the study of the liberal arts, particularly philosophy, the inconsistency of the religion of Mani, Augustine did not take up with the church nor with any other school of philosophers, "because they were without the saving

29. The *Confessions* are divided into two parts: the first part (1–9) describes Augustine up to the time of his conversion and the death of his mother; the second part (10–13), added at a later date, describes Augustine's thoughts during the time of the writings (cf. *Confessions* 10.4–6). The unity of the work is to be found in the central theme of the praise of God "for the good things and for the bad," and in the autobiographical aspect, which was also present in the second part. The *Confessions* were begun after April 4, 397 (the death of Ambrose) and completed around 400. See A. Pincherle, "The 'Confessions' of St. Augustine," *AugSt* 7 (1976): 119–33; *Augustine's Confessions: The Odyssey of Soul* (Cambridge: Cambridge University Press, 1969).

30. Augustine *Confessions* 4.2.2.

31. Ibid., 5.14.24.

name of Christ."[32] Instead, he fell into the temptation of skepticism, with academics at the helm of his life.

The road to his conversion began at Milan with the preaching of Ambrose (ca. A.D. 339–397), which dispersed the Manichaean difficulties and provided the key for the interpretation of the Old Testament with the use of allegorical hermeneutics. Under Ambrose's influence, Augustine's difficulties about the Bible began to be resolved, and the process was accelerated by his discovery of neo-Platonist philosophy, in which he could find confirmation of much that was in the Gospel of John.[33] On the eve of his conversion, Pontitianus, Augustine's Christian friend, found him studying the Epistles of Paul. The following day, Augustine was dramatically converted:

> I probed the hidden depths of my soul and wrung its pitiful secrets from it, and when I gathered them all before the eyes of my heart, a great storm broke within me, bringing with it a great deluge of tears. . . . For I felt that I was still enslaved by my sins, and in my misery I kept crying, "How long shall I go on saying 'Tomorrow, tomorrow'? Why not now? Why not make an end of my ugly sins at this moment?"
>
> I was asking myself these questions, weeping all the while with the most bitter sorrow in my heart, when all at once I heard the sing-song voice of a child in a nearby house. Whether it was the voice of a boy or a girl I cannot say, but again and again it repeated the chorus, "Take it and read, take it and read." At this I looked up, thinking hard whether there was any kind of game in which children used to chant words like these, but I could not ever remember hearing them before. I stemmed my flood of tears and stood up, telling myself that this could only be God's command to open my book of Scripture and read the first passage on which my eyes should fall. . . .
>
> So I hurried back to the place where Alypius was sitting, for when I stood up to move away I had put down the book containing Paul's Letters. I seized it and opened it, and in silence I read the first passage on which my eyes fell: "No orgies or drunkenness, no immorality or indecency, no fighting or jealousy. Take up the weapons of the Lord Jesus Christ; and stop giving attention to your sinful nature, to satisfy its desires." I had no wish to read more and no need to do so. For in an instant, as I came to the end of the sentence, it was as though the light of faith flooded into my heart and all the darkness of doubt was dispelled.[34]

32. Ibid.

33. Ibid., 7.5.7; 7.9.13; 7.10.16. On Ambrose's influence on Augustine, see F. Homes Dudden, *The Life and Times of St. Ambrose,* 2 vols. (Oxford: Oxford University Press, 1935).

34. Ibid., 8.12; cf. W. Mallard, "The Incarnation in Augustine's Conversion," *RAug* 15 (1980): 80–98; E. Kevane, "Philosophy, Education and the Controversy on Saint Augustine's Conversion," *Studies in Philosophy and the History of Philosophy* 2 (1963): 61–103.

He continued his personal reflection on the necessity of faith to arrive at wisdom. This reflection terminated in the conviction that the authority on which faith rested was the Scriptures, the Scriptures guaranteed and read by the church. Now he was convinced that the way which led to Christ was precisely the church.

Augustine's conversion took place in A.D. 386, at which time he authored *Against the Skeptics.* He was baptized in 387, ordained as a priest in 391, appointed as coadjutor bishop, and was consecrated a bishop of Hippo Regius in 395. His numerous writings included polemical works against the Manichaeans, the Donatists, and the Pelagians, in addition to important theological works such as *The Trinity* and *The City of God.*[35] During this time a stream of biblical commentaries also flowed from his pen, including works on Genesis, the Sermon on the Mount, Romans, Galatians, and John.[36] Between 414 and 417 Augustine reached a high point in expository writing with his sermons on the Psalms and the Johannine writings, which established his reputation as preacher and exegete. As Gerald Bonner has noted: "The effect of this close and devoted application to the text of scripture in Augustine's early years as a priest and bishop may be seen in his later writings, both exegetical and controversial, with their constant citations which, on occasion, produce what is virtually a mosaic of scripture texts perfectly welded together."[37]

His Hermeneutical Approach

Many of Augustine's commentaries, like those of Chrysostom, were expository sermons preached to his congregation at Hippo; therefore they were more practical than grammatical and critical. After covering the first five verses of the first chapter of Romans, Augustine found his comments so elaborate that he withdrew from his task.[38] Augustine's other writings abound in quotations, and his polemical works evidence his knowledge of the Bible and his skill in its use. This was especially so in his theological treatises *On Christian Doctrine* and *The City of God.*

The City of God, whose title was taken by Augustine from the Psalms, was designed, from book 11 onwards, to indicate how the whole Bible

35. Cf. G. G. Willis, *St. Augustine and the Donatist Controversy* (London: SPCK, 1950); Gerald Bonner, *Augustine and Pelagianism in the Light of Modern Research* (Philadelphia: Westminster, 1973).

36. For a discussion of the dating of these works, see M. Le Landais, "Deux annees de predication de saint Augustin," in *Etudes Augustiniennes,* by H. Rondet, M. Le Landais, A. Lauras, and C. Coutourier (Paris: Cerf, 1953), 19–95.

37. Gerald Bonner, "Augustine as Biblical Scholar," *CHB,* 1:544.

38. W. Babcock, "Augustine's Interpretation of Romans (A.D. 394–396)," *AugSt* 10 (1979): 55–74.

was the story of two cities: the heavenly and the earthly. Augustine's approach downplayed the division between the Old and New Testaments. The Old Testament was not considered a preparation for the establishment of the heavenly kingdom of Christ, though Augustine recognized that Christ's coming brought significant changes. The Old Testament was not about blessings in the present earthly world as opposed to the New Testament's offering of heavenly blessings. Instead, both Testaments simultaneously described both cities from their inception to their end. The city of God was equally present in the Israel of the Old Testament as it was with the church in the New.[39] Thus Augustine presented a unified and canonical approach to the Bible that still allowed for the significance of the coming of Jesus Christ, while maintaining the essential unity of the two Testaments.[40] From this canonical framework, Augustine developed his hermeneutical approach.

In this approach, Augustine was able to interpret both literally and symbolically. After tracing the establishment of the two cities from their heavenly and earthly points of view in books 11–15 of *The City of God,* he traced their history up to and through the flood account (Gen. 6–9) and on into Israelite history (Gen. 12–50). When dealing with the history of Israel, Augustine demonstrated most clearly what he meant when he said that biblical history was primarily prophetic rather than simply an inspired and correct record of past events.[41] Also, Augustine contextualized his view of the relation between the historical and spiritual interpretation, and between prophecy that had both heavenly and earthly aspects.[42] In books 15 and 16 Augustine made it clear that the primary function of Old Testament history was to point to the existence of the city of God by anticipating the coming of Christ, who made possible for all humanity the reversal of the curse of the disobedience of Adam (cf. Rom. 5:12–21).[43]

Augustine accepted the historical account of the creation story and the flood story in Genesis.[44] On common-sense grounds, Augustine argued that the days and years referred to in the genealogy (Gen. 5) should be no different from the days and years of the flood narrative, and it was clear that ordinary days and years were meant in the flood story. There was no reason to suggest that Methuselah's 969 years (cf. Gen. 5:27) were

39. Cf. R. H. Barrow, *Introduction to St. Augustine's 'The City of God'* (London: Faber and Faber, 1950).

40. Augustine *The City of God* 10.25.

41. Ibid., 17.3.

42. Ibid., 17.4.

43. Ibid., 15.8; 16.2.

44. Cf. M. M. Gorman, "A Study of the Literal Interpretation of Genesis" (Ph.D. diss., University of Toronto, 1975).

anything other than normal years.[45] While arguing for a literal interpretation, he acknowledged the difficulty of explaining the fact that some patriarchs in Genesis 5 did not father children until they were over one hundred years old.[46]

Yet, Augustine did offer spiritual meanings of many of the events reported in Genesis. He commented that the door of Noah's ark (Gen. 8:13) was representative of the wound made in the side of Christ at his crucifixion.[47] He maintained that Abraham, in fathering a son through Hagar, his wife's servant (Gen. 16), was not to be blamed, because this action was not accomplished with lust. His marriage to Keturah, his second wife (Gen. 25), was also not the result of fleshly lusts, but a foreshadowing of "the carnal people" who thought they belonged to the New Covenant (cf. Jer. 31; 2 Cor. 3).[48] He contended that Jacob did not act fraudulently when he deprived Esau of his blessing (Gen. 27), since his action enabled Christ to be proclaimed to the nations when Isaac blessed him.[49] One additional example demonstrates Augustine's spiritualizing tendency. Augustine claimed that when Jacob anointed the stone after his heavenly vision (Gen. 28), he was not practicing idolatry but was foreshadowing Christ.[50] This spiritualizing methodology was closer to Chrysostom's typological exegesis than Origen's allegorizing.

Augustine recognized the importance of one's presuppositions when interpreting Holy Scripture. He was perhaps the greatest of the Christian Platonists.[51] The integration of biblical data and Platonic philosophy can be seen in Augustine's famous maxim: *Credo ut intelligam* (I believe in order that I may understand). Augustine derived the biblical foundation of this principle from the Latin version of the Septuagint translation of Isaiah 7:9, *nisi credideritis non intelligetis* (unless you believe, you shall not understand). The philosophical foundation came from the Platonic notion of innate first principles, which enabled persons to understand particulars in this world.[52] In Augustine's work *On Free Will*, he declared:

45. Augustine *Exposition of Genesis According to the Letter* 11.15.20.

46. Augustine *The City of God* 15.23.

47. Ibid., 15.26.

48. Ibid., 16.25.

49. Ibid., 16.37.

50. Ibid., 16.38. For a thorough analysis of Augustine's exegesis in *The City of God*, see R. A. Markus, *Saeculum: History and Society in the Theology of St. Augustine* (Cambridge: Cambridge University Press, 1970).

51. A. Hilary Armstrong, *St. Augustine and Christian Platonism* (Villanova, Penn.: Villanova University Press, 1967), 1–2. Armstrong, 288–94, notes that "Augustine's limited knowledge of Greek [forced him to] read the Platonists and Neoplatonists through the Latin translations of Victorinus."

52. Cf. R. A. Markus, "St. Augustine," *EP*, 1:198–99.

> You remember the position we adopted at the beginning of our former discussion. We cannot deny that believing and knowing are different things, and that in matters of great importance, pertaining to divinity, we must first believe before we seek to know. Otherwise the words of the prophet would be vain, where he says: "Except ye believe ye shall not understand" (Isa. 7:9 LXX). Our Lord himself, both in his words and by his deeds, exhorted those whom he called to salvation first of all to believe. And no one is fit to find God who does not first believe what he will afterwards learn to know.[53]

Augustine recognized that the realm of the eternal and the realm of the temporal are known differently. The priority clearly rested with the eternal in Augustine's scheme. The knowledge of the eternal precedes and helps to illumine the realm of the temporal. Since knowledge from the realm of the eternal is accepted in faith and leads to understanding of both eternal and temporal realms, then biblical interpretation begins with faith. For example, in expounding the Gospel of John, he observed, "For we believe in order that we may know, we do not know in order that we may believe."[54] The precedence of faith to understanding, for Augustine, corresponded to the biblical distinction between "walking by faith and not by sight" (cf. 2 Cor. 5:7). He maintained that those who had embraced the God-given revelation in Scripture by faith could be enabled by reason in the quest for full understanding. The "things below" could function to help the individual come to a fuller knowledge of "things above."[55]

Long before the insights of contemporary semiotics or semantics, Augustine recognized that things in the created world could function as "signs" or "symbols" through which God was understood.[56] Understanding is possible because of the illumination afforded by the uncreated light of God. Augustine believed that for the mind to see God it must be illumined by God, and this results in (1) a faith that believes that what we look for, when seen, ought to make us blessed; (2) a hope that is assured that vision will follow right looking; (3) and a love which longs to see and to enjoy.[57]

Bernard Ramm has noted that Augustine spoke of natural objects that were percepts but not signs, such as pieces of metal or wood. He next spoke of things which signified other things. A tree could signify forestry service, a

53. Augustine *On Free Will* 2.4.6.

54. Augustine *Tractates on the Gospel of St. John* 40.9.

55. Augustine *On the Trinity* 1.1; see also Robert E. Cushman, "Faith and Reason," in *A Companion to the Study of St. Augustine,* ed. Roy W. Battenhouse (New York: Oxford University Press, 1955), 290–94.

56. Bernard Ramm, *Protestant Biblical Interpretation: A Textbook of Hermeneutics,* 3d rev. ed. (Grand Rapids: Baker, 1970), 34–35; Belford D. Jackson, "Semantics and Hermeneutics in Saint Augustine's *De doctrina Christiana*" (Ph.D. diss., Yale University, 1967), 171–87.

57. Avery Dulles, *A History of Apologetics,* Theological Resources, ed. Jaroslav Pelikan and John P. Whalen (New York: Corpus, 1971), 61, citing *Soliloquies* 1.6.13 and *The City of God* 8.8.

shoe a shoemaker, and an anvil the blacksmith guild. Then, there were things whose primary, if not sole, function was to signify other things, such as words.[58] Augustine defined a sign as "a thing which apart from the impression that it presents to the sense, causes of itself some other thing to enter our thoughts."[59] These signs are conventional or natural. Smoke is an obvious sign of fire. Conventional signs, according to Augustine, are those which "living creatures give to one another."[60] From this he proceeded to discuss sounds and speech. This included God's method of communication to women and men through speech, and speech incarnate in the written Scriptures. Such insight was typical of the genius of Augustine, concerning a subject that was not developed until over one thousand years after his time.

Having recognized the place of faith and the significance of signs in Augustine's hermeneutics, we will also examine the influence of Tyconius, the Donatist, on Augustine and others in North Africa. The first hermeneutical treatise written in the Latin West was Tyconius's *Book of Rules,* written about 380. Even though he functioned in the schismatic Donatist community, he drew respect from Christians as a competent theologian and exegete. Augustine, in *On Christian Doctrine,* interacted favorably with Tyconius's *Book of Rules.*

In the "Prologue" to the *Book of Rules,* Tyconius stated,

> I thought it necessary before anything else which occurred to me to write providing something like keys and windows to the secrets of the law. For there are certain mystical rules which govern the depth of the entire law and hide the treasures of truth from the sight of some people. If the logic of these rules is accepted without prejudice as we set it down here, every closed door will be opened and light will be shed on every obscurity. Guided, as it were, by these rules in paths of light, a person walking through the immense forest of prophecy may well be defended from error.
>
> These rules are as follows:
>
> 1. Of the Lord and His Body
> 2. Of the Lord's Bipartite Body
> 3. Of Promises and the Law
> 4. Of Species and Genus
> 5. Of Times
> 6. Of Recapitulation
> 7. Of the Devil and His Body.[61]

58. Ramm, *Protestant Biblical Interpretation,* 34–35.

59. Augustine *On Christian Doctrine* 2.1.1.

60. Ibid., 2.2.3.

61. Tyconius *The Book of Rules of Tyconius* 1; for a full discussion of Augustine's use of Tyconius, see chapter 1 in James Samuel Preus, *From Shadow to Promise: Old Testament Interpretation from Augustine to the Young Luther* (Cambridge: Harvard University Press, 1969).

Augustine quoted the prologue but disagreed with the claim that these rules would solve "all obscurities" in the law. This was followed by a detailed summary of each of the seven rules. The second and third rules, according to Augustine, were wrongly labeled, but apart from these minor points and a warning about Tyconius's Donatist presuppositions, his review was positive and enthusiastic. Tyconius's hermeneutics began with the principle that all exegesis has an ecclesiological goal: The Bible illustrates and interprets the struggles of the contemporary church. His thoroughly symbolic interpretation of the last book of the New Testament, the Apocalypse of John, brought about a shift from a traditional millenarian reading, which Augustine also adopted. This hermeneutical concentration on the situation of the church militant between the ages was the feature which appealed to Augustine and the generations after him.

Tyconius approached the hermeneutical task by giving careful attention to the peculiarities of the biblical text. The emphasis was upon the biblical text rather than the biblical author; thus, the texts themselves offered the clue to their ecclesiological meaning. As Karlfried Froehlich described, Tyconius began "with the observation that the wording of biblical passages often shows rhetorical patterns which point to several subjects governing a single sentence or to a transition from one subject to another in the same verse."[62] The third rule rehearsed the distinction between law and promise, developing the concept that the true church always includes the people of God, but the visible church includes children of the devil as well. This true church would manifest itself as the false brethren were revealed. The vision of history as the battleground of the true and false church, of course, found its lasting expression in Augustine's two cities characterized in his *City of God*.[63] His hermeneutics was a commentary on a theme also adopted from Tyconius. The goal of all biblical interpretation should prioritize the love of God and neighbor (cf. Matt 22:37–39), the ordering of the Christian life toward its heavenly home.[64]

Thus far we have seen that Augustine emphasized the entire biblical canon, the priority of faith, the significance of signs, the biblical text, and the goal of love. Lastly, we must briefly examine the place of allegorical interpretation in Augustine.

Augustine commended the method of interpreting obscure passages by the light of passages already understood, and, as we might expect, this was preferred before the interpretation by reason. Also, he stressed the spirit of the text more than verbal accuracy or critical acumen. Even the

62. Karlfried Froehlich, *Biblical Interpretation in the Early Church* (Philadelphia: Fortress, 1984), 27–28.

63. Ibid., 28.

64. Augustine *On Christian Doctrine* 1.35–36.

mistakes of an exegete, properly disposed, suggested Augustine, may confirm religious faith and establish character. He said,

> If the mistaken interpretation tends to build up love, which is the end of the commandment, the interpreter goes astray in much the same way as a man who, by mistake, quits the high road, but yet reaches, through the fields, the same place to which the road leads.[65]

Augustine did not hesitate to put more than one interpretation on a text, especially the Psalms, and no one was more elaborate in comparing Scripture with Scripture than was he.[66]

We have noted that the goal of biblical interpretation for Augustine was to increase love for God and for one's neighbor.[67] Augustine asserted, "What is read should be subjected to diligent scrutiny until an interpretation contributing to the reign of charity is produced."[68] It was this hermeneutical theme that determined when Augustine used spiritual or figurative interpretation. He recommended this guideline: "Whatever there is in the word of God that cannot when taken literally be referred to purity of life or soundness of doctrine, you may set down as figurative."[69] Thus Augustine did not limit Scripture to just one sense. When he approached the Bible, he first asked theological rather than historical questions.[70]

As Augustine explained, it was his spiritual father, Bishop Ambrose, who opened the method of allegorical exegesis for him:

> I listened with delight to Ambrose, in his sermons to the people, often recommending this text most diligently as a rule: "The letter kills, but the spirit gives life" (2 Cor 3:6), while at the same time he drew aside the mystic veil and opened to view the spiritual meaning of what seemed to teach perverse doctrine if it were taken according to the letter.[71]

This proof-text for 2 Corinthians 3:6 was a misreading of that text. Nevertheless, despite Augustine's dislike for crude literalism, he did not ignore

65. Ibid., 1.36–41.

66. David Schley Schaff, "St. Augustine as an Exegete," *NPNF*, 6:xi.

67. J. Burnaby, "Amor in St. Augustine," in *Philosophy and Theology of Anders Nygren*, ed. Charles W. Kegley (Philadelphia: Westminster, 1974), 174–86; also see O. O'Donovan, *The Problem of Self-Love in St. Augustine* (New Haven: Yale University Press, 1989).

68. Augustine *On Christian Doctrine* 3.15.

69. Ibid., 3.10.

70. See Beryl Smalley, *The Study of the Bible in the Middle Ages*, 2d ed. (Oxford: Blackwell, 1952), 22–23.

71. Augustine *Confessions* 6.4.6; 5.14.24. I noted that it was only after he discovered the allegorical method of interpreting the Bible, especially for dealing with the complex moral problems in the Old Testament, that he was able to become a Christian.

the historical sense of the text.[72] He was concerned with the historical meaning in biblical texts, but he did not disavow the historical sense even as he simultaneously offered an allegorical one. His approach to this dual sense was described and defended by explaining: "There is no prohibition against such exegesis, provided that we also believe in the truth of the story as a faithful record of historical fact."[73] In reality Augustine suggested not a twofold sense of Scripture but a fourfold sense that would be adopted later by medieval theologians. These four senses were (1) literal, (2) allegorical, (3) tropological or moral, and (4) anagogical. Augustine worked with a different list for the Old Testament, based on the Greek technical terms of a rhetorical analysis of language: (1) historical (*historia*), (2) aetiological (*aetiologia*), (3) analogical (*analogia*), and (4) allegorical (*allegoria*).[74]

As with Origen, anything that might be dishonoring to God must be interpreted figuratively, because the words of Scripture were viewed by Origen as the expression of eternal truth.[75] The allegorical method was also to be employed to explain seemingly insignificant details. Thus he allegorized every detail in John 2:1–11, the story of the wedding at Cana. The six waterpots represented the six ages from Adam to Christ, while the two or three measures indicated all humanity, the two measures pointed to the circumcision and uncircumcision, and the three measures were viewed as the three sons of Noah, the ancestors of the human race. Perhaps Augustine's most famous allegorical interpretation was his understanding of the story of the good Samaritan (Luke 10).

The great mind of Augustine, however, could not rest in a simple allegorism. He successfully offered some guidelines for the use of allegorical exegesis, yet, like those before him, he was unable to develop an all-inclusive system to determine what was to be interpreted allegorically and what was not. Like Jerome, in the course of his theological development he began to emphasize more strongly the literal and historical sense of Scripture, though for Augustine, the theological was always primary. Augustine was no simple traditionalist, but he gladly upheld the authority of the rule of faith. Thus he suggested that if the interpreters were troubled and could not distinguish between the literal and figurative interpretation, they should consult the

72. This was not dissimilar to Chrysostom. In fact, it was much closer to Theodoret and the later Antiochenes than the Alexandrians.

73. Augustine *City of God* 13.22.

74. Cf. Robert E. McNally, *The Bible in the Early Middle Ages* (Westminster, Md.: Newman, 1959), 50–54.

75. For examples of Augustine's practice see questions 52–83 in St. Augustine, *Eighty-Three Different Questions*, trans. David L. Mosher, *Fathers of the Church*, vol. 70 (Washington, D.C.: Catholic University of America Press, 1977), 88–220.

rule of faith.[76] Excesses in Augustine's interpretation were thereby modified by his concern for a Catholic interpretation faithful to the authority of the church and creed. He went so far as to acknowledge, "I should not believe the gospel except as moved by the authority of the Catholic Church."[77]

The goal of scriptural exegesis for Augustine was to induce love for God and neighbor, but he felt that these were found in their true form only in the church. To counter the various heretical sects who emphasized their own private interpretations, Augustine stressed the need for the authority of the church in interpreting the Bible.[78] Thus, Augustine's genius could hold together creativity and creed; author, text, and interpreter; the historical and figurative; faith and intellect.

In sum, Augustine stressed the priority of faith for understanding the Bible. He thought much of the Bible was to be understood both literally and allegorically, yet the historical was never to be disavowed. Scripture was to be interpreted canonically, allowing Scripture to interpret Scripture. The entire canon served as the context for each unit of Scripture. Allegorical interpretation was profitable to deal with difficulties and details, as well as to discover the theological meaning of the passage being studied. What Augustine always stressed was that the entire canonical text should produce love for God and for neighbor in the lives of those in the church.

Theodoret of Cyrus

His Background

Theodoret of Cyrus (ca. A.D. 393–466) was the last of the major representatives of the Antiochene school. He has been generally regarded as one of the great exegetes of the Greek church. J. W. D. Wand described Theodoret as "the Augustine of the East."[79] He noted his importance by saying, "He was a great pastor as well as a first-class theologian, who had won back ten thousand Marcionites to the Catholic fold."[80] His contributions did not display much originality, yet he moved beyond the traditional Antiochene paradigm with his openness to allegorical exegesis. His work can be described as eclectic and encyclopedic. Jean Daniélou has observed that in this sense Theodoret was more representative of all Greek learning than of just the Antiochene school.[81]

76. Augustine *On Christian Doctrine* 3.2. In 3.5, he referred to it as the *praescriptio fidei.*

77. Augustine *Against the Epistle of Manichaeus Called Fundamental* 5.6.

78. Jack B. Rogers and Donald K. McKim, *The Authority and Interpretation of the Bible. An Historical Approach* (Grand Rapids: Eerdmans, 1979), 34.

79. J. W. C. Wand, *A History of the Early Church to A.D. 500.* (London: Methuen, 1937), 239.

80. Ibid., 240.

81. Jean Daniélou with A. H. Couratin and John Kent, *Historical Theology,* vol. 2 of *The Pelican Guide to Modern Theology,* ed. R. P. C. Hanson, 3 vols. (Middlesex, England: Penguin, 1969), 107–8.

Theodoret (whose name means "given by God") was born and educated in Antioch where he spent his initial twenty-three years of life. He then left for the monastery in Nicerte in 416. Theodoret spoke only sparingly of his formative years, but it is probable that he was raised in a home of moderately wealthy Christian parents. This can be deduced from his discussion of his family having employed persons to work the family land.[82] He also noted his mother's work among the monks. Moreover, the following telling remark indicates his Christian heritage: "Even before my conception my parents promised to devote me to God; from my swaddling bands they devoted me according to their promise and educated me accordingly."[83] He was elected Bishop of Cyrus, a small town near Antioch, a diocese for which he provided oversight with great wisdom and zeal for thirty-five years.

Like his predecessors in the Antiochene school, Theodoret demonstrated intellectual resources of remarkable depth which enabled him to meet the challenges which needed to be addressed in exegeting the Scriptures and expounding church doctrine. It is clear from Theodoret's writing that he was quite accomplished in Greek as well as Syriac.[84] When working with the Jewish Scriptures he relied essentially on the Septuagint, displaying only a modest acquaintance with Hebrew.

His writings evidence classical training and a familiarity with a wide spectrum of classical Greek poets, philosophers, and orators. Theodoret himself, while Bishop of Cyrus, encouraged the children of the wealthy in Cyrus to attend the schools of the rhetoricians. His education also included training in Christian theology through the church, his family, and particularly through the writings of Diodore, Chrysostom, and Theodore of Mopsuestia. He said, "From my mother's breath I have been nurtured on Apostolic teaching."[85] The family traditionally had played an important role among Christian Antioch, a role which received its classic expression in the fourth-century work of John Chrysostom, *On Vainglory and the Education of the Young*.[86]

Theodoret evidences a heavy debt to the Antiochene tradition. By Theodoret's time, this instruction was conveyed to believers through cate-

82. Theodoret *Letters* 113. See N. N. Glubokowski, *The Blessed Theodoret: His Life and His Works* (Moscow, 1890) as noted from the Russian edition in Quasten, *Patrology*, 3:536–38.

83. Theodoret *Letters* 81.

84. Cf. Ramsay Macmullen, "Provincial Languages in the Roman Empire," *AJP* 87 (1966): 1–17.

85. Cf. Peter Brown, "The Rise and the Function of the Holy Man in Late Antiquity," *JRomSt* 61 (1971): 80–101.

86. On the influence of the Alexandrian and Antiochene schools in the fifth century, see H. I. Marrou, *Education in Late Antiquity*, trans. George Lamb (New York: Sheed and Ward, 1956), 328.

chetical instruction and preaching while those seeking ordination were often trained by learned church leaders. The indirect influence of the Antiochene giants was obviously felt by the time of Theodoret. In *Letter* 16, Theodoret mentioned Diodore and Theodore as his teachers (*tous didaskalous*), but the context of the statement and the fact that Diodore was probably dead at the time of Theodoret's birth, coupled with the fact that Theodore had moved to Mopsuestia by 393, suggests that Theodoret was making reference to indirect influence rather than actually sitting under their tutelage.[87] Thus it was the Antiochene tradition, more than direct teaching by the Antioch theologians, that shaped Theodoret's exegesis.

His Hermeneutical Approach

Theodoret's exegesis, like that of Origen, Chrysostom, and Augustine, was shaped by his pastoral context. In a letter addressed to the monks of Constantinople (ca. 449), Theodoret commented on his labors as Bishop of Cyrus:

> My task has been to contend on behalf of the apostolic decrees to bring the pasture of instruction to the Lord's flocks, and to this end I have written 35 books interpreting the divine scriptures and proving the falsehood of the heresies . . . not on behalf of a duality of sons, but of the only begotten Son of God, against the heathen, against the Jew. I have never ceased to struggle trying to convince the heathen that the Eternal Son of the ever living God is creator of the universe, and the Jew that about him the prophets uttered their predictions.[88]

Here we see Theodoret's framework for his exegetical efforts: (1) his pastoral orientation, and (2) his theological concerns.

Theodoret was dependent almost entirely on the Greek text for his commentaries. Occasional references to a Hebrew or a Syriac reading indicate some familiarity with Hebrew and Syriac texts, but Theodoret showed no interest in confirming a text's reading based on the *hebraica veritas* (reliability of the Hebrew). Theodoret apparently utilized the original text most frequently to clarify an obscure Greek word or biblical name or to illuminate a discrepancy between versions of the Septuagint or between the Septuagint and Syriac. There are a few examples where Theodoret used the Hebrew as a corrective device in order to establish a more defensible text. He was certainly aware that the Hebrew lacked many psalm titles that appeared in the Septuagint. Yet, he consistently upheld the inclusion of the titles and emphasized the heading *eis to telos* (toward the completion or unto the end) as pointing to the connection between the psalmist's words and the

87. Theodoret *Letters* 16.
88. Ibid., 146.

Christian age. The bishop's work as textual critic indicate that his primary work as an interpreter was to explain and clarify the text for a Christian readership, underlying his pastoral concerns and frameworks.[89]

Theodoret's primary audience for his biblical interpretation was clearly Christian and primarily the believers in his diocese. The fundamental reason for writing the commentaries was Theodoret's concern to nourish the flock. His commentaries were for the purpose of elucidating and enhancing the faith of his Christian readers. Such a purpose placed him in a path more consistent with the aspect of the Antiochene tradition shaped by the preacher John Chrysostom than that of Theodore of Mopsuestia. Theodore had established this distinction, as noted by Maurice F. Wiles:

> I judge the exegete's task to be to explain words that most people find difficult; it is the preacher's task to reflect also on words that are perfectly clear and to speak about them. For the latter there are times when excess is valuable, but the former must give the meaning and do it concisely.[90]

Theodoret's self-definition and his ethical exhortations, exemplified by his characteristic usage of *opheleia* (benefits), placed him in a position that James Barr classified as a "mediator between text and context of meaning."[91] Thus the crucial point for Theodoret's interpretation involved his thoroughgoing commitment to interpreting the Scriptures for the benefit of the church. His exegesis was intended to bring the reader into the presence of the blessings and benefits which the Word of God provided.

Having surveyed his purposes and framework for the interpretative task, we must now look at Theodoret's hermeneutical methodology for accomplishing his work. As was the case with other biblical interpreters in the early church, the elements which made up Theodoret's approach to the Scriptures were multifaceted. His exegetical approach has consistently been evaluated in terms of the exegetical tradition of the Antiochene school. Certainly his interpretation of the Old Testament manifested the Antiochene typological exegesis of finding correlations to Christ or the church.[92] Also, there was in Theodoret a strong historical orientation con-

89. Cf. C. Thomas McCollough, "Theodoret of Cyrus as Biblical Interpreter and the Presence of Judaism in Later Roman Syria" (Ph.D. diss., University of Notre Dame, 1984), 117–18. I am deeply dependent on McCollough's insights at this point and in what follows. His work on Theodoret is one of the most thorough and insightful to date.

90. Maurice F. Wiles, "Theodore of Mopsuestia as Representative of the Antiochene School," *CHB*, 1:491.

91. James Barr, *Old and New in Interpretation: A Study of the Two Testaments* (London: SCM, 1966), 39.

92. Cf. G. W. Ashby, *Theodoret of Cyrhus as Exegete of the Old Testament* (Grahamtown, South Africa, 1972), cited in J. Stewardson, "The Christology of Theodoret of Cyrus According to His Eranistes" (Ph.D. diss., Northwestern University, 1972). This typological approach was consistent

cerned with the historical context for the prophet's words and actions. Theodoret included outlines of the historical situation in his commentaries of the biblical prophets useful for historical exegesis of the text, because Theodoret understood history to be the stage on which God's revelation to the created order was unfolded. Contrary to the Alexandrians, the historical reading of the text was not simply an accommodation to the immature (*sarkikoi*) of the congregation but a genuine encounter with revelation. Theodoret's historical concerns parallel those of Lucian, Diodore, Chrysostom, and Theodore. Yet his interests in typology exceeded the Antiochenes, even those of the homiletician Chrysostom. Theodoret's range for identifying typologies was broader than his predecessors, as exemplified in the following quotations from his commentaries. In his commentary on Zechariah he claimed,

> The ancient events were a type for us. But it is imperative that there should be a resemblance between the archtype and the image itself, so that what is true of the latter case (the antitype) is also true of the Jews. For the latter is the prefiguration of the former.[93]

In the initial remarks of the preface to his *Questions on Joshua,* comparing his interpretation of Joshua to Paul's statements in Galatains 4, he commented,

> And Paul wrote these things not that we should reject history but that we should compare the type to the antitype: Abraham with God; two wives with two testaments . . . so also the law as Moses; and Joshua to the Saviour as indeed they even have the same name.[94]

Also, he recognized Old Testament foreshadowings of the future in the Psalms:

> Because in truth the ancient events are a type of the things of the New Testament, so as the body has alongside it the shadow, we must set forth this affinity. There the pious king Hezekiah, and here Christ, the helmsman of piety. . . . There the war against and destruction of Assyria, here the attack on and ruin of demons.[95]

We can see Theodoret's fondness for typological interpretation and his great flexibility in his employment of it. Verbal resemblances, as with the names of Joshua and Jesus, were enough to argue that the Old Testament

with the correlative concerns of historical events as evidenced also in Theodore of Mopsuestia. See Rowan A. Greer, *Theodore of Mopsuestia: Exegete and Theologian* (London: Faith, 1961), 94.

93. Theodoret *Commentary on Zechariah* 9.16.

94. Theodoret *Questions on Joshua* preface, i.

95. Theodoret *Commentary on Psalms* 28.1.

writer was prefiguring some portion of the messianic age.[96] Johannes Quasten has observed that Theodoret, after consulting numerous works on the Psalms, some extremely allegorical and others explaining messianic prophesies as referring to events of the past, regarded it as his duty to avoid either extreme.[97] Whatever referred to history, he explained historically, but matters that could be understood as typologically pointing to Christ, the church, or the preaching of the apostles were so interpreted.

Theodoret's typological exegesis served a role in establishing an orthodox Christology as well. It was readily utilized to identify the historical aspect of Christ, the man from the seed of David, as well as God the Word. He, therefore, emphasized the fullness of both the human and divine natures of Christ: *theon teleion kai anthropon teleion* (fully God and fully man).[98] He commented that Zechariah believed the "one out of David" according to the flesh was God the Word who took the form of a servant. The prophet's expectation of one who would "overcome his enemies" was read typologically as

> the victory of Christ . . . who has destroyed the demons for us and taken to himself our thoughts and all of us are utterly enslaved by the body by descending and taking on the burden of the holy servant. . . . He was not as God but as man. For as God he is equal to the Father. . . . Yet he was sent as man, carrying out the plan of God.[99]

This emphasis in Theodoret's exegesis typifies the concerns raised by the christological debates in the fifth century. While demonstrating more flexibility and an equal or greater concern for theological orthodoxy, Theodoret was nevertheless a faithful representative of the Antiochene tradition. But what about Theodoret's response to allegorical hermeneutics, loved by the Alexandrians and loathed by the elders of the Antioch school?[100]

Cyril, Bishop of Alexandria, a contemporary of Theodoret, wrote commentaries on the Minor Prophets that, at many points, offered historical interpretations much like those of the Antiochenes. Interestingly, Theodoret's work showed numerous similarities with Cyril's, even occa-

96. See Francis S. Rossiter, "Messianic Prophecy According to Theodoret of Cyrus and Antiochene *Theoria*" (Ph.D. diss., Pontifical Gregorian University, Rome, 1949).

97. Quasten, *Patrology*, 3:540.

98. Kevin McNamara, "Theodoret of Cyrus and the Unity of the Person in Christ," *ITQ* 22 (1955): 313–28.

99. Theodoret *Zechariah* 2.8–9.

100. Eustathius, Bishop of Antioch (A.D. 324–326), went so far in his only surviving work as to identify Origen as the "Witch of Endor," in a sermon on 1 Kings 28. See Quasten, *Patrology*, 3:302–5; R. V. Sellers, *Eustathius of Antioch and His Place in the Early History of Christian Doctrine* (Cambridge: Cambridge University Press, 1928).

sionally adopting figurative practices. This seems to indicate eclectic methodologies merging toward a hermeneutical synthesis in the fifth-century church. Undoubtedly, the christological and soteriological factors of the time influenced the convergence between the Alexandrians (Cyril) and the Antiochenes (Theodoret).

An example of Theodoret's comments on Zephaniah 2 is illustrative of his flexibility. Theodore of Mopsuestia interpreted the prophet's description of the approaching disaster for Judah and Assyria as a reference to the historical period of the reign of Josiah and to the warnings of God against those among the tribes of Judah and the adversaries of Judah who insulted God through false worship. Whereas Theodoret was aware of Theodore's historical exegesis, he chose to see it figuratively as pointing to the remnant called to follow the apostles. The passage reads:

> And the coast will be
> For the remnant of the house of Judah,
> They will pasture on it.
> In the houses of Ashkelon they will lie down at evening;
> For the Lord their
> God will care for them
> And restore their fortune.
>
> [Zeph. 2:7 NASB]

Theodoret commented:

> These things happen after the return. For in the books of the Maccabees we read Jonathan and Simon led them to capture Gaza and Askelon and Ptolemais and they prevailed over their houses. But the indubitable and precise purpose (*telos*) of the prophet is to show the time after the ascension of our Saviour and the holy apostles, the God of the universe visits the nations, freeing them from their servitude and captivity.
>
> But the precise purpose is given through the Holy Apostles and through the holy things the apostles accomplished; and the holy apostle called them the remnant. For when setting forth the prophecies, precisely it is this which is proclaimed, "though the Israelites be countless as the sands of the sea, only a remnant will be saved" (Romans 9:27). He [Paul] explains the prophecy, saying, "So in this time a remnant has come into being, chosen by the grace of God" (Romans 11:5). For God has said this through the blessed Zephaniah, the remnant of my people shall possess them.[101]

101. Theodoret *Commentary on Zephaniah* 2:7–10.

The motivations for this spiritualized interpretation were his pastoral concerns and his interest in expounding the text in its most beneficial fashion. We can see the influence of Theodoret's theological presuppositions and his context, as well as his self-understanding, as critical elements in shaping his interpretation of Scripture.

Theodoret's work did not evidence originality, yet there were marks of a creative synthesis with other traditions. In his hermeneutical approach he adopted a middle course, avoiding the radical historicism of Theodore of Mopsuestia and his consistent literalism. Where possible, Theodoret offered broad typological interpretations, even allowing for figurative explanations on occasion. He was an heir to the theological and hermeneutical traditions of Antioch, yet his self-understanding as pastor of the flock and his own cultural and theological horizons were seen to be influential factors in his exegetical practices. Beginning with different starting points than contemporaries such as Jerome, Augustine, or Cyril of Alexandria, he nevertheless demonstrated an eclectic hermeneutic representative of the canonical and Catholic concerns of the fifth-century church.

Conclusion

It has been observed that the theological concerns that dominated the christological controversies of the fifth century strongly influenced the hermeneutical approaches of this period.[102] We have observed the practices of three diverse interpreters of this era, yet we discovered a common convergence toward a theological and hermeneutical synthesis. Jerome, the great translator, Augustine, the superior theologian, and Theodoret, the model pastor, each showed elements of literal and figurative exegesis. Each showed concerns to communicate the canonical meaning of Scripture. By this we mean that a text was not to be interpreted apart from its larger context, the entire biblical canon. We also noticed that the rule of faith, whether emphasizing providential, christological, or soteriological concerns, also played a dominant role, especially in the work of Augustine and Theodoret.[103] While Jerome and Augustine showed development from a figurative to a literal hermeneutic, Theodoret's movement went the

102. Robert L. Wilken, "Tradition, Exegesis and the Christological Controversies," *CH* 34 (1965): 123–45.

103. Note how these three basic concerns reflect the three major challenges of Gnosticism that continued to be concerns for the church after the third century. For an alternative to the synthesis offered in this chapter see David W. Johnson, "The Myth of the Augustinian Synthesis," in *Biblical Hermeneutics in Historical Perspective*, ed. Mark S. Burrows and Paul Rorem (Grand Rapids: Eerdmans, 1991), 100–114.

other direction. What can be seen here is that neither the allegorical practices of Alexandria nor the historical emphases of Antioch dominated. A balanced and multifaceted hermeneutic emerged that influenced hermeneutical practices in the Middle Ages as well as in post-Reformation times. In sum we can see that this balanced hermeneutic was influenced by (1) pastoral and theological concerns, (2) presuppositions that viewed the text from the standpoint of faith, and (3) interpretations that produced edification among the saints (Jerome), love toward God and neighbor (Augustine), and benefit and blessing for the church (Theodoret). Having concluded our survey of the hermeneutical practices of the early church from Jesus to the Chalcedonian era, we must see how, if at all, these observations can help untangle the hermeneutical knots and answer the interpretative questions raised in our own time.

6

Biblical Interpretation Then and Now

The title of this volume indicates that our concern is not only to describe the development of hermeneutical models in the early church, but also to understand its significance for our day. In this final chapter we will review the findings of our earlier work and offer a brief survey of interpretative approaches from the middle of the fifth century to the middle of the twentieth century. We shall then focus our attention on the trends, models, and methods represented in contemporary hermeneutics. It is possible that such a method might appear anachronistic, and we are aware of the problems of a complete incorporation of early church hermeneutics into a different culture and time period. Thus our purpose is to let the insights and synthesis of the early church serve as a window through which we can view the present situation. In this we are following the suggestions of many "post-critical" theologians who, after tracing the routes offered by modern movements and trends, have called for the church to once again listen to its classic voices.[1]

1. Cf. Thomas C. Oden, *Agenda for Theology: Recovering Christian Roots* (San Francisco: Harper and Row, 1979); idem, *The Living God: Systematic Theology*, vol. 1 (San Francisco: Harper and Row, 1987); Charles M. Wood, *The Formation of Christian Understanding: An Essay in Theological Hermeneutics* (Philadelphia: Westminster, 1981); Mark I. Wallace, "The New Yale Theology," *CSR* 17 (1987): 154–70.

The Early Church in Review

In this section we shall summarize views of biblical authority and interpretation in the second through the fifth centuries.[2] In general, Scripture was seen as a gift from God given primarily to the people of God to be expounded to his people and the people of the world. Because it was a gift of God, it had its origin not just in the prophets and apostles, but in God himself. Irenaeus acknowledged that the Bible could sometimes be obscure, yet he maintained that its nature was completely spiritual.[3] Origen remained convinced that a divine purpose rested behind each passage, even those that presented him intellectual difficulty.[4] Gregory of Nyssa, representative of the Cappadocians, found the Holy Spirit in every statement of Holy Scripture (cf. 2 Tim. 3:16).[5]

Similarly, the major representatives of the Antioch school confessed the divine origin of Scripture. Theodore of Mopsuestia, one of the first critical interpreters in the early church, also emphasized the human aspect of Scripture. He thus distinguished various types of inspiration, yet equally attributed all of Scripture to the work of the Holy Spirit.[6] His fellow elder, John Chrysostom, affirmed the full inspiration and thus recognized the spiritual value of all biblical statements.[7] The great theologian Augustine noted historical and textual difficulties, yet strongly affirmed his belief in divine inspiration. He described inspiration as the work of God whereby Christ gave the church his written Word by using his apostles as if they were his own hands.[8]

Since the written Word of God was given by the Spirit of God, Scripture had a primacy in the life, teaching, and mission of the church. This had reference to the Old Testament as well as the New. The Old Testament was authoritative by virtue of its prophetic testimony to the coming Messiah. This authority applied also to the New Testament because the apostles witnessed to Jesus Christ, who had come in fulfillment of the promises of the prophets. Generally, the early church considered all of Scripture true and maintained that God's people must accept and abide by its teaching.

As these statements suggest, the Bible was the primary divine authority for the early church. Yet this was true for Marcion, the Gnostics, the

2. A succinct survey of these and other matters can be found in G. W. Bromiley, "The Church Fathers and Holy Scripture," in *Scripture and Truth,* ed. D. A. Carson and John Woodbridge (Grand Rapids: Zondervan, 1983), 199–212.

3. Irenaeus *Against Heresies* 2.28.2.

4. Origen *On First Principles* 4.3.1.

5. Gregory of Nyssa *Against Eunomius* 7.1.

6. Theodore of Mopsuestia *Commentary on Minor Prophets* 1.1.

7. Chrysostom *Homily on John* 11.

8. Augustine *Harmony of the Gospels* 1.35.54.

Monatists, and the Judaizers as well. Thus, the church's ecclesiastical authority and its rule of faith were also raised to a similar level of authority within the orthodox tradition. As we have seen, various questions and different answers arose as Scripture, the source of the church's authority, was interpreted in light of rival authorities and hermeneutical models. While there were definite differences among the Fathers regarding their understanding of the literal-historical sense of Scripture, as well as the typological and allegorical, there existed a general consensus that Scripture should be interpreted christologically.

The diversity, dissensions, and heresies did not obscure the agreement shared by all from Clement and Ignatius to Jerome, Augustine, and Theodoret. The church recognized that the fulfillment of the Old Testament events, promises, and prophecies was centered in Christ. Whether viewed functionally, typologically, or allegorically, this was so. As G. W. Bromiley has so aptly stated, "The Old Testament and the New Testament were seen together in indissoluble unity as the one book of the one God inspired by the one Spirit and testifying to the one Son."[9] The themes of unity and fulfillment for the Fathers were focused in the conviction that Christ was the true and final subject of Scripture.

What can we surmise about the early church's use of Scripture? They gladly acknowledged its divine origin and authority, yet apart from the Antiochenes there was insufficient attention given to Scripture's human and historical aspects. We noted that all of the Fathers gave assent to the literal sense of Scripture, but a contextual, grammatical, and historical interpretation was emphasized by Theodore and Chrysostom, with a developing convergence in that direction with Jerome, Augustine, and Theodoret. We also saw that scriptural authority was consistently affirmed by all, but in practice it was sometimes usurped by a creedal authority that limited creativity in interpretation or by fanciful interpretation that yielded to a secondary authority such as philosophical concerns. The struggle between *sola scriptura* and the church's confessional stance, and philosophical challenges, has continued to the present day. The dogmas and creeds of the church must not develop, in the patristic or the contemporary church, at the hermeneutical level, into a body of teaching equal in status to Holy Scripture. Yet the rule of faith, even as a relative and historical interpretation, must speak to and inform the church's attempt to interpret Scripture. Likewise, while the church must interpret the Bible in light of its current philosophical milieu, the goal of interpreting Scripture for the church must remain primary. The developing hermeneutical models in the early church converged in the fifth century to emphasize (1) the pri-

9. Bromiley, "Church Fathers and Holy Scripture," 212.

macy of the literal sense of Scripture; (2) an allowance for a deeper or a multiple sense of Scripture; (3) the need for faith presuppositions in interpretation; (4) the canonical context for interpretation, that is, Scripture should be interpreted by Scripture; (5) Scripture should be interpreted for the edification of the church to produce a greater knowledge of, and love for, God; (6) the interpretation should not be out of line with the church's rule of faith; and (7) Scripture should be interpreted christologically.

It will be helpful to identify the early church methodologies with the following models or handles:[10] (1) the "pietistic" or "functional" model of the apostolic fathers; (2) the "dogmatic" or "authoritative" model of the apologists; (3) the "allegorical" or "reader-oriented" model of the Alexandrians; (4) the "literal-historical" or "author-oriented" model of the Antiochenes; and (5) the "canonical" or "text-oriented" model of Augustine and Theodoret. Before examining these models from a contemporary perspective, it is necessary to trace briefly what transpired in the hermeneutical field from the fifth to the twentieth century.

Medieval, Reformation, and Post-Reformation Hermeneutics

Medieval Hermeneutics

From the time of Augustine, the church, following the lead of John Cassian (d. ca. 433), subscribed to a theory of the fourfold sense of Scripture.[11] The literal sense of Scripture could and usually did nurture the virtues of faith, hope, and love, but when it did not, the interpreter could appeal to three additional virtues, each sense corresponding to one of the virtues. The allegorical sense referred to the church and its faith—what it should believe. The tropological sense referred to individuals and what they should do—corresponding to love. The anagogical sense pointed to the church's future expectation—corresponding to hope. Bernard of Clair-

10. By the term *model* or *handle* we refer to the use of an image employed reflectively and critically to deepen one's theoretical understanding of a reality. See Patrick R. Keifert, "Mind Reader and Maestro: Models for Understanding Biblical Interpreters," *Word & World* 1 (1980): 153–68; Avery Dulles, *Models of the Church* (Garden City, N.Y.: Doubleday, 1978), 19–37; also see idem, *Models of Revelation* (Garden City, N.Y.: Doubleday, 1983); I. T. Ramsey, *Religious Language* (New York: Macmillan, 1963); idem, *Models and Mystery* (New York: Oxford University Press, 1964); Max Black, *Models and Metaphors* (Ithaca, N.Y.: Cornell University Press, 1962); Ian G. Barbour, *Myths, Models, and Paradigms* (London: SCM, 1974).

11. See Beryl Smalley, *The Study of the Bible in the Middle Ages*, 2d ed. (Oxford: Blackwell, 1952), 26–36. Cf. Gillian R. Evans, *The Language and Logic of the Bible: The Earlier Middle Ages* (Cambridge: Cambridge University Press, 1984); G. W. H. Lampe, ed., *The Cambridge History of the Bible 2: The West from the Fathers to the Reformation* (Cambridge: Cambridge University Press, 1969).

vaux (1090–1153), in the twelfth century, clearly explicated and practiced this fourfold approach. In the fourteenth century Nicholas of Lyra (1265–1349) summarized this medieval hermeneutical theory in a much-quoted rhyme:

> Littera gesta docet,
> (The letter teaches facts)
> Quid credas allegoria,
> (allegory what one should believe)
> Moralis quid agas,
> (tropology what one should do)
> Quo tendas anagogia.
> (anagogy where one should aspire).

For example, the city of Jerusalem, in all of its appearances in Scripture, was understood literally as a Jewish city, allegorically as the church of Christ, tropologically as the souls of women and men, and anagogically as the heavenly city.[12]

Thomas Aquinas (1224–1274) wanted to establish the spiritual sense more securely in the literal sense than had been the case in earlier medieval thought. He returned to the distinction between things and signs as in Augustine, but because of his Aristotelianism preferred "things" and "words."[13] In Scripture, the things designated by words can themselves have the character of a sign. He maintained that the literal sense of Scripture has to do with the sign-character of words; the spiritual sense, with the sign-character of things. Thus, he was able to demonstrate that the spiritual sense of Scripture was always based on the literal sense and derived from it.[14] Thomas also equated the literal sense with the meaning of the text intended by the author.[15] The medieval exegetes and theologians admitted that the words of Scripture contained a meaning in the historical situation in which they were first uttered, but overall these scholars denied

12. See James Houston's introduction in Bernard of Clairvaux, *The Love of God and Spiritual Friendship*, ed. with an introduction by James Houston (Portland: Multnomah, 1983), 32–33. Also see John Rogerson, Christopher Rowland, and Barnabas Lindars, vol. 2 of *The History of Christian Theology*, ed. Paul Avis, 3 vols. (Grand Rapids: Eerdmans, 1988); Beryl Smalley, "The Bible in the Middle Ages," in *The Church's Use of the Bible Past and Present*, ed. D. E. Nineham (London: Macmillan, 1963), 60.

13. David C. Steinmetz, "The Superiority of Precritical Exegesis," *ThT* 27 (1980): 31–32.

14. Ibid.; cf. Thomas Aquinas, *On Interpretation*, trans. J. T. Oesterle (Milwaukee: Marquette University Press, 1962).

15. B. Moeller, "Scripture, Tradition and Sacrament in the Middle Ages and in Luther," in *Holy Book and Holy Tradition*, ed. F. F. Bruce and E. G. Rupp (Manchester: Manchester University Press, 1968), 120–22. Cf. E. Gilson, *The Christian Philosophy of St. Thomas Aquinas*, trans. L. K. Shook (London: Victor Gollancz, 1957), 20–21.

that the final and full meaning of those words were restricted to what the first audience thought or heard.

Reformation Hermeneutics

Martin Luther (1483–1546), the great Reformer, started out using the allegorical method, but later claimed to have abandoned it.[16] Yet, it was Erasmus (1466–1536), more than Luther, who through the influence of John Colet (1466–1519) rediscovered the priority of the literal sense.[17] John Calvin (1509–1564), the greatest exegete of the Reformation, more than anyone else developed the trend toward using thc grammatical-historical exegetical method as the foundation for developing the spiritual message from the text. Yet, it was Luther's emphasis on a fuller sense located in the christological meaning of Scripture that linked the Reformers with Jesus, the apostles, and the early church.[18]

Post-Reformation Hermeneutics

It is commonly believed that the followers of the Reformers shrank from the exegetical freedom employed by Luther and Calvin. They instead conducted their exposition along newly established theological boundaries, establishing a new Protestant scholasticism.[19] The followers of Luther and Calvin in the sixteenth and seventeenth centuries tended to systematize their exegesis into a philosophical mold.[20] This new form of scholasticism exercised an authoritative and dogmatic hermeneutic, coupled with the rise of the Enlightenment that rejected both authoritative and dogmatic approaches, and issued in two reactions: (1) a newfound pietism in Philip Jakob Spener (1635–1705) and August Herman Franke (1663–1727),[21] and (2) a historical-critical method that stressed the importance of the his-

16. Cf. Raymond Larry Shelton, "Martin Luther's Concept of Biblical Interpretation in Historical Perspective" (Ph.D. diss., Fuller Theological Seminary, 1974).

17. Louis Bouyer, "Erasmus in Relation to the Medieval Biblical Tradition," *CHB*, 2: 492–505; cf. J. H. Bentley, *Humanist and Holy Writ* (Princeton, N.J.: Princeton University Press, 1983), 115–26; A. Rabil, *Erasmus and the New Testament: The Mind of a Christian Humanist* (San Antonio: Trinity University Press, 1972), 43–45.

18. David S. Dockery, "Martin Luther's Christological Hermeneutics," *GTJ* 2 (1983): 189–203.

19. J. K. S. Reid, *The Authority of Scripture: A Study of Reformation and Post-Reformation Understanding of the Bible* (London: Methuen, 1962).

20. John Patrick Donnelly, "Calvinist Thomism," *Viator* 7 (1976): 441–51.

21. See J. O. Duke, "Pietism versus Establishment: The Halle Phase," *CQ* 72 (1978): 3–16; K. J. Stein, "Philip Jacob Spener's Hope for Better Times: Contribution in Controversy," *CQ* 73 (1979): 3–20. Spener, in *Pia Desideria* (*Pious Wishes*, 1675) offered six proposals for reform which became a short summary of pietism: (1) There should be a more extensive use of the Word of God among us. The Bible must be the chief means for reform. (2) There must be a renewal of the spiritual priesthood of all believers (calling for a return to Luther's emphasis).

torical, over against the theological, interpretation of the New Testament pioneered by Johann Salamo Semler (1725–1791) and Johann David Michaelis (1717–1791).[22] Both of these movements were responses within Lutheranism, but they soon spread across denominational and geographical lines as well. Whereas many scholars of this period were interested primarily, if not exclusively, in the historical-critical approach, Friedrich E. D. Schleiermacher (1768–1834), a mystical pietist, a philosopher, and a theologian, manifested a new hermeneutical concern. Schleiermacher granted that the historical-critical approach helped disclose the intention of the biblical writers in the context of their day, but he questioned what their message means to readers and hearers in a different age and culture. In doing so, he became not only the "Father of Theological Liberalism," but also the "Father of Modern Hermeneutics."

The Beginning of Modern Hermeneutics

Schleiermacher argued that interpretation consisted of two categories: grammatical and psychological.[23] Prior to Schleiermacher, hermeneutics

---

(3) He appealed for the reality of Christian practice and argued that Christianity is more than a matter of simple knowledge. (4) Spener urged restraint and charity in religious controversies. He asked his readers to love and pray for unbelievers and the erring, and to adopt a moderate tone in disputes. (5) He stressed the need of reform in the education of ministers, calling for training in piety and devotion as well as in academic subjects. (6) He implored ministers to preach edifying sermons, understandable by the people.

22. It is beyond our scope in this chapter to examine the developments in historical-critical methodologies which include the following: literary criticism, source criticism, form criticism, tradition criticism, redaction criticism, structuralism, and canonical criticism. See David Alan Black and David S. Dockery, eds., *New Testament Criticism and Interpretation* (Grand Rapids: Zondervan, 1991), and Mark A. Noll, *Between Faith and Criticism* (San Francisco: Harper and Row, 1986). The rise of criticism corresponded with the rise of historicism. J. A. Turretini, a Reformed theologian from Geneva, largely dependent on John Locke, set forth his approach to interpretation in *De Sacrae Scripturae interpretation methodo* (1728). The hermeneutic can be summarized in four statements: (1) Since the God who gave revelation in the Bible also endowed people with the rational faculty necessary for receiving communication, the Bible's communication is to be grasped in the same way as other communications. (2) Since the Bible presumes the validity of the law of contradiction, which states that a thing cannot be both true and not true at the same time, no biblical interpretation can be accepted as true that clashes with what is already known to be true. (3) Since it is a historical book, the Bible must be understood from the vantage point of its writers as they lived in their own times and places, rather than from any modern vantage point. (4) Since the Bible is to speak for itself like any other book, the mind, subject to the law of contradiction, must come to the Bible as a *tabula rasa,* emptied of all cherished concepts derived from the modern view of life. See W. G. Kümmel, *The New Testament: The History of the Investigation of Its Problems,* trans. S. MacLean Gilmour and Howard Clark Kee (Nashville: Abingdon, 1970), 58–60.

23. See F. E. D. Schleiermacher, *Hermeneutics: The Handwritten Manuscripts,* ed. H. Kimmerle, trans. James Duke and H. J. Forstman (Missoula, Mont.: Scholars, 1977), 66–68.

was understood as special hermeneutics (*hermeneutica sacra*) and general hermeneutics (*hermeneutica profana*). Special hermeneutics was concerned with how the Bible ought to be interpreted and general hermeneutics was used to interpret other kinds of literature. Schleiermacher, however, insisted that the understanding of linguistic symbols, whether biblical, legal, or literary texts, should be derived from a consideration of how understanding in general takes place, thus a shift from special hermeneutics to general hermeneutics.

The Primacy of the Author

Schleiermacher saw that what was to be understood must, in a sense, be already known. Acknowledging that this appeared circular or even contradictory, he maintained that this very account of understanding remained true to the facts of everyday experience. This was emphasized in his comment that "every child arrives at the meaning of a word only through hermeneutics."[24] The child must relate the new word to what is already known; otherwise, the word remains meaningless. On the other side, the child must assimilate "something alien, universal, which always signifies a resistance for the original vitality. To that extent it is an accomplishment of

---

Schleiermacher's grammatical hermeneutics were largely dependent upon the work of Ernesti's *Institutio interpretis Novi Testament* (1761). Moses Stuart translated the latter in 1822 and noted it in "Are the Same Principles of Interpretation to Be Applied to the Scripture as to Other Books?" *The Biblical Repository* 2 (1832): 124–37. Stuart is cited by Walter C. Kaiser, Jr., "Legitimate Hermeneutics," in *Inerrancy,* ed. Norman L. Geisler (Grand Rapids: Zondervan, 1979), 117–47. Ernesti's rules were as follows: (1) Master the *usus loquendi* (the use which speakers/writers made of their words). (2) The sense of words is regulated by usage. (3) The sense is not totally determined by standard linguistic conventions because each writer has personal style. (4) The interpreter needs to immerse himself in linguistic usage of the writer's place and time and then in the writer's own characteristics. (5) The aim is to establish literal sense of the utterance, unless there are clear indications for nonliteral understanding. (6) The interpreter must be aware that the verbal sense is often ambiguous and may have to appeal to indirect evidence such as a) author's purpose, b) analogies, and c) common sense. (7) It should be remembered that the author has freedom in usage of words but cannot stray too far from the conventional, or it becomes unintelligible. (8) The interpreter must never begin anywhere other than with words of the text and with the attempt to establish their sense. The hermeneutical task ends when the verbal sense has been discovered. (9) Scripture cannot be understood theologically until it has been understood grammatically. (10) There are two requisites of the competent interpreter: a) an acuteness of understanding (*subtilitas intelugendi*) to discern the sense of a passage, and b) an acuteness of skill (*subtilitas explicandi*) to exhibit that sense to the public. (11) Hermeneutics is the science which teaches us to find in an accurate and judicious manner the meaning of an author and appropriately to explain it to others.

24. Schleiermacher, *Hermeneutics,* 40. My understanding of the modern period has been greatly enhanced by James Duke's class lecture/notes on this subject (Texas Christian University), as well as those of Daniel Fuller (Fuller Theological Seminary) and Lenore Langsdorf (University of Texas).

hermeneutic."[25] Schleiermacher added that since understanding new subject matter depended on positive relations to the interpreter's own known horizons, lack of understanding was never completely removed. Therefore, understanding constituted a progressive process, not simply an act that can be definitively completed.[26]

Schleiermacher contended for a preunderstanding that must take place before interpretation can happen. For Schleiermacher, understanding was related to the author's intention. In his section on grammatical interpretation, the early Schleiermacher articulated some of the most incisive statements found in all hermeneutical literature on the principles useful in grasping what an author willed to communicate. But the grammatical meaning was not enough for him. He argued that the theme of an author's text was a product of the author's nature. The ultimate aim, therefore, was to get through to an author's unique individuality, a psychological interpretation.[27] Understanding required a knowledge of grammatical concerns, but also intuition through empathy with and imagination of the author's experience. The goal was for the author and interpreter to share a life-relationship. Thus the interpreter is to seek an immediate knowledge of the author's individuality. Understanding, then, involved more than rethinking what an author thought; it included reexperiencing what was in the life of the author who generated the thought. Schleiermacher was thus able to contend that if this reexperiencing could take place, the interpreter could understand the author's work as well as or even better than the author.[28]

The Schleiermacher tradition was continued and expanded by his biographer, Wilhelm Dilthey (1833–1911). In "The Development of Hermeneutics," Dilthey made the goal of interpretation to understand a life not native to oneself. He postulated the idea of a universal nature that could make this possible, yet he admitted that an author's personality could not be fully grasped (*individuum est ineffable*).[29] In hermeneutics, Dilthey envisioned the possibility of a foundation for the humanities that would make them truly *Geisteswissenschaften* (sciences of the spirit or human sciences). Hermeneutics was expanded beyond the Schleiermacher model of understanding so that the task of interpretation was to understand the expression

25. Hans-Georg Gadamer, "The Problem of Language in Schleiermacher's Hermeneutic," *JTC* 7 (1970): 70.

26. Schleiermacher, *Hermeneutics*, 141.

27. Anthony C. Thiselton, *Two Horizons: New Testament Hermeneutics and Philosophical Description* (Grand Rapids: Eerdmans, 1980), 103–6.

28. Cf. R. E. Palmer, *Hermeneutics* (Evanston, Ill.: Northwestern University Press, 1969), 84–97.

29. Wilhelm Dilthey, "The Development of Hermeneutics," in *Selected Writings*, ed. and trans. H. P. Rickman (Cambridge: Cambridge University Press, 1976), 192–219.

of the inner life of humans. Meaning for Dilthey involved knowing human experience from within. Understanding was achieved through a mystical process of mental transfer; these experiences were preconceptual acts of human consciousness prior to becoming rational concepts. The goal of hermeneutics consisted of three aspects: experience, expression, and understanding. Thus, he sought the plausibility of a universal human nature manifested in every human being past and present so that no radical difference could exist between an author in the past and an interpreter in the present.[30]

This reshaped concept still concentrated on the intention of the author. It was described by Dilthey as the process in which the interpreter grasped the mind (*Geist*) of the author. He thought that understanding took place by the transposition of the interpreter into the author via an act of imagination at the level of the lived experience.[31] But as we have indicated, Dilthey admitted that an interpreter could never fully grasp an author's personality. This was so because sentiment associated with certain words cannot be fully communicated by the author or grasped by the interpreter.[32] In summarizing the Schleiermacher-Dilthey approach, T. F. Torrance has observed:

> It is all the more necessary that the interpreter should divine the seminal determination in the consciousness of the biblical author in order to reconstruct and reproduce it as a determination in his own consciousness and so to remodel it in his own understanding. This is of course consistent with Schleiermacher's fundamental approach to Christian doctrine in his effort to transpose it into another conceptual form and so to make it understandable in the culture of modern Europe.[33]

Development toward Existential Hermeneutics

From Schleiermacher the history of modern hermeneutical theory followed the trail beyond Dilthey to Gottlob Frege (1848–1925),[34] Edmund

30. Cf. Palmer, *Hermeneutics,* 98–113.

31. Thomas W. Gillespie, "Biblical Authority and Interpretation: The Current Debate on Hermeneutics," in *A Guide to Contemporary Hermeneutics,* ed. Donald K. McKim (Grand Rapids: Eerdmans, 1986), 211–12.

32. Ibid. For example, the particular nuance associated with the word *effort* carries different connotations depending on whether a person is a professor or a ballplayer. And each of these manifest an individual style so that, for instance, what is conceived of as effort by the professor cannot be communicated fully to the ballplayer or vice versa.

33. T. F. Torrance, "Hermeneutics according to Schleiermacher," *SJT* 21 (1968): 262; see also James Torrance, "Interpretation and Understanding in Schleiermacher's Theology: Some Critical Questions," *SJT* 21 (1968): 268–82.

34. Cf. Gottlob Frege, "On Sense and Reference," in *Translations from the Philosophical Writings of Gottlob Frege,* trans. Peter Geach and Max Black (Oxford: Blackwell, 1966), 56–78.

Husserl (1857–1939),[35] Ludwig Wittgenstein (1889–1951),[36] and Martin Heidegger (1889–1976).[37] It is important to note the development that took place from an emphasis on epistemology in Schleiermacher to existential emphases with Heidegger. Picking up on Dilthey's recognition of the radical historicality of human life, Heidegger subjected human-being (*Dasein*) to a thoroughgoing analysis in his magnum opus, *Being and Time.* That Heidegger studied with Husserl but could not agree with his mentor that an objective interpretation or objective knowledge was possible is most significant. Heidegger was skeptical that it was possible to achieve determinate meaning in textual interpretation. While Schleiermacher, Dilthey, Frege, Husserl, and the early Wittgenstein opted for the possibility of an objective interpretation, Heidegger, Rudolf Bultmann, and Hans-Georg Gadamer moved away from this position, away from the possibility of determinate meaning and objectivity. Heidegger shifted the emphasis from historical concerns of the text to the *a priori* concerns of the interpreter.[38] Indeed understanding was generated from the interpreter's existential awareness of human possibilities.[39] From this level of awareness, understanding moved from cognition to expression in the use of language. Heidegger affirmed that what came to expression in discourse was the projection of an understanding of the possibility of human-being (*Dasein*).[40] The interpreter became the source of meaning as emphasis shifted from the author to the reader, indeed, even to the "care" of the reader's being.[41]

35. Cf. Edmund Husserl, *Ideas: General Introduction to Pure Phenomenology,* trans. W. R. B. Gibbon (New York: Collier, 1962); see also Lenore Langsdorf, "Husserl on Judging" (Ph.D. diss., State University of New York at Stony Brook, 1977).

36. Cf. Ludwig Wittgenstein, *Tractatus Logico-Philosophicus* (London: Routledge and Kegan Paul, 1961); idem, *Philosophical Investigations* (1936–1949), 3d ed. (Oxford: Blackwell, 1967); also Jerry H. Gill, "Wittgenstein and Religious Language," *ThT* 21 (1964): 59–72.

37. Martin Heidegger, *Being and Time,* trans. John Macquarrie (Oxford: Blackwell, 1962); idem, *On the Way to Language,* trans. Peter D. Hertz (New York: Harper and Row, 1971).

38. The best discussion of the hermeneutical development in Heidegger is found in Thiselton, *Two Horizons,* 143–204, 327–56; see also Michael Gelvin, *A Commentary on Heidegger's "Being and Time"* (New York: Harper and Row, 1970).

39. Heidegger, *Being and Time,* 67ff. Heidegger used the hyphenated form *ek-sistenz* particularly in his later writings, employing etymology to describe his fuller meaning, something he frequently did.

40. John McGinley, "Heidegger's Concern for the Lived-World in His Dasein-Analysis," *PhT* 16 (1972): 92–116. In this article, McGinley identifies three important differences between the conception of *Dasein* in Heidegger and Husserl. (1) Husserl made knowledge and its certitude the fundamental problem, while Heidegger established the question of Being as fundamental (p. 102). (2) Husserl made a radical distinction between consciousness and reality, whereas Heidegger rejected this kind of duality (p. 103). (3) Husserl examined pure consciousness as an abstraction from its world, but for Heidegger, involvement with the environment was an indispensable characteristic of human subjectivity.

41. Heidegger, *Being and Time,* 220–22; cf. John Macquarrie, *An Existentialist Theology: A Comparison of Heidegger and Bultmann* (London: SCM, 1955), 105–11.

That Rudolf Bultmann (1884–1976) was primarily responsible for Heidegger's hermeneutical insights entering the field of biblical studies is well known.[42] What was important for Bultmann was not the objectifying language of the New Testament, but the existential possibilities of human-being projected through it. One such possibility obviously rested in the New Testament concept of faith. The New Testament was written from the vantage point of faith and called for faith from its readers. Bultmann drew attention to the considerable diversity of theological interests in the primitive church and denied the coherence of an objective doctrinal norm. As he theologized in his *New Testament Theology*, "In the beginning, faith is the term which distinguishes the Christian congregation from Jews and the heathen, not orthodoxy (right doctrine). The latter along with its correlate, heresy, arises out of the differences which develop within the Christian congregations."[43] By faith, New Testament doctrine, couched in the objectifying mode of language, which Bultmann called "myth," was to be interpreted in terms of the primordial possibilities of human-being. What Bultmann intended by his radical program of demythologizing was not the removal of myth but rather its existential interpretation.

Bultmann stood in the Schleiermacher-Dilthey-Heidegger hermeneutical tradition, even though his proposals were major modifications of it.[44] He wished not to reject this tradition, for he remained convinced that the chief interest in reading many texts, particularly philosophical and theological ones, was to have a personal encounter with authors. His objection lay in the tradition's one-sidedness in supposing that grasping the author's individual personality was the only goal in interpreting texts. The broader goal of interpretation, according to Bultmann, included gaining the possibilities of human-being as they exist in relation to the concrete historical world.[45] Understanding, then, may occur when the existential possibilities of the language of faith are appropriated by faith and result in a new self-understanding (*selbst verstandnis*) or understanding of existence (*existenz verstandnis*).[46]

The presupposition that made such understanding possible was that both the interpreter and author share the same historical world as humans. In this, human-being occurs as being in an environment, in understanding

42. Cf. Thiselton, *Two Horizons*, 205–51, for the influences on Bultmann of Heidegger and others including Schleiermacher, Dilthey, Kant, Gogarten, and the Lutheran traditions.

43. Rudolf Bultmann, *Theology of the New Testament*, trans. Kendrik Grobel, 2 vols. (New York: Scribners, 1955), 135.

44. Thiselton, *Two Horizons*, 234–44.

45. Rudolf Bultmann, "The Problem of Hermeneutics," in *Essays Philosophical and Theological*, trans. and ed. James Greig (London: SCM, 1955), 238–43.

46. See the careful discussion of Bultmann's hermeneutics in Paul Ricoeur, *Essays on Biblical Interpretation*, ed. L. S. Mudge (Philadelphia: Fortress, 1980), 49–70.

discourse with objects, as well as with other women and men. Bultmann amplified:

> Such an investigation of the possibilities of human being is always guided by a prior understanding of "human being"—by a particular understanding of human existence, which may be naive, but from which in general in the first instance the categories develop, which make an investigation possible—for example, the question of salvation—of the "meaning" of personal life, or of the "meaning" of history—of the ethical norms of action, the order of human community life and such like. Without such a prior understanding and the questions initiated by it, the texts are mute.[47]

Thus, Bultmann thought biblical exegesis without prior understanding an impossibility.[48] By deemphasizing the cognitive aspects of the biblical text, and shifting the notion of interpretation to existential encounter, Bultmann redirected the focus of New Testament interpretation in the twentieth century.

The Marburg scholar argued that exegesis without presuppositions is impossible. The interpreter must approach the text with specific questions or with a specific way of raising questions, bringing to the text a certain idea of the subject matter with which the text is concerned. Bultmann raised significant points, awakening scholarship from its Cartesian dogmatic slumbers, but his approach was not accepted by all contemporary theologians or interpreters.[49]

Karl Barth (1886–1968), for example, argued that what dropped out of Bultmann's hermeneutical method was a serious consideration of the intended reference of the discourse, the *Sache,* which may and often does transcend both language and the user of the language.[50] Bultmann seemed to imply that no matter what the biblical texts spoke about, their ultimate subject matter was human existence. All would agree that the biblical texts arose from human existence, but when interpretation was exclusively oriented toward human existence, the theological and cognitive aspects were reduced. When Bultmann demythologized Jesus and the apostolic writings by conforming them to these existential categories, he was not letting the New Testament texts speak for themselves. He seemed neither

47. Bultmann, "The Problem of Hermeneutics," 253.

48. So he brilliantly articulated in his classic article, "Is Exegesis without Presuppositions Possible?" *Existence and Faith,* ed. Shubert M. Ogden (London: Hodder and Stoughton, 1961), 289–96.

49. See Helmut Thielicke, *Prolegomena,* vol. 1 of *The Evangelical Faith,* trans. G. W. Bromiley, 3 vols. (Grand Rapids: Eerdmans, 1974), 38–218. He sketches two basic hermeneutical types: Cartesian and non-Cartesian.

50. Cf. Karl Barth, *Rudolf Bultmann: Ein Versuch ihn zu Verstehen,* Theologischen Studien und Kritiken 34 (Zurich: Evangelischer Verlag, 1952).

open nor responsive to other possibilities of understanding human existence besides those set forth by Heidegger. Munich theologian Wolfhart Pannenberg (1928–) responded to Bultmann:

> Although there is no intention of dimming down the particular content of the text [in Bultmann], but rather of making it visible precisely for contemporary understanding, nevertheless that content is narrowed down from the outset; anything other than the possibilities of human existence cannot become relevant for existential interpretation. . . . Now, it is rather doubtful that the text which is to be interpreted on the basis of such handling, can still say what it has to say on its own: the New Testament texts for example, are concerned, at least explicitly, with many things other than the possibilities of understanding human existence, although everything with which they are concerned will also be an element of the understanding of the existence of the New Testament author.[51]

From Existential to Ontological Hermeneutics: Toward a Hermeneutics of Conversation

At this point, Gadamer (1900–) attempted to move the discussion beyond the contributions of his mentors, Heidegger and Bultmann,[52] by orienting hermeneutics to language and its subject matter rather than to an existential understanding of the author objectified in the biblical text. Gadamer sought not to recreate the moment of life when an author composed a text, as did Schleiermacher, nor to rethink the meaning an author intended to communicate; instead, he sought to grasp the vital knowledge of the subject matter that, under certain conditions, emerges from a text's language.[53] By subject matter (*die Sache*), Gadamer referred to that which takes place when two people, engaged in conversation, come to agreement. This concept was developed in his classic volume *Wahrheit und Methode* (*Truth and Method*).[54]

Gadamer rejected the idea that a text, and the biblical text in particular, is a fixed repository of stable content. He advocated that the text is not a depository of meaning, but a mediation of meaning. The reader's task is not

51. Wolfhart Pannenberg, "Hermeneutics and Universal History," in *History and Hermeneutics*, ed. R. W. Funk (Tübingen, Mohr, 1967) 132; cf. R. C. Roberts, *Rudolf Bultmann's Theology* (Grand Rapids: Eerdmans, 1977).

52. See Gadamer's contribution to his former teachers in "Von Zirkel des Verstehens," in *Festschrift Martin Heidegger zum Siebzigsten Geburstag* (Pfullingen: Neske, 1959), 24–34; idem, "Martin Heidegger und die Marburger Theologie," *Zeit und Geeschicte: Dankesgabe an Rudolf Bultmann zum 80*, ed. E. Dinkler (Tübingen: Mohr, 1964), 479–90.

53. Gadamer, "Problem of Language in Scheiermacher's Hermeneutic," 90–92.

54. Hans-Georg Gadamer, *Wahrheit und Methode* (Tübingen: Mohr, 1960), trans. and ed. Garrett Borden and John Cumming as *Truth and Method* (New York: Sheed and Ward, 1975).

to determine the author's meaning when the text was penned, but to understand what the text says to the present reader.[55] The reader's task is pictured by Gadamer as a conversation in which two people attempt to come to a common understanding about some matter which is of interest to both. The goal is not so much understanding each other, but understanding that about which they are talking. Gadamer maintained that the text is an exposition of something that exceeds itself.[56] Language thus serves as a functioning structure of meanings which are always polyvalent and analogous. This means, therefore, that a text has a fullness of meaning which by its very nature can never be exhausted. Not only is it possible but always it is the case that the meaning mediated by the text actually exceeds the conscious intention of the author.[57]

Gadamer also insisted that there is a great distance of time and culture that separates the interpreter from the original author. Similarly, he recognized the tradition established as a result of that distance of time that impinges upon the way an interpreter reads the biblical text.[58] According to Gadamer, there can be no such thing as "pure objectivity" in biblical interpretation any more than there is in other scientific exegesis. This has led many to conclude that historical-biblical exegesis is impossible.[59] Granting Gadamer's points concerning distance and tradition, how can a synthesis be converged to hurdle the seeming impasse? What can be learned from the early church that will speak to contemporary concerns?

Hermeneutics in the Contemporary Church

As we have noted, the present state of biblical studies is seemingly headed toward a hermeneutical impasse. The problem of interpreting Scripture is one for which all would like to find a simple key, an easy for-

55. Gadamer, *Truth and Method,* 253.

56. Ibid., 330.

57. Ibid., 264.

58. See the summary of these matters in Thiselton, *Two Horizons,* 304–19.

59. For those who suggest the limitations of science in general, in addition to "scientific exegesis," see J.-F. Lyotard, *The Post-Modern Condition: A Report on Knowledge,* trans. G. Bennington and B. Massummi (Minneapolis: University of Minnesota Press, 1984); Paul Feyerabend, *Against Method* (London: Thretford, 1975). This response has been intensified by the influence of Jacques Derrida, who has attempted to show the limits of all these approaches. See Jacques Derrida, *Speech and Phenomena,* ed. and trans. D. B. Allison (Evanston, Ill.: Northwestern University Press, 1973); idem, *Of Grammatology,* trans. Gayatri Chakravorty Spivak (Baltimore: Johns Hopkins University Press, 1974); idem, *Writing and Difference* (Chicago: University of Chicago Press, 1978). His influence in biblical studies is evidenced by the fact that an entire issue of *Semeia* was devoted to Derrida; see "Derrida and Biblical Studies," *Semeia* 23 (1982), passim, ed. Robert Detweiler. See also David Tracy, *Plurality and Ambiguity: Hermeneutics, Religion, Hope* (San Francisco: Harper and Row, 1987).

mula that would enable us to approach a text and quickly and certainly establish its meaning. Unfortunately, there is no simple answer. It is, however, possible to indicate three diverse perspectives that will enable the contemporary church to wrestle with the biblical text. From these perspectives we can suggest a healthy synthesis built on the strengths represented in the various viewpoints. These perspectives include what we shall call (1) an "author-oriented" perspective, (2) a "reader-oriented" perspective, and (3) a "text-oriented" perspective. To these approaches we now turn our attention.

Author-Oriented Perspective

The prominent approach to biblical studies in both Protestant and Roman Catholic schools of interpretation until the middle of this century was an author-oriented approach. This view has been known as either the "literal-grammatical," "historical-contextual," or "historical-critical" method of interpretation. Advocates of this position such as Krister Stendahl[60] and John L. McKenzie,[61] writing in the *Journal of Biblical Literature* (1958), defined this approach to interpretation as determining the meaning intended by the human author and understood by the original readers. This approach considered the meaning of texts to be stable and univocal, and its meaning in the original setting is where meaning is located. Stendahl suggested that to "furnish the original," to reconstruct the transaction of the author to the original audience by way of the text, is the task of interpretation. In "Contemporary Biblical Theology" (1962), Stendahl distinguished between what a text meant and what it means.[62] In an earlier edition of Robert M. Grant's *Short History of the Interpretation of the Bible,* Grant affirmed a very similar position, even while recognizing the widespread influence of Heidegger and Bultmann:

> It would appear that the primary task of the modern interpreter is historical, in the sense that what he is endeavoring to discover is what the texts and contexts he is interpreting meant to their authors in their relationships with their readers.[63]

In 1967, a literary scholar from the University of Virginia, E. D. Hirsch, Jr. (1928–), published a major work, *Validity in Interpretation,* advocating

60. Krister Stendahl, "Implications of Form Criticism and Tradition Criticism for Biblical Interpretation," *JBL* 77 (1958): 33–38.

61. John L. McKenzie, "Problems of Hermeneutics in Roman Catholic Exegesis," *JBL* 77 (1958): 197–204.

62. Krister Stendahl, "Contemporary Biblical Theology," *IDB,* 1:419–20.

63. Robert M. Grant, *A Short History of the Interpretation of the Bible* (New York: Macmillan, 1963), 186.

an author-oriented, normative hermeneutic. He followed this in 1976 with his *Aims of Interpretation*.[64] Working within the Schleiermacher-Dilthey tradition of general hermeneutics, Hirsch called for a grammatical interpretation that attempts to grasp the meaning an author intended to convey in what is written. His influence in biblical interpretation is praised by many scholars of diverse theological traditions.

Hirsch distanced himself from the Schleiermacher tradition by maintaining that it is not the task of the interpreter to have access to the mental processes by which an author produced a work.[65] He affirmed that the author's verbal meanings can be grasped because the interpretation of texts is concerned with sharable meanings. Hirsch contended that an author chooses language conventions which will also bring to mind in others the things he or she is attempting to communicate; so also the reader can know what the writer wanted to share with his or her audience by words.[66] Language is efficient in transmitting these meanings because it consists of conventions and elements that the society agreed should stand for all its various aspects of common experience. Thus, "an author's verbal meaning is limited by linguistic possibilities but is determined by his actualizing and specifying some of these possibilities."[67] The meaning of words are thus limited by a context that has been determined by the author. Interpreters cannot, then, understand what a writer meant except by what he or she has actually written.[68] With reference to biblical studies, G. B. Caird summarized,

> We have no access to the mind of Jeremiah or Paul except through their recorded words. A fortiori, we have no access to the Word of God in the Bible except through the words and the minds of those who claim to speak in his name. We may disbelieve them, that is our right; but if we try, without evidence, to penetrate to a meaning more ultimate than the one the writers intended, that is our meaning, not theirs or God's.[69]

To summarize Hirsch's position concerning an author-oriented interpretation, we can note that he claimed the task of the interpreter is to understand what an author meant at the time of the writing. This is pos-

64. E. D. Hirsch, Jr., *Validity in Interpretation* (New Haven, Conn.: Yale University Press, 1967).

65. E. D. Hirsch, Jr., *The Aims of Interpretation* (Chicago: University of Chicago Press, 1976).

66. Ibid., 17–18.

67. Ibid., 47.

68. Ibid., 48.

69. G. B. Caird, *The Language and Imagery of the Bible* (Philadelphia: Westminster, 1980), 61. Caird has discussed the concept of "meaning" and discovering "meaning" in Scripture as carefully as anyone (see pages 32–61). He distinguishes between meaning^R (referent), meaning^S (sense), meaning^V (value), meaning^E (entailment), and meaning^I (intention). Obviously in our discussion at this point we are concerned with meaning^I (intention) and meaning^S (sense).

sible because the text's meaning is controlled by language conventions which exist between the speaker and hearer, or author and reader.[70] Hirsch acknowledged that this process may take the form of a guess, and although there are no rules for making good guesses, there are methods for validating guesses, as Hirsch elucidated: "The act of understanding is at first a genial (or a mistaken) guess and there are no methods for making guesses, no rules for generating insights; the methodological activity of interpretation commences when we begin to test and criticise our guesses."[71] Addressing this issue, Paul Ricoeur has noted,

> As concerns the procedures of validation by which we test our guesses, I agree with Hirsch that they are closer to a logic of probability than a logic of empirical verification. To show that an interpretation is more probable in light of what is known is something other than showing that a conclusion is true. In this sense, validation is not verification. Validation is an argumentative discipline comparable to the juridical procedures of legal interpretation. It is a logic of uncertainty and of qualitative probability. . . . A text is a quasi-individual, the validation of an interpretation applied to it may be said, with complete legitimacy, to give a scientific knowledge of the text.[72]

Before moving to a discussion of the "reader-oriented" approach, it will be informative to note biblical scholar Walter C. Kaiser's amplification of Hirsch's approach. Kaiser has taken the insights from Hirsch's theory of general hermeneutics and applied them specifically to biblical interpretation. Kaiser's writings are prolific and he has consistently maintained Hirsch's important distinction between "meaning" and "significance."[73] Meaning is

70. Ibid., 60–61. What we can observe in Caird is a concern for the author's meaning as located in the text. Others who, like Hirsch, have grounded or at least discussed the "author's intention" with "meaning in the text" include William E. Cain, *The Crisis in Criticism* (Baltimore: Johns Hopkins University Press, 1984); Suresh Ravel, *Metacriticism* (Athens, Ga.: University of Georgia Press, 1981); Geoffrey Thurley, *Counter-Modernism in Current Critical Theory* (New York: St. Martin's, 1983); K. K. Ruthven, *Critical Assumptions* (Cambridge: Cambridge University Press, 1979); Susan R. Horton, *Interpreting Interpreting* (Baltimore: Johns Hopkins University Press, 1979); Lenore Langsdorf, "Current Paths Toward an Objective Hermeneutic," *CTR* 2 (1987): 145–54; P. D. Juhl, *Interpretation* (Princeton, N.J.: Princeton University Press, 1980). A helpful study with concern for authorial intention and the meaning of metaphor is Janet Martin Soskice, *Metaphor and Religious Language* (Oxford: Clarendon, 1985).

71. Hirsch, *Validity in Interpretation*, 19–20; quote from 25. Hirsch, then, does not argue that the interpreter can know the author's meaning better than the author, as was posited by Schleiermacher and Dilthey.

72. Paul Ricoeur, *Hermeneutics and the Human Sciences*, ed. and trans. John B. Thompson (Cambridge: Cambridge University Press, 1986), 212; cf. William J. Abraham, "Intentions and the Logic of Interpretation," *AJT* 4 (1988): 11–26.

73. Cf. Walter C. Kaiser, Jr., *Toward an Exegetical Theology* (Grand Rapids: Baker, 1981); *The Uses of the Old Testament in the New* (Chicago: Moody, 1985). See also Grant Osborne, *The Hermeneutical Spiral: Meaning and Significance* (Downers Grove, Ill.: InterVarsity, 1991); Elliot Johnson, *Expository Hermeneutics* (Grand Rapids: Zondervan, 1989).

what the writer meant in the writing addressed to the original readers. There is only one normative meaning for a text, but there are many significances. The significance of the text includes all the various ways that a text can be read and applied beyond the author's intention. The significance is understood to be descriptive and not normative. Perhaps his major contribution in his vast writings has been the development of the principle that no additional meaning can be understood in any text than the meaning that would have been available to the author through previous revelation.[74] Later revelation can be interpreted in light of earlier revelation, but one cannot read the meaning of later revelation back into earlier revelation. In light of the way the early church read earlier revelation through the vehicles of typological and allegorical exegesis, plus the developments of *sensus plenior* and the analogy of faith since the time of Augustine, such a view is quite controversial. This raises questions about a text's fuller meaning and its hermeneutical significance in the full biblical canon. The matters will be addressed in our evaluation at the end of this section.

Reader-Oriented Perspective

The difficulty of the task described has been underscored by contemporary theorists who think that discovering the author's intention is most problematic, even fallacious.[75] As noted earlier, chief among these has been Gadamer. Reader-oriented hermeneuticians stress the distance that separates interpreters from the original authors of a text in terms of time, culture, and language. The goal of interpretation is for the reader to come to a common understanding about something of interest to both reader and author. A presupposition underlying this approach is that all texts

74. Walter C. Kaiser, Jr., *Toward an Old Testament Theology* (Grand Rapids: Zondervan, 1978), section 2. At this point he moves beyond Hirsch, who does not always limit the intention of the author to a single meaning. In fact Hirsch suggests that the more important or meaningful a text, the greater the possibility of deeper meanings. See the criticism of Kaiser in Raju D. Kunjummen, "The Single Intent of Scripture—Critical Examination of a Theological Construct," *GTJ* 7 (1986): 81–110. However, see Kaiser, "The Promise to David in Psalm 16 and Its Application in Acts 2:25–33 and 13:32–37," *JETS* 23 (1980): 219–29. Here he apparently does not rule out the possibility of intentional multivalence of meaning.

75. See the criticism of Hirsch in David Couzens Hoy, *The Critical Circle: Literature and History in Contemporary Hermeneutics* (Berkeley: University of California Press, 1978), 11–35; also Philip B. Payne, "The Fallacy of Equating Meaning with the Human Author's Intention," *JETS* 20 (1977): 243–52. The classic contribution on this matter published prior to Hirsch's writings is the chapter by William K. Wimsatt and Monroe C. Beardsley, "The Intentional Fallacy," in *The Verbal Icon: Studies in the Meaning of Poetry* (Lexington: University of Kentucky Press, 1954). See the critique of Wimsatt and Beardsley in Colin Lysa's "Personal Qualities and the Intentional Fallacy," vol. 6 of *Philosophy and the Arts*, The Royal Institute of Philosophy Lectures (New York: St. Martin's, 1973), 194–210.

have a fullness of meaning, which by its very nature can never be exhausted. Thus it is not only possible, but is always the case that the meaning which is communicated to the reader exceeds and is broader than the meaning that the author intended to convey.[76] This framework constitutes the basic philosophy behind the rise in biblical interpretation of the "new hermeneutic."[77] In the contemporary church, the reader-response model has been adopted by many interested in liberation[78] and feminist theologies.[79]

Text-Oriented Perspective

A text-oriented approach has been ably expounded by Paul Ricoeur (1913–)[80] and to a lesser extent by Graeme Nicholson.[81] Nicholson contends that authorial meaning may be judged to be identical with textual meaning.[82] Ricoeur is so important for the contemporary discussion because he manages to combine theoretically the legitimate concerns of both Hirsch and Gadamer. As noted, Ricoeur agrees with Hirsch that it is possible to reach a valid interpretation of a text. The goal of a text-oriented approach is not so much to discover the "author's intention," but the "author's results." Text-oriented hermeneutics concerns itself with what the author achieved. Ricoeur has stressed that generally when one reads a text, the author is not present to be questioned about ambiguous

76. In addition to Gadamer, see Wolfgang Iser, *The Act of Reading: A Theory of Aesthetic Response* (Baltimore: Johns Hopkins University Press, 1978).

77. Chief advocates of the "new hermeneutic" are Gerhard Ebeling and Ernst Fuchs. See Gerhard Ebeling, *Introduction to a Theological Theory of Language* (London: Collins, 1973); Ernst Fuchs, *Marburge Hermeneutik* (Tübingen: Mohr, 1968); idem, *Hermeneutik* (Tübingen: Mohr, 1970); Paul J. Achtemeier, *An Introduction to the New Hermeneutic* (Philadelphia: Westminster, 1969). The most even-handed response of the "new hermeneutic," recognizing both strengths and weaknesses, are Anthony C. Thiselton, "The Use of Philosophical Categories in New Testament Hermeneutics," *Churchman* 87 (1973): 87–100; idem, "The New Hermeneutic," in *New Testament Interpretation*, ed. I. Howard Marshall (Grand Rapids: Eerdmans, 1975), 308–33; idem, "Understanding God's Word Today," in *Christ the Lord*, ed. John R. W. Stott (London: Collins Fontana, 1977). Thiselton finds the strength of this approach in interpreting genres of poetry and parables. See Thiselton, "The Parables as Language-Event," *SJT* 23 (1970): 437–68.

78. See the chapter "Hermeneutics, Truth, and Praxis," in José Miguez Bonino, *Doing Theology in a Revolutionary Situation* (Philadelphia: Fortress, 1975), 86–105.

79. Cf. Carol P. Christ and Judith Plaskow, *Womanspirit Rising: A Feminist Reader in Religion* (New York: Harper and Row, 1979); also Elisabeth Schüssler Fiorenza, "Toward a Feminist Biblical Hermeneutics: Biblical Interpretation and Liberation Theology," in *The Challenge of Liberation Theology: A First World Response*, ed. Brian Mahan and C. Dale Richesin (Maryknoll: Orbis, 1981), 91–112.

80. Paul Ricoeur, *Interpretation Theory: Discourse and the Surplus of Meaning* (Fort Worth: Texas Christian University Press, 1976); idem, *Essays on Biblical Interpretation.*

81. Graeme Nicholson, *Seeing and Reading* (Atlantic Highland: Humanities, 1984).

82. Ibid., 226.

meaning in the text.[83] This, of course, is the case with the human authors of the biblical text.[84]

In contrast to Gadamer, Ricoeur does maintain that a text's meaning is intelligible across historical and cultural distance. Because of the nature of writing, the text opens up a possible world to the interpreter (the text-world); the interpreter may enter into that world and appropriate the possibilities which it offers. When that occurs, the meaning of the text is actualized in the interpreter's understanding. What is understood or appropriated, then, is not necessarily the author's intended meaning, or the historical situation of the original author or readers, but the text itself.[85] In many ways this closely parallels Gadamer's fusion of horizons which occurs when the text is disclosed to the reader. The fusion is brought about through the ideality of the textual sense. Thus, a convergence takes place so that understanding seems to occur on a variety of levels, including that of author (following Hirsch), reader (following Gadamer), and text (following Ricoeur).[86] This model has been appropriated in biblical interpretation by newer fields of linguistics,[87] structuralism,[88] and the new narrative and literary approaches to the biblical text.[89] Having examined the contemporary approaches to biblical and philosophical hermeneutics, we must explore how our findings from the early church inform this discussion.

83. Ricoeur, *Interpretation Theory,* 1–24; cf. Wayne C. Booth, *Critical Understanding: The Power and Limits of Pluralism* (Chicago: University of Chicago Press, 1979), 260.

84. Ricoeur discusses this under the heading "Distanciation and Appropriation" in *Hermeneutics and Human Sciences,* 131–44, 182–93.

85. Paul Ricoeur, *The Conflict of Interpretations: Essays in Hermeneutics,* Studies in Phenomenology and Existential Philosophy, ed. Paul D. Ihde (Evanston, Ill.: Northwestern University Press, 1974), 142–50; cf. Peter Homans, "Psychology and Hermeneutics," *JR* 60 (1975): 327–47; William L. Hendricks, "Learning from Beauty," *SWJT* 29 (1987): 19–27.

86. Cf. Raymond E. Brown, "Hermeneutics," in *Jerome Biblical Commentary,* ed. Raymond E. Brown, Joseph A. Fitzmyer, and Roland E. Murphy (Englewood, N.J.: Prentice-Hall, 1968) offers a rapprochement between reader-oriented hermeneutics' emphasis on letting a text speak its contemporary message to contemporary readers, and the way the primitive church's original authors and readers understood the New Testament itself; cf. idem, *Biblical Exegesis and Church Doctrine* (New York: Paulist, 1985). See also Robert E. C. Johnston, "Text and Text-Interpretation in the Thought of Paul Ricoeur" (licentiate diss., Katholieke Universiteit te Leuven, 1977).

87. Cf. Robert E. Longacre, *Grammar of Discourse* (New York: Plenum, 1983); David Alan Black, *Linguistics for Students of New Testament Greek* (Grand Rapids: Baker, 1988); Richard J. Erickson, "Linguistics and Biblical Language," *JETS* 26 (1983): 257–63; Max Turner and Peter Cottrell, *Linguistics and Biblical Interpretation* (Downers Grove, Ill.: InterVarsity, 1989).

88. Cf. Daniel M. Patte, *Structural Exegesis: From Theory to Practice* (Philadelphia: Fortress, 1978); idem, *The Gospel According to Matthew: A Structural Commentary on Matthew's Faith* (Philadelphia: Fortress, 1987); W. Stancil, "Structuralism and New Testament Studies," *SWJT* 22 (1980): 41–59.

89. Cf. R. Alan Culpepper, "Story and History in the Gospels," *RevEx* 81 (1984): 467–78; also Peter W. Macky, "The Coming Revolution: The New Literary Approach to New Testament

Toward a Hermeneutical Synthesis

A Review of Hermeneutical Models

The survey of the various models represented in the early church helps us to see that the contemporary hermeneutical problem is not entirely new. The five models of the early church find similar parallels on the contemporary scene. The "functional" model is present with the pietists; the "authoritative" with the scholastics; the "author" perspective of Antioch, with Hirsch and the historical-critics; the "reader" perspective of the Alexandrians, with contemporary existential, liberation, new hermeneutic, and feminist models; and the "text" perspective associated with Augustine and Theodoret, with Ricoeur and the linguistic/literary approaches.

The functional/pietistic approach is common among all who read the Bible devotionally, but who really are not concerned with exegesis based on the historical context of the passage or hermeneutical questions beyond moral responses. The authoritative/dogmatic approach is necessary for all who attempt to interpret Scripture in a confessional setting, whether Jewish, Catholic, Protestant, Orthodox, or Free Church. One of the strengths of this approach is that parameters are set to guard against what each community perceives as heresy. But its weaknesses need to be noted: (1) answers are sometimes offered before questions are asked; (2) creativity can be threatened; and (3) often, as with Tertullian, challenges are met with anti-intellectual or separatist responses. This brings us to the three models to which the majority of this chapter has been devoted.

Toward a Textual, Canonical, and Confessional Hermeneutic

Sensus Plenior

The question of deeper meanings, normative meanings, and limits or parameters of a text's meaning can be shaped and informed, though not fully answered, by the biblical canon itself. Borrowing from Ricoeur, we can suggest that the biblical text, in its canonical context, contains a surplus of meaning which is not unlike what has traditionally been called *sensus plenior*. This indicates a fuller meaning in the text than that possibly intended

---

Interpretation," *TE* 9 (1979): 32–46; Leland Ryken, *Words of Delight: A Literary Introduction to the Bible* (Grand Rapids: Baker, 1987); idem, *Words of Life: A Literary Introduction to the New Testament* (Grand Rapids: Baker, 1988); Tremper Longman III, *Literary Approaches to Biblical Interpretation* (Grand Rapids: Zondervan, 1987); Edgar V. McKnight, *The Bible and the Reader: An Introduction to Literary Criticism* (Philadelphia: Fortress, 1985). Perhaps most helpful in this regard is Patrick R. Keifert, "Mind Reader and Maestro: Models for Understanding Biblical Interpreters," *Word & World* 1 (1980): 153–68, who shows how different paradigms within linguistic and literary approaches function. He offers the paradigms of "mind reader," "maestro," "player-card," "deliberator," and "story teller."

or known by the author.[90] The more significant the text, the greater the possibility for a fuller meaning.

To illustrate, let us use the example of the "seed" as it is used in Scripture. The seed promised to Abraham and Sarah (Gen. 12–22) had an objective, normative meaning to them, the original historical hearers. It meant that God had promised to give them a son. This is an interpretation that can be validated, but the meaning of the seed is deeper. Its use in Genesis 12 with Abraham and Sarah is a resignification of the promise concerning the seed in Genesis 3:15, where Eve was promised a seed. Historically, the seed referred to the immediate children born to Eve and Sarah. But beyond that, seed is given a broader canonical meaning in the Davidic covenant in 2 Samuel 7, where there is a promise to David that his seed would sit on the throne of Israel forever. Paul, in Galatians 3:16–29, reveals the depth of the theological concept of the seed, whose fullest meaning is found in the Lord Jesus Christ. It is unlikely that the original historical figures, the biblical authors, or the original readers understood seed in Genesis, 3 and 12 or in 2 Samuel 7 as Jesus Christ. Yet from a canonical perspective, we see that the meaning of seed goes beyond, but does not ignore, the meaning understood by the original readers. Eve had a son, as did Sarah. David's son, Solomon, and his sons as well, sat on the throne of Israel. Because of its canonical shape and divine nature, the biblical text may have a surplus of meaning or a full depth of meaning which by its very nature can never be exhausted.[91] It is thus possible, though not always the case, that the meaning of a text may actually exceed the conscious intention of the original authors or the understanding of the original readers.

Following the Antiochene influence and the affirmations of Hirsch, we can affirm that the biblical author's intended meaning is the objective meaning of a text. This is discovered not by identifying the author's mental process, but by the achievements of the author which is the text itself. Despite Gadamer's pessimism concerning distanciation, it seems plausible

90. William Sanford LaSor, "The *Sensus Plenior* and Biblical Interpretation," in *Scripture, Tradition and Interpretation,* ed. W. Ward Gasque and William Sanford LaSor (Grand Rapids: Eerdmans, 1978), 260–77. A critique of *sensus plenior* can be found in Douglas J. Moo, "The Problem of *Sensus Plenior,*" in *Hermeneutics, Authority and Canon,* ed. D. A. Carson and John Woodbridge (Grand Rapids: Zondervan, 1986), 175–211. The history of the discussion can be traced in B. Bierberg, "Does Scripture Have a *Sensus Plenior*?" *CBQ* 10 (1948): 182–95; Raymond E. Brown, "The History and Development of the Theory of *Sensus Plenior,*" *CBQ* 15 (1953): 141–62; idem, "The *Sensus Plenior* in the Last Ten Years," *CBQ* 25 (1963): 262–85.

91. See Vern Poythress, "Divine Meaning of Scripture," *WTJ* 48 (1986): 241–79. Bruce K. Waltke has suggested very similar ideas using Psalm 110 and its varied uses in the canon. See "A Canonical Process Approach to the Psalms," in *Tradition and Testament,* ed. J. S. Feinberg and P. D. Feinberg (Chicago: Moody, 1981), 3–32.

that through determined and dedicated effort the interpreter may reach back and read the text in light of its original context, culture, and setting. Yet, we would suggest that Gadamer has helpfully reminded us of the difficulty of that task, a task not to be taken lightly. Moreover, he has identified the problems associated with our traditions and prejudices that keep us from reading the text objectively. It also is exciting to think that, as Gadamer suggests, every reading of a text, because of its full meaning, can be a new reading. In this sense we have much to learn from the Alexandrians, who approached the text expectantly seeking to find a new meaning in the text's deeper meaning.

How can these fuller meanings be validated? What parameters exist to limit fanciful excesses? Are all these meanings normative? We would suggest that there are indicators in the text's verbal meaning and linguistic possibilities that enable us to limit the range of meaning and help us validate our interpretations.[92] Also, the parameters are located in the text and the full biblical canon, though the church's confessional tradition cannot be ignored. Finally we would suggest that a text's meaning must be consistent with the overall canonical message. In this sense the eclectic and broader concerns of Augustine and Theodoret provide a window to unravel contemporary difficulties. These include (1) approaching the text with right presuppositions, which Augustine identified as faith[93] (following Peter Stuhlmacher, over against Jacques Derrida, this can be identified as a hermeneutics of consent instead of a hermeneutics of suspicion); (2) recognizing that the historical and literal meaning of a text is the primary meaning, but not the limit of meaning; (3) acknowledging the possibility of a deeper meaning in the prophetic-apostolic witness; (4) affirming the human authorship of the text, as well as its divine origin; (5) regarding the biblical text, more than the author's mind, as the place where meaning is concentrated; (6) understanding that a text rests in its historical, literary, and canonical context; (7) viewing Scripture as a commentary on Scripture, thus affirming the analogy of faith and the *sensus plenior* of Scripture; (8) expecting illumination for enablement in interpretation; and (9) expecting the text to speak to the reader's contemporary concerns. Let me briefly suggest how these matters might be addressed.

92. E.g., Kenneth L. Pike and Evelyn G. Pike, *Grammatical Analysis*, SIL Publications in Linguistics 53 (Dallas: Summer Institute of Linguistics and University of Texas at Arlington Press, 1977); Robert E. Longacre, "The Discourse Structure of the Flood Narrative," *JAAR* 41 (1979): 89–133; John H. Sailhamer, "Exegesis of the Old Testament as a Text," in *A Tribute to Gleason Archer*, ed. Walter C. Kaiser, Jr., and Ronald Youngblood (Chicago: Moody, 1986), 279–96, whose bibliographic material on this matter is most extensive. Also note Vern Poythress, "Analysing a Biblical Text: Some Important Linguistic Distinctions," *SJT* 32 (1979): 113–37.

93. See Vern Poythress, "God's Lordship in Interpretation," *WTJ* 50 (1988): 27–64.

Text and Context Markings

It is true that all reading is perspectival; that is, the reader participates in understanding the text, but the reader is not the determiner of meaning. We would suggest there are indicators in the text itself, contextual markers, that are not there by accident but to guide us toward an objective meaning. An objective meaning is thus mediated by the text itself. The text's indicators limit the possibilities so that the number of meanings available to the reader is not infinite. While stressing the historical meaning of the text, we cannot neglect the concerns of the contemporary reader. The concept of the text's significance, in this way, is as important as its meaning, though not equated with it.[94]

Focusing meaning in the biblical text, rather than in the author or reader, acknowledges that a text's verbal meaning can be construed only on the basis of its own linguistic possibilities. These are not given from some other realm, but must be learned or guessed at; this is a process which is entirely intrinsic to a particular social and linguistic system. Ricoeur maintains that what has to be appropriated for understanding to be completed is nothing other than the power of disclosing the "text-world" that is the reference of a text. The gulf between reader and author has been bridged by the text itself. A text is indeed historical in its origin, but it is also present in its power to communicate its sense and to open a world to its reader by its reference. It is in this sense that Ricoeur can suggest that the letters to the Romans, Galatians, Corinthians, and Ephesians, as well as the other books, are addressed to contemporary readers as much as to the original readers.

Canonical Context

Therefore the historical meaning and the contemporary understanding belong together in a single canon of Scripture. These two coexist, and their interaction is shaped by canonical meaning. We must wrestle with both sides of the problem, the then and now communicated to us by the canonical text itself. But the distinctive emphases within the canon must not be reduced or flattened out in the interests of superficial harmonizations, ecclesiastical confessions, or contemporary "rules of faith."[95] Nor can we

94. See David M. Scholer, "Issues in Biblical Interpretation," *EQ* 88 (1988): 5–22.

95. Craig Blomberg, "The Legitimacy and Limits of Harmonization," in *Hermeneutics, Authority and Canon,* ed. D. A. Carson and John Woodbridge (Grand Rapids: Zondervan, 1986), 135–73; Daniel P. Fuller offers guidelines for harmonizing and comparing texts with other texts (the analogy of faith) including helpful warnings in "Biblical Theology and the Analogy of Faith," in *Unity and Diversity in New Testament Theology,* ed. R. Guelich (Grand Rapids: Eerdmans, 1978), 195–96. Texts must be compared with other texts by the same author before making comparisons with other writers. Paul must be compared with Paul, John with John, and Luke with Luke before other comparisons can be made. It is also useful to examine texts by the

develop a "canon within a canon" in an attempt to silence the more challenging sections of Holy Scripture. Our synthesis of these two concerns must maintain the full biblical unity of the biblical canon without ignoring the diversity evident in the historical situations.

In this sense the canon becomes the interpreter's primary rule of faith. The question of limits for the possible meanings of a text are, however, determined both by the canon and the church's theology. The canon establishes a permissable range of "resignification." Resignification is the new meaning given to the concepts, teachings, and figures as they are reintroduced in the progress of revelation through the Bible. The text is not a mere ancient document, but because it has canonical shape it has ongoing meaning and authority for the believing community. This approach to hermeneutics not only looks for all the traditions, texts, and precursors that flow into a passage studied but also seeks to determine how that tradition functioned in the text and the interpretive principles by which it did so. Because the Scripture is a canonical word for the community, we can also read the prophets or the apostles for the present members of the believing fellowship. Both horizons, as Thiselton brilliantly contends, must be maintained.[96]

The project then is characterized by two interrelated phases: (1) literary-historical analysis, and (2) canonical-theological analysis. The first deals primarily with the external features of the text and the situation in which the text has been placed by its author. The second is concerned with the inner life of the text, that is, how the text impinges on the members of the believing community, past and present. In this view, the norms and principles essential to historical and literary methodologies are incorporated into the theological interpretation, serving to guide and oversee theological application. Our task then is to go "there and back again," to go to the text's meaning in the historical situation before coming back again to speak to the present.

Normative Canon

In what sense is meaning in a text normative? We would suggest that the text's significance beyond the canonical meaning is primarily descriptive. Within the canon, however, there are passages where meaning is limited to the initial readers because of their historical or cultural setting.[97]

---

same author in chronological manner so that matters of development may be observed. Secondly, texts must be compared with texts of a similar genre. Epistles should be compared with other epistles prior to comparing texts from Gospels, narratives, Acts, or apocalyptic literature.

96. Thiselton, *Two Horizons*, 439–45.

97. Cf. David Hesselgrave, "Contextualization and Revelational Epistemology," in *Inerrancy and Hermeneutics*, ed. E. Radmacher and R. Preus (Grand Rapids: Zondervan, 1984), 693–764.

But most passages within the canon, because of their canonical status, can be understood in a normative manner. If the biblical text is regarded as completely descriptive, it might lead to the conclusion that the student of Scripture is little more than an antique keeper who displays the exhibits to the best possible advantage of the audience, but cannot demonstrate any relevance. But this approach is unacceptable and lacks all the dynamic of the experience of New Testament Christianity. It should be asked if the real question is not, To what extent is Scripture normative for the contemporary church? Granted that the cultural background and environment have changed since the first century, the canonical message may need to be contextualized or further resignified. Even though there are many contextual and cultural changes, the changes in the human nature have not changed. It is at the point of contextual application that the canonical word can still speak powerfully to contemporary men and women. The canonical message speaks authoritatively to the human condition. This does not mean the contemporary understanding of the biblical message is merely a repetition of early Christian beliefs, but it is a principled restatement, understanding cultural considerations, that awakens twentieth-century readers to an awareness that the Bible can speak in a relevant way to contemporary needs. By illumination, contemporary interpreters can appropriate the meaning of the biblical canon for themselves.[98]

Illumination

The idea of illumination as enablement for understanding the text in this manner (see 1 Cor. 2:10–16) has at times disappeared from the contemporary discussion. We need to realize that we search not only for the external meaning of the text but for its inner meaning as well. We are suggesting that discovering Scripture's meaning involves not only examining the author's result in the written text, but also the Holy Spirit's work of illuminating the reader's mind to interpret the text. With the enablement of the Spirit, discerning a text's meaning and significance is not only possible but plausible. That a text may have deeper meanings, especially in genres like parables and poetry, is implied, but objective meaning is nevertheless present and discoverable.[99] Our goal as interpreters is to seek to determine the text's meaning in both its historical and canonical contexts and to communicate its meaning to contemporary men and women.

98. See Millard Erickson, *Christian Theology,* 3 vols. (Grand Rapids: Baker, 1983–86), 1:253–56. For an alternative view, see Daniel P. Fuller, "The Holy Spirit's Role in Biblical Interpretation," in *Scripture, Tradition and Interpretation,* ed. Ward W. Gasque and William Sanford LaSor (Grand Rapids: Eerdmans, 1978), 189–98.

99. See Craig Blomberg, *Interpreting the Parables* (Downers Grove, Ill.: InterVarsity, 1989).

Conclusion

We have concentrated in this final chapter on contemporary hermeneutical theory and the diversity of hermeneutical models. We have seen that a synthesis of "author-," "reader-," and "text-" oriented models can converge into a canonical synthesis, not unlike the approach of Augustine and Theodoret in the fifth century.[100] In this way, the early church serves as a window for the concerns of contemporary hermeneutical theorists and practitioners.

In conclusion, we have learned that the contributions, variety, and development of the early church's hermeneutical approaches are reflected in the diversity represented among contemporary hermeneutical approaches. We learned there are three primary models among contemporary approaches: (1) "author-oriented" perspectives; (2) "reader-oriented" perspectives; and (3) "text-oriented" perspectives. We concluded that meaning is found in the author's achievement, identified as the text itself, though of course the background behind the text is extremely informative. We noted the legitimate concerns of Gadamer and those in the "reader" model. We can agree that distance, tradition, and perspective hinder the possibility of a purely objective interpretation. Yet, with Hirsch and those emphasizing the primacy of the author in interpretation, we can maintain, along with the Antioch school, Theodoret, and Augustine, the plausibility of determining a text's normative meaning. This meaning can be validated by linguistic and literary keys in the text. Thus the author's meaning is available only in the text, not by making contact with the author's mental patterns.

We observed that the canonical concerns Augustine had previously emphasized should be reinstituted, or at least reconsidered. By seeing the canon as normative for the early church as well as contemporary readers, both horizons confronting the interpreter can be addressed. These different horizons are brought together by canonical emphases. In this way the historical emphases of the Antiochenes, the concerns of others for deeper meaning in Scripture, and the church's past and present concerns for hermeneutical (theological) parameters are brought together. Their coexistence and interaction shape the text's canonical meaning. Concern for these levels of meaning are addressed and informed by the impressive, but varied, contributions of the third-, fourth-, and fifth-century church.

Contemporary biblical hermeneutics is thus able to wrestle with both sides of a single problem. The Old Testament and the New must be inter-

100. A contemporary model of this synthetic or symphonic approach can be found in Vern Poythress, *Symphonic Theology: The Validity of Multiple Perspectives in Theology* (Grand Rapids: Zondervan, 1987).

preted in their separate contexts. Each passage speaks to a particular historical context. But a fuller meaning is provided when the complete revelation of the canon informs these passages, which is a broader and deeper understanding than a historical interpretation alone can provide.

Likewise, in the New Testament, the writings of Paul and James must be interpreted on their own terms. Each speaks to a particular pastoral and historical situation concerning faith and works. But their distinctive contributions within the canon must not be reduced or flattened out in the interest of superficial harmonizations. Neither can one be eclipsed by elevating the other as the key to the whole gospel message. How the interpreter can best avoid these pitfalls, while emphasizing the full canonical meaning of the text, remains a challenge. Full justice must be given to both the primary and plenary meanings. Moreover, we must give equal attention to the unity and diversity of the biblical canon, without ignoring or deemphasizing either.

Finally, we recognize that several far-reaching disciplines should be incorporated in biblical interpretation: history, philosophy, theology, language and linguistic studies, literature, rhetoric, sociology, and anthropology among others. While concern for biblical interpretation must remain primarily the concern of the communities of faith, we cannot adopt the mindset of Tertullian and try to shield the Bible's interpretation from the broader interdisciplinary questions raised by the perspectives of the various disciplines. Thus, the early church serves as an important window, not only for positive insights for contemporary hermeneutical matters, but also as a means to avoid the pitfalls and failures of the past. We must look to those upon whose shoulders we stand to gain insight, knowledge, and motivation to address the hermeneutical challenges raised by theologians and biblical interpreters of our day. In conclusion, following the thoughts of Emilio Betti, a hermeneutic theorist whose primary work was done earlier in this century and who suggested that hermeneutics are vital to the well-being of society, we can affirm that hermeneutical understanding is vital to the well-being of society, the academy, and particularly the church.

Glossary

Adoptionist Christology. An adoptionist Christology is a belief that Jesus was in nature a man who became God by adoption. This theory maintained that Jesus was a virtuous man chosen by God, and with him the Spirit of God was united. He was an obedient man, doing even more than commanded. Therefore, he was by divine decree adopted to great power and lordship. Adherents of this Christology were declared heretics in the third century.

Alexandrian School. Alexandria was a center of great learning. Here Philo developed his allegorical hermeneutics. The school of thought represented in Alexandria had streams of Platonic, neo-Platonic, and Gnostic thought, and these streams of thought influenced the way Judaism and Christianity were articulated. At the beginning of the third century A.D. Alexandria became important as a seat of Christian theology. The school was characterized by its dependence upon neo-Platonic philosophy and its application of the allegorical method of biblical interpretation.

Allegorical Interpretation. That kind of interpretation which assumes that the text to be interpreted says or intends to say something other than its literal wording suggests. It seeks to draw out a deeper, mystical sense not derivable from the words themselves.

Already/Not Yet Tension. The belief that the eschatological life may be enjoyed here and now in the "already," but that the full consummation of this life is "not yet" complete and awaits a future fulfillment. There is an indeterminate interval between Christ's resurrection and second coming. During this interval the age to come overlaps the present age. Believers "already" live spiritually in the new age, though temporally they do "not yet" live in that age. This dialectic is called the "already/not yet" tension.

Antiochene School. An approach to or school of biblical interpretation and theology popular from the third to the eighth centuries A.D. that developed in Antioch of Syria. The approach tended to be rational, historical, and literal, in contrast to that which had previously developed in Alexandria. Interpreters who followed this approach seemed to be critical in their methodology, with some dependence upon Aristotle and that philosophical tradition.

Apocalyptic Literature. A collective term to designate those ancient visionary writings or parts of writings that, like the Book of Revelation, claim to reveal the mystery of the end of the age and the glories of the age to come. It is a distinctly Jewish and Christian phenomenon that goes back to the sixth century B.C., but it flourished between 200 B.C. and A.D. 100.

Apostolic Fathers. A group of early Christian writers believed to have had direct contact with the apostles of the early church. The term is used to describe the earliest noncanonical writings of the late first and early second centuries.

Arius/Arianism. Arius (A.D. 250–336) was an elder in an urban parish in Alexandria (A.D. 318–325). He taught that God the Father alone is God. This God could not possibly have communicated his essence to any other; thus the Son is a being created by the will and power of the Father. Unlike the Father, Jesus was not without beginning. Arianism was declared heretical at both the Council of Nicea (A.D. 325) and the Council of Constantinople (A.D. 381).

Authoritative Hermeneutics. A way of interpreting Scripture to point out the false beliefs of heretics. This was accomplished by establishing the correct theological meaning of Scripture by the authority of the bishop or the *regula fidei* (rule of faith).

Canon/Canonical. The tern *canon* refers to the group of books acknowledged by the early church as the rule of faith and practice. Both Jews and Christians have canons of Scripture. The Jewish canon consists of thirty-nine books called the Old Testament or Hebrew Scriptures. The Christian canon consists of sixty-six books (thirty-nine Old Testament and twenty-seven New Testament) for Protestants and eighty books for Catholics, whose canon includes the Apocrypha.

Chalcedonian Christology. The belief about Jesus Christ adopted at the Council of Chalcedon (A.D. 451) and considered by most today as the foundation of classical orthodox Christology. The confession affirms Jesus as the one and the same Christ, Son, Lord, Only Begotten—to be acknowledged in two natures, without confusion, without change, without division, without separation; the distinction of the natures being in no way abolished because of the union, but rather the characteristic property of each one being preserved, and concurring into one person and one being.

Christocentric Interpretation. A term often used synonymously with "christological," but more specific or focused, seeing Jesus Christ as central to all interpretation of the Old Testament.

Christological Interpretation. The Greek word *Christos* means "anointed one" and is the equivalent of the Hebrew *Mashiah* (Messiah). Christological interpretation reads the Old Testament in light of the belief that Jesus of Nazareth is the Messiah/Christ and the fulfillment of the Old Testament promises and prophecies.

Christology. The word refers to the teaching of Christ, his person and natures. In earlier times, Christology also included the work of Christ, now usually treated under the doctrine of salvation.

Dead Sea Scrolls. The name given mainly to parchment and papyrus scrolls written in Hebrew, Aramaic, or Greek and discovered in eleven caves along the northwestern coast of the Dead Sea between 1947 and 1956. The scrolls date from 250 B.C. to A.D. 68 and are assigned to an Essene community located at the site or area know as Qumran.

Early Church. A rather broad and somewhat ambiguous term used to describe the Christian church from its inception through its development in the first five centuries. Sometimes the terms *earliest church, earliest Christianity, primitive church,* or *primitive Christianity* are more focused upon the first-century church.

Exegesis. Exegesis means "to explain the meaning of a text in its original context." In Christian theology, exegesis is based on the presupposition that the Bible is in some sense the Word of God and that humanity is the recipient of its message. Exegesis and hermeneutics are sometimes used synonymously, but we can distinguish that exegesis asks, What did a text mean to the original sender or receiver? while hermeneutics asks, What does a text mean for the present reader?

Functional Hermeneutic. A way of describing how readers apply biblical text to their own context and situation without attention to its original context or situation. Meaning is thus bound up with Scripture's functional application.

Gemara. A commentary work of the rabbis known as Amoraim (expounders). It developed primarily in two centers, Babylon and Palestine (Tiberias) from the third to the fifth centuries.

Hermeneutic. The name ascribed by scholars to a school of thought beginning principally with the so-called later Heidegger but whose roots go back to Dilthey and Schleiermacher, sometimes called ontological hermeneutics. It differs from traditional hermeneutics in that it is no longer equated with a theory of exegetical method, but is a description of what constitutes the phenomenon of understanding as such. It rejects the idea that a text has meaning autonomous of the interpreter.

Hermeneutics. From the Greek *hermeneuein*: to express, to explain, to translate, to interpret. It is variously defined, but refers to a theory of interpretation. Traditionally, hermeneutics sought to establish the principles, methods, and rules needed in the interpretation of written texts, particularly sacred texts.

Indicative/Imperative. The shape of New Testament theology and ethics. It recognizes that often the New Testament writers explain the individual believer's or the church's position before God (in the indicative mood). This is followed by an exhortation to live out this teaching in practical terms (in the imperative mood). For example, in Romans 6, Paul says, "Anyone who has died has been freed from sin. . . . Therefore do not let sin reign in your mortal body" (6:7, 12).

Late Judaism. Judaism from the closing of the Old Testament to the third century A.D., specifically its different groups (Pharisees, Sadducees, Essenes, and Zealots) during the intertestamental period and the first century A.D.

Literal Interpretation. An attempt to understand Scripture in its plain and ordinary sense without seeing a deeper or spiritual meaning.

Meaning. Meaning is a highly ambiguous term, and the only safe way of handling it is to identify the various senses in which it is used. One way of discussing meaning is by use of the terms *sense* and *referent.* The sense is what is being said and the referent is what is being talked about. Meaning can also be discussed in terms of *value* and *entailment.* Meaning as value does not imply a greater understanding of a subject, but instead a greater appreciation. For instance, we can say that Paul means more to one person than does John. This person may not understand Paul better, but she or he does prefer Paul to John. By entailment, we are not indicating that meaning expresses synonymous relationships between two ideas, but that one idea leads inexplorably to the other. When we discuss meaning in terms of the author's intentions or results, it is more than understanding why writers say what they say. To understand why writers say what they do is not the same thing as understanding what they are saying. The author's results can be discussed in terms of historical meaning, objective meaning, and normative meaning. Historical meaning is grounded in the historical sense of the text. When the genre so indicates, the historical meaning also refers to the historicity of the event behind the text. An objective meaning is a meaning deter mined primarily by the author or text, rather than the reader. An objective meaning refers to the interpreter's attempt to ground meaning in either the author's intention or the author's result (the text itself). Often the historical meaning and the objective meaning are identified as synonymous concepts, but this is not mandatory. A normative meaning suggests that the interpreter's findings have authority for the interpreter and may even be binding upon the interpreter.

Midrash. Jewish interpretation of Scripture; more precisely, a commentary that contemporizes Scripture for current and practical situations.

Mishna. From the Hebrew *shanah*: to learn, to repeat. The Mishna was an authoritative collection of rabbinic halakic (legal or procedural) material developed within the oral traditions of pharisaic and rabbinic Judaism, arranged and revised by Judah ha-Nasi in the first decades of the third century. The Mishna provides the foundation for the structure of the Talmud and is of great significance for understanding the Judaism of the intertestamental and early church period.

Nestorian Christology. The teaching about Jesus associated with Nestorius of Antioch. Nestorianism maintained that Christ was a conjunction (*synapheia*) of two distinct natures. It was believed that before the union, there had been the Son of God, with his divine nature, and a human embryo, with his human nature. The Son of God entered the human fetus at the moment of conception, but did not mix with it in any way. God and man were linked in symmetrical union in which the whole was greater than its parts. The whole was the person of Christ, the appearance of a union which could theoretically be dissolved without destroying either the Son of God or the man Jesus. Nestorius and his teaching were condemned at the Third Ecumenical Council (Ephesus, A.D. 431) and again at Chalcedon (A.D. 451).

Nicene Christology. The teaching of the fourth-century church derived from the Council of Nicea (A.D. 325) and confirmed at Constantinople (A.D. 381). This teaching was articulated by Athanasius (ca. A.D. 297–373). The Council of Nicea condemned Arius by insisting that the Son was not simply the "firstborn of all creation," but was indeed "of one essence with the Father." Against Arius, Athanasius sought to uphold the unity of essence of the Father and Son by basing his argument not on a philosophical doctrine of the nature of the Logos, but on the nature of the redemption accomplished by the Word in the flesh. Only God himself, taking on human flesh and dying and rising in human flesh, can effect a redemption that consists in being saved from sin and corruption and death, and in being raised to share the nature of God himself. After Nicea, it became apparent that there were two main schools of thought in the church, centered in Alexandria and Antioch respectively. In doctrinal terms, Alexandria claims priority, and Antioch is best regarded as a reaction against what were believed to be Alexandria's excesses.

Patristics. The study of the fathers of the church. The leaders, particularly the bishops, were known as the Fathers. More specifically, the term has come to be applied to the first Christian writers of acknowledged eminence. The outstanding thinkers and theologians of the first six centuries of the church have come to be regarded as the Fathers and the study of these leaders is known as patristics.

Pericope. A term adopted from Hellenistic rhetoric and used to refer to a short section or passage of Scripture. It was first used in Christian circles by Jerome to designate a portion of Scripture. This usage preceded the division of Scripture into chapters. In contemporary biblical criticism, the term is used to refer to any self-contained unit of Scripture.

Pesher. An approach to commenting on Scripture, particularly the Old Testament prophets, by the Qumran sectarians who believed themselves to be living in the last days. Pesher is a divinely illuminated interpretation of the divine mysteries of Scripture, relating such texts to the last days.

Pharisees. An important Jewish group which flourished in Palestine from the late second century B.C. to the late first century A.D. The Pharisees were strongly committed to the daily application and observance of the law. They accepted the traditional elaborations of law, making specific and daily application possible. They believed in the existence of spirits and angels, the resurrection, and the coming of a Messiah.

Qumran. The name given to the ruins of an Essene community of fanatic Jewish monastics on the northwestern coast of the Dead Sea. It was first occupied in approximately 150 B.C. and destroyed in A.D. 68 by Rome during the first Jewish revolt.

Rabbinic Literature. Commentary and prescriptive writings based on Scripture for the various Jewish communities. "Rabbi" is a title used to honor Jewish religious teachers. As the title given to teachers of the law in the Jewish community, it passes on from teacher to pupil by ordination, qualifying one who has the proper training to function as preacher, teacher, and pastor in the Jewish synagogue. The writings of the rabbis are broadly grouped under the title *rabbinic literature.*

Redaction Criticism. From the German *Redaktionsgeschichte,* the term refers to a method of biblical criticism that seeks to determine the theological perspectives of a biblical writer by analyzing the editorial and compositional techniques and interpretations employed in shaping and framing the written and oral traditions about Jesus (see Luke 1:1–4).

Sensus Plenior. A Latin term for the fuller meaning of a passage of Scripture intended by God, but not clearly understood by the human author or the original hearers/readers.

Shema. The common name given to the three prayers offered daily by pious Jews of the first century A.D. The prayers are based upon Deuteronomy 6:4–9; 11:13–21; and Numbers 15:37–41.

Soteriology. The term referring to the church's teaching about salvation of humans from the power and effects of sin. From the Greek term *soteria,* it relates to the comprehensive doctrine of salvation—past, present, and future.

Talmud. From the Hebrew *lamad:* study or instruction. Talmud is the comprehensive term for the Mishna and its accompanying commentary, the Gemara (the teaching). The Gemara contains a wide variety of material bearing directly or remotely on the subjects of the Mishna (proverbs, tales, custom, folklore, etc.) as well as strict exposition of the text. The structure of the Talmud is therefore that of the Mishna, having six orders divided into sixty-three tractates, the form it obtained by the third century.

Targum. In broad terms, the word *Targum* means "translation or interpretation"; more specifically it refers to Aramaic translations of the Old Testament. In rabbinic literature it often refers to Aramaic phrases that are found in the Old Testament books of Ezra, Nehemiah, and Daniel. The Targum developed from the synagogue practice of translating the Hebrew Scriptures into Aramaic, for the Aramaic-speaking Jews, usually with an accompanying commentary or expanded paraphrase.

Typological Interpretation. From the Greek *typos:* pattern or archetype. It is an approach to biblical interpretation in which persons, events, or things of the Old Testament are interpreted as being foreshadowings or prototypes of persons, events, or things in the New Testament. Typological differs from allegorical interpretation in that the latter sees the hidden, spiritual meaning of a text whereas the former understands a revelatory connection between two historically distinct but religiously significant persons or events.

Bibliography

Abraham, William J. "Intentions and the Logic of Interpretation." *ATJ* 4 (1988): 11–26.

Achtemeier, Elizabeth. "Typology." *IDB* Supplement, 926–27.

Achtemeier, Paul J. *An Introduction to the New Hermeneutic.* Philadelphia: Westminster, 1969.

Ackroyd, Peter R., and C. F. Evans, eds. *The Cambridge History of the Bible: From Beginnings to Jerome,* vol. 1. Cambridge: Cambridge University Press, 1970.

Adler, Mortimer J. *How to Read a Book.* New York: Simon and Schuster, 1940.

Akers, Randy Lee. "The Perfected Soul as an Exegetical Goal in Origen's Writings on the Song of Songs." Ph.D. dissertation, Northwestern University, 1984.

Aldridge, J. W. *The Hermeneutics of Erasmus.* Richmond: John Knox, 1966.

Aleith, E. "Paulus verstandnis des Johannes Chrysostomus." *ZNW* 38 (1939): 181–88.

Alexander, James N. S. "The Interpretation of Scripture in the Ante-Nicene Period." *Int* 12 (1958): 272–80.

Allen, Leslie C. "The Old Testament in Romans I–VIII." *VE* (1964): 6–41.

Altaner, Berthold. *Patrology.* Translated by Hilda C. Graef. 2d ed. New York: Herder and Herder, 1961.

Amerigen, Thomas E. *The Stylistic Influence of the Second Sophistic on the Panegyrical Sermons of St. John Chrysostom: A Study in Greek Rhetoric.* Washington, D.C.: Catholic University of America Press, 1921.

Ammundsen, V. "The Rule of Truth in Irenaeus." *JTS* 13 (1912): 574–80.

Aquinas, Thomas. *On Interpretation.* Translated by J. T. Oesterle. Milwaukee: Marquette University Press, 1962.

Argyle, A. W. "Philo and the Fourth Gospel." *ExT* 63 (1951–52): 385–86.

Armstrong, A. Hilary. *St. Augustine and Christian Platonism.* Villanova, Penn.: Villanova University Press, 1967.

Arnold, E. *The Early Christians.* Translated and edited by the Society of Brothers at Rifton, New York. Grand Rapids: Baker, 1972.

Athanasius. *De Incarnatione.* Edited by F. L. Cross. London: Macmillan, 1939.

Attwater, Donald. *St. John Chrysostom: Pastor and Preacher.* London: Harvill, 1959.

Augustine, *Against the Manichaens and Against the Donatists.* Translated by Richard Stothert, A. H. Newman, and J. R. King. Revised by C. D. Hartranft. Vol. 4 of *Nicene and Post-Nicene Fathers,* 1st series. Reprint. Grand Rapids: Eerdmans, 1983.

______. *City of God, and Christian Doctrine.* Translated by M. Dods and J. F. Shaw. Vol. 2 of *Nicene and Post-Nicene Fathers,* 1st series. Reprint. Grand Rapids: Eerdmans, 1988.

______. *Eighty-Three Different Questions.* Translated by David L. Mosher. In *Fathers of the Church.* Washington, D.C.: Catholic University of America Press, 1977. Vol. 70, 80–220.

______. *Homilies on the Gospel of John and the First Epistles of John.* Translated by J. Gibb and H. Browne. Edited by J. H. Myers. Vol. 7 of *Nicene and Post-Nicene Fathers,* 1st series. Reprint. Grand Rapids: Eerdmans, 1986.

______. *Homilies on the Psalms.* Translated by T. Scratton. Vol. 8 of *Nicene and Post-Nicene Fathers,* 1st series. Reprint. Grand Rapids: Eerdmans, 1976.

______. *On Christian Doctrine.* Translated by D. W. Robertson, Jr. Vol. 80 of *Library of Liberal Arts.* New York: Liberal Arts, 1958.

______. *On the Holy Trinity, Doctrinal Treatises and Moral Treaties.* Translated by A. W. Hadden et al. Revised by W. G. T. Shedd. Vol. 3 of *Nicene and Post-Nicene Fathers,* 1st series. Reprint. Grand Rapids: Eerdmans, 1980.

______. *Sermon on the Mount, Harmony of the Gospels and Homilies on the Gospels.* Translated by W. Findlay, D. S. Salmond, and R. G. MacMullen. Edited by D. S. Schaff, M. B. Riddle, and P. Schaff. Vol. 6 of *Nicene and Post-Nicene Fathers,* 1st series. Reprint. Grand Rapids: Eerdmans, 1980.

______. *Writings Against the Pelagians.* Translated by P. Holmes and R. G. Wallis. Revised by B. B. Warfield. Vol. 5 of *Nicene and Post-Nicene Fathers,* 1st series. Reprint. Grand Rapids: Eerdmans, 1987.

Aune, David E. *The New Testament in Its Literary Environment.* Philadelphia: Westminster, 1987.

Ayer, J. C., ed. *A Sourcebook for Ancient Church History.* New York: Scribners, 1913.

Ayers, Robert H. *Language, Logic and Reason in the Church Fathers: A Study of Tertullian, Augustine and Aquinas.* New York: Oxford University Press, 1979.

Babcock, W. "Augustine's Interpretation of Romans (A.D. 394–396)." *AugSt* 10 (1979): 55–74.

Baker, D. L. *Two Testaments, One Bible: A Study of Some Modern Solutions to the Theological Problem of the Relationship Between the Old and New Testament.* Downers Grove, Ill.: InterVarsity, 1976.

Balas, David L. "Marcion Revisited: A Post-Harnack Perspective." *In Text and Testaments,* edited by E. March, 95–108, San Antonio: Trinity University Press, 1980.

Banks, Robert. *Reconciliation and Hope.* Grand Rapids: Eerdmans, 1974.

Barbour, Ian G. *Myths, Models, and Paradigms.* London: SCM, 1974.

Barclay, William. "A Comparison of Paul's Missionary Preaching and Preaching to the Church." In *Apostolic History and the Gospel,* edited by W. Ward Gasque and Ralph P. Martin, 165–75. Grand Rapids: Eerdmans, 1970.

______. "Romans V.12–21." *ExT* 70 (1958–59): 132–35.

Bardenhewer, Otto. *Geschicte der Altkirschlichen Literatur.* 5 vols. Darmstadt: Wissenschaftliche Buchgesellschaft, 1962.

Bardy, G. "Theodoret." *DTC* 15 (1950): 299–325.

Bardy, J. "Aux origines de l' ecole d'Alexandria." *RSR* 21 (1933): 430–50.

Barkley, Gary W. "Origen's *Homilies on Leviticus:* An Annotated Translation." Ph.D. dissertation, The Southern Baptist Theological Seminary, 1984.

Barnard, L. W. "The Background of St. Ignatius of Antioch." *VC* 17 (1963): 193–206.

______. *Justin Martyr: His Life and Thought.* Cambridge: Cambridge University Press, 1967.

______. "Justin Martyr in Recent Study." *SJT* 22 (1969): 152–64.

______. "The Old Testament and Judaism in the Writings of Justin Martyr." *VT* 14 (1964): 395–406.

______. *Studies in the Apostolic Fathers and Their Background.* New York: Schocken, 1966.

Barnes, Timothy David. "The Chronology of Montanism." *JTS* n.s. 21 (1970): 403–8.

______. *Tertullian: A Historical and Literary Study.* Oxford: Clarendon, 1971.

Barnes, W. E. "The Third Century and Its Greatest Christian: Origen." *ExT* 44 (1932–33): 295–300.

Barr, James. *Holy Scripture: Canon, Authority, Criticism.* Philadelphia: Westminster, 1983.

______. *Old and New in Interpretation: A Study of the Two Testaments.* London: SCM, 1966.

______. "St. Jerome's Appreciation of Hebrew." *BJRL* 49 (1966–67): 281–302.

Barrett, C. K. *The Epistle to the Romans.* HNTC. New York: Harper and Row, 1957.

______. "The Eschatology of the Epistle to the Hebrews." In *The Background of the New Testament and Its Eschatology,* edited by W. D. Davies and David Daube, 363–93. Cambridge: Cambridge University Press, 1954.

______. *First Epistle to the Corinthians.* HNTC. New York: Harper and Row, 1968.

______. "The Interpretation of the Old Testament in the New." In *Cambridge History of the Bible,* vol. 1, edited by P. R. Ackroyd and C. F. Evans, 377–411. Cambridge: Cambridge University Press, 1970.

Barrow, R. H. *Introduction to St. Augustine's 'The City of God'.* London: Faber and Faber, 1950.

Barth, Karl. *Rudolf Bultmann: Ein Versuch ihn zu Verstehen.* Theologischen Studien und Kritiken 34. Zurich: Evangelischer Verlag, 1952.

Barth, Marcus. "The Old Testament in Hebrews." In *Current Issues in New Testament Interpretation,* edited by W. Klassen and G. F. Snyder, 65–78. New York: Harper and Row, 1962.

Bassler, J. M. "Alexandria." *HBD,* 20–21.

Bate, H. N. "Some Technical Terms of Greek Exegesis." *JTS* 24 (1922–23): 59–66.

Bauer, Walter. *Der Wortgottesdienst der alesten Christen.* Tübingen: Mohr, 1930.

______. *Orthodoxy and Heresy in Earliest Christianity.* Edited by Robert Kraft and Gerhard Krodel. Philadelphia: Fortress, 1971.

Baur, Chrysostomus. *John Chrysostom and His Time.* Translated by M. Gonzaga. 2 vols. Westminster, Md.: Newman, 1959.

Baus, Karl, Hans-Georg Beck, Eugen Ewig, and Herman Josef Vogt. *The Imperial Church from Constantine to the Early Middle Ages,* translated by Anselm Biggs. In *History of the Church,* edited by Hubert Jedin and Paul Dolan. 10 vols. New York: Seabury, 1980.

Beare, F. W. "Canon of the New Testament." *IDB,* 1:334–58.

Beasley-Murray, G. R. *Baptism in the New Testament.* Grand Rapids: Eerdmans, 1973.

Bebis, G. S. "Concept of Tradition in the Fathers of the Church." *GOTR* 15 (1970): 22–55.

Beckwith, Roger. *Confessing the Faith in the Church of England Today.* Latimer Studies 9. Oxford: Oxford University Press, 1981.

Beekman, John, and John Callow. *Translating the Word of God.* Grand Rapids: Zondervan, 1974.

Beker, J. Christiaan. *Paul the Apostle: The Triumph of God in Life and Thought.* Philadelphia: Fortress, 1980.

Bell, Harold Idris. *Cults and Creeds in Graeco-Roman Egypt.* Liverpool: At the University Press, 1954.

Benoit, A. *Saint Irenee: Introduction a l'etude de sa theologie.* Paris: Cerf, 1960.

Bentley, J. H. *Humanist and Holy Writ.* Princeton, N.J.: Princeton University Press, 1983.

Bentley-Taylor, David. *Augustine: Wayward Genius.* Grand Rapids: Baker, 1980.

Berkhof, L. *The History of Christian Doctrine.* Grand Rapids: Baker, 1937.

Berkouwer, G. C. *Studies in Dogmatics: Holy Scripture.* Translated and edited by Jack B. Rogers. Grand Rapids: Eerdmans, 1975.

Bernard of Clairveaux. *The Love of God and Spiritual Friendship.* Edited with an introduction by James Houston. Portland: Multnomah, 1983.

Berthouzoz, R. *Liberte et grace suivant la theologie d'Irenee de Lyon.* Paris: Cerf, 1980.

Bethune-Baker, J. F. *An Introduction to the Early History of Christian Doctrine to the Time of the Council of Chalcedon.* London: Methuen, 1903.

Bettensen, Henry, ed. *Documents of the Christian Church.* Oxford: Oxford University Press, 1963.

Betz, Hans Dieter. *Galatians.* Hermeneia. Philadelphia: Fortress, 1979.

Bienert, Wolfgang. *"Allegoria" and "Anagoge" bei Didymos dem Blinden von Alexandria.* Berlin: de Gruyter, 1972.

Bierberg, B. "Does Scripture Have a *Sensus Plenior?*" *CBQ* 10 (1948): 182–95.

Bigg, Charles. *The Christian Platonists of Alexandria.* Oxford: Clarendon, 1886.

Bihlmeyer, Karl. *Church History.* Revised by H. Tuchle. Translated by V. E. Mills. 3 vols. Westminster, Md.: Newman, 1968.

Birdsall, R. Scott. "The Naasene Sermon and the Allegorical Tradition: Allegorical Interpretation, Syncretism and Textual Authority." Ph.D. dissertation, Claremont Graduate School, 1984.

Black, David Alan. *Linguistics for Students of New Testament Greek.* Grand Rapids: Baker, 1988.

Black, David Alan, and David S. Dockery, eds. *New Testament Criticism and Interpretation.* Grand Rapids: Zondervan, 1991.

Black, Matthew. "The Christological Use of the Old Testament in the New Testament." *NTS* 18 (1971): 1–14.

______. "The Pauline Doctrine of the Second Adam." *SJT* 7 (1954): 170–79.

______. *Romans.* NCB. London: Marshall, Morgan and Scott, 1973.

Black, Max. *Models and Metaphors.* Ithaca, N.Y.: Cornell University Press, 1962.

Blackman, E. C. *Marcion and His Influence.* London: SPCK, 1948.

Blair, H. A. "Two Reactions to Gnosticism." *CQR* 152 (1951): 141–58.

Bloch, Renee. "Midrash." In *Approaches to Ancient Judaism: Theory and Practice,* edited by W. S. Green, translated by Mary Howard Calloway. Brown Judaic Studies 1. Missoula, Mont.: Scholars, 1978.

Blomberg, Craig. *Interpreting the Parables.* Downers Grove, Ill.: InterVarsity, 1987.

______. "The Legitimacy and Limits of Harmonization." In *Hermeneutics, Authority and Canon,* edited by D. A. Carson and John Woodbridge, 135–73. Grand Rapids: Zondervan, 1986.

Bock, Darrell L. "Evangelicals and the Use of the Old Testament: Part 1." *BibSac* 142 (1985): 209–23.

______. "Evangelicals and the Use of the Old Testament: Part 2." *BibSac* 142 (1985): 306–19.

______. *Proclamation from Prophecy and Pattern.* Sheffield: JSOT, 1987.

Boer, H. R. *A Short History of the Early Church.* Grand Rapids: Eerdmans, 1976.

Boer, W. de. "Hermeneutic Problems in Early Christian Literature." *VC* 1 (1947): 150–67.

Bokser, Ben Z. "Justin Martyr and the Jews." *JQR* 64 (1973): 97–122.

______. "Justin Martyr and the Jews." *JQR* 64 (1974): 204–11.

Bonino, José Miguez. *Doing Theology in a Revolutionary Situation.* Philadelphia: Fortress, 1975.

Bonner, Gerald. *Augustine and Pelagianism in the Light of Modern Research.* Philadelphia: Westminster, 1973.

______. "Augustine as Biblical Scholar." *CHB,* 1:541–63.

______. *St. Augustine of Hippo: Life and Controversies.* 2d ed. Philadelphia: Westminster, 1986.

Bonsirven, Joseph. *Exegese rabbinique et Exegese paulinienne.* Paris: Beauchesne et Ses Fils, 1938.

Booth, Wayne C. *A Rhetoric of Irony.* Chicago: University of Chicago Press, 1974.

______. *Critical Understanding: The Power and Limits of Pluralism.* Chicago: University of Chicago Press, 1979.

Borchert, Gerald L. "Gnosticism." *EDT,* 444–47.

______. "Insights into the Gnostic Threat to Christianity as Gained Through the Gospel of Philip." In *New Directions in New Testament Study,* edited by Richard N. Longenecker and Merrill C. Tenney, 79–96. Grand Rapids: Zondervan, 1975.

Bornkamm, Gunther. "The Revelation of Christ to Paul on the Damascus Road and Paul's Doctrine of Justification and Reconciliation." In *Reconciliation and Hope,* edited by Robert Banks, 90–103. Grand Rapids: Eerdmans, 1974.

Bornkamm, H. *Luther and the Old Testament.* Edited by V. I. Gruhn. Philadelphia: Fortress, 1966.

Boullvec, Allain Le. "Ya-t-il des traces de la pol emique antignostique d'Irenee dans le *Peri Archon* d'Origene?" In *Gnosis and Gnosticism: Papers Read at the Seventh International Conference on Patristic Studies,* 138–47. Leiden: Brill, 1977.

Bowe, Barbara Ellen. "A Church in Crisis: Ecclesiology and Paranesis in Clement of Rome." Th.D. dissertation, Harvard University, 1986.

Bowker, J. *The Targums and Rabbinic Literature.* Cambridge: Cambridge University Press, 1969.

Boyd, W. J. P. "Origen on Pharoah's Hardened Heart: A Study of Justification and Election in St. Paul and Origen." *StPat* 7 (1966): 434–42.

Brackett, John K. "An Analysis of the Literary Structure and Forms in Protrepticus and Paidagogus of Clement of Alexandria." Ph.D. dissertation, Emory University, 1986.

Braude, W. G., ed. *Midrash on Psalms.* 2 vols. Yale Judaica Series. New Haven, Conn.: Yale University Press, 1959.

Braun, H. "The Meaning of New Testament Christology." In *Existence and Providence,* edited by R. W. Funk. New York: Harper and Row, 1968.

Bray, Gerald L. *Creeds, Councils and Christ.* Downers Grove, Ill.: InterVarsity, 1984.

______. *Holiness and the Will of God.* London: Marshall, Morgan and Scott, 1978.

Breck, John. "Theoria and Orthodox Hermeneutics." *SVTQ* 20 (1976): 195–219.

Bright, W., ed. *The Orations of St. Athanasius Against the Arians.* Oxford: Oxford University Press, 1873.

Bromiley, G. W. "The Church Fathers and Holy Scripture." In *Scripture and Truth,* edited by D. A. Carson and John Woodbridge, 199–220. Grand Rapids: Zondervan, 1983.

______. *Historical Theology: An Introduction.* Grand Rapids: Eerdmans, 1978.

Brown, Colin. "Parable." *NIDNTT,* 2:751–56.

Brown, Harold O. J. *Heresies.* Garden City, N.Y.: Doubleday, 1984.

Brown, Milton Perry. *The Authentic Writings of Ignatius.* Durham, N.C.: Duke University Press, 1963.

Brown, Peter. *Augustine of Hippo.* Berkeley, Calif.: University of California Press, 1967.

______. "The Rise and the Function of the Holy Man in Late Antiquity." *JRomSt* 61 (1971): 80–101.

Brown, Raymond E. *Biblical Exegesis and Church Doctrine.* New York: Paulist, 1985.

______. "Hermeneutics." In *Jerome Biblical Commentary,* edited by Raymond E. Brown, Joseph A. Fitzmyer, and Roland E. Murphy. Englewood Cliffs, N.J.: Prentice-Hall, 1968.

______. "The History and Development of the Theory of a *Sensus Plenior.*" *CBQ* 15 (1953): 141–62.

______. *Peter in the New Testament.* Minneapolis: Augsburg, 1973.

______. "The *Sensus Plenior* in the Last Yen Years." *CBQ* 25 (1963): 262–85.

______. *The Sensus Plenior of Sacred Scripture.* Baltimore: St. Mary's University, 1955.

Brownlee, William H. *The Midrash Pesher of Habakkuk.* SBLMS 24. Missoula, Mont.: Scholars, 1979.

Bruce, F. F. *Biblical Exegesis in the Qumran Texts.* Grand Rapids: Eerdmans, 1959.

______. *The Books and the Parchments.* 3d rev. ed. Westwood, N.J.: Revell, 1963.

______. *The Canon of Scripture.* Downers Grove, Ill.: InterVarsity, 1988.

______. *The English Bible.* Oxford: Oxford University Press, 1961.

______. *The Epistle to the Hebrews.* NIC. Grand Rapids: Eerdmans, 1964.

______. "Galatian Problems: The Other Gospel." *BJRL* 53 (1970–71): 253–71.

______. "The History of New Testament Study." In *New Testament Interpretation,* edited by I. Howard Marshall, 21–59. Grand Rapids: Eerdmans, 1975.

______. "Interpretation." *IBD,* 2:695–96.

______. "New Light on the Origins of the New Testament Canon." In *New Dimensions in New Testament Study,* edited by Merrill C. Tenney and Richard N. Longenecker, 3–18. Grand Rapids: Zondervan, 1974.

______. *New Testament Development of Old Testament Themes.* Grand Rapids: Eerdmans, 1968.

______. *Paul: Apostle of the Heart Set Free.* Grand Rapids: Eerdmans, 1977.

______. *Tradition: Old and New.* Grand Rapids: Zondervan, 1970.

Buckley, E. R. "Justin Martyr's Quotations from the Synoptic Tradition." *JTS* 36 (1935): 173–76.

Bultmann, Rudolf. *"Ginosko." TDNT,* 1:689–719.

______. "Is Exegesis without Presuppositions Possible?" In *Existence and Faith,* edited by Shubert M. Ogden, 289–96. London: Hodder and Stoughton, 1961.

______. *Jesus Christ and Mythology.* London: SCM, 1960.

______. *Kerygma and Myth.* Edited by H.-W. Bartsch. London: SCM, 1953.

______. *Presence of Eternity: History and Eschatology.* New York: Harper and Row, 1957.

______. "The Problem of Hermeneutics." In *Essays Philosophical and Theological.* Translated and edited by James Greig. London: SCM, 1955.

______. *Theology of the New Testament.* Translated by Kendrick Grobel. 2 vols. New York: Scribners, 1955.

Burghardt, Walter J. "On Early Christian Exegesis." *TS* 11 (1950): 78–116.

______. "Saint Jerome." *TNEB* 6 (1985): 535–36.

Burkill, T. A. *The Evolution of Christian Thought.* Ithaca, N.Y.: Cornell University Press, 1971.

Burkitt, F. C. *Church and Gnosis: A Study of Christian Thought in the Second Century.* Cambridge: Cambridge University Press, 1932.

______. "Justin Martyr and Jeremiah 11:19." *JTS* 33 (1932): 371–74.

______. *The Religion of the Manichees.* Cambridge: Cambridge University Press, 1925.

Burleigh, J. H. S. *The City of God.* London: Nisbet, 1949.

Burnaby, J. *Amor Dei: A Study of the Religion of St. Augustine.* London: Hodder and Stoughton, 1938.

______. "Amor in St. Augustine." In *Philosophy and Theology of Anders Nygren,* edited by Charles W. Kegley, 174–86. Philadelphia: Westminster, 1974.

Burton, E. D. *A Critical and Exegetical Commentary on the Epistle to the Galatians.* ICC. New York: Scribners, 1920.

Buschel, Friedrich. *"Allegoreo." TDNT,* 1:260–63.

Butterworth, G. W. "Clement of Alexandria." *JTS* 17 (1916): 68–76.

______. "Clement of Alexandria's Protrepticus and the Phaedrus of Plato." *CQ* 10 (1916): 198–205.

Cadiou, Rene. *Introduction au systeme d'Origene.* Paris: Societe d'edition "Les belles lettres," 1932.

______. *Origen.* Translated by J. A. Southwell. St. Louis: Herder, 1944.

Cain, William E. *The Crisis in Criticism.* Baltimore: Johns Hopkins University Press, 1984.

Caird, G. B. "The Exegetical Method of the Epistle to the Hebrews." *CanJTh* 5 (1959): 44–51.

______. *The Language and Imagery of the Bible.* Philadelphia: Westminster, 1980.

Campenhausen, Hans von. *Ecclesiastical Authority and Spiritual Power in the Church of the First Three Centuries.* London: Black, 1969.

______. *The Fathers of the Greek Church.* Translated by Stanley Godman. New York: Pantheon, 1959.

Carey, G. L. "Clement of Alexandria." *NIDCC,* 234.

______. "Theophilus." *NIDCC,* 967.

Carlston, Charles. "The Vocabulary of Perfection in Philo and Hebrews." In *Unity and Diversity in New Testament Theology,* edited by R. Guelich, 133–60. Grand Rapids: Eerdmans, 1978.

Carpenter, H. J. "Popular Christianity and the Theologians in the Early Centuries." *JTS* n.s. 14 (1963): 294–310.

Carson, D. A. "Hermeneutics: A Brief Assessment of Some Recent Trends." *Themelios* 5:2 (January 1980): 12–20.

______. "Matthew." In vol. 8 of *The Expositor's Bible Commentary.* Edited by Frank E. Gaebelein. Grand Rapids: Zondervan, 1984.

Carson, D. A., and H. G. M. Williamson, eds. *It Is Written: Scripture Citing Scripture. Essays in Honour of Barnabas Lindars.* Cambridge: Cambridge University Press, 1988.

Carson, D. A., and John D. Woodbridge, eds. *Hermeneutics, Authority and Canon.* Grand Rapids: Zondervan, 1986.

Carter, R. E. "Chrysostom's Ad Theodorum lapsum and the Early Chronology of Mopsuestia." *VC* 16 (1962): 87–107.

______. "The Future of Chrysostom Studies." *StPat* 10 (1970): 14–21.

Casey, R. P. "Clement of Alexandria and the Beginning of Christian Platonism." *HTR* 18 (1925): 39–101.

Cayre, F. *Manual of Patrology and History of Theology.* Translated by H. Howitt. 2 vols. Paris: Desclee and Co., 1935.

Chadwick, Henry. *Augustine.* Oxford: Oxford University Press, 1986.

______. *The Circle and the Ellipse: Rival Concepts of Authority in the Early Church.* Oxford: Clarendon, 1959.

______. *Early Christian Thought and the Classical Tradition.* Oxford: Clarendon, 1966.

______. "The Fall of Eustathius of Antioch." *JTS* 49 (1948): 27–35.

______. "Origen, Celsus and the Resurrection of the Body." *HTR* 41 (1948): 83–102.

______. "Philo and the Beginnings of Christian Thought." *CHLGEMP,* 137–42.

______. "St. Paul and Philo." *BJRL* 48 (1965–66): 286–307.

Chadwick, Owen, *From Bossuet to Newman: The Idea of Doctrinal Development.* Cambridge: Cambridge University Press, 1957.

______. "Did the Translation of St. Irenaeus Use a Latin New Testament?" *RBen* 2 (1924): 34–157.

Chadwick, Owen, ed. *Oxford Early Christian Texts.* Multiple vols. Oxford: Oxford University Press, 1970– .

Charles, R. H., ed. *Apocrypha and Pseudepigrapha of the Old Testament in English.* 2 vols. Oxford: Clarendon, 1913.

Chase, G. H. *Chrysostom: A Study in the History of Biblical Interpretation.* Cambridge: Deighton, Bell and Co., 1887.

Christ, Carol P., and Judith Plaskow. *Womanspirit Rising: A Feminist Reader in Religion.* New York: Harper and Row, 1979.

Christiansen, Irmgard. *Die Technik der allegorischen Auslegungswissenschaft bei Philon von Alexandrien.* Tübingen: Mohr, 1969.

Clabeaux, John James. "The Pauline Corpus Which Marcion Used." Ph.D. dissertation, Harvard University, 1983.

Clark, Elizabeth A. *Clement's Use of Aristotle: The Aristotelian Contribution to Clement of Alexandria's Refutation of Gnosticism.* New York: Edwin Mellen, 1988.

______. *Jerome, Chrysostom and Friends.* New York: Edwin Mellen, 1979.

Clark, F. L. "Citations of Plato in Clement of Alexandria." *TPAPA* 33 (1902): 13–20.

Clark, William Kemp Lowther. *St. Basil the Great: A Study in Monasticism.* Cambridge: Cambridge University Press, 1913.

Cochrane, Charles Norris. *Christianity and Classical Culture.* New York: Oxford University Press, 1972.

Coleman-Norton, P. R. "Saint John Chrysostom and the Greek Philosophers." *CPhil* 25 (1930): 305–17.

Colson, H. "Notes on Justin Martyr's Apology I." *JTS* 23 (1922): 161–71.

Combrink, H. J. B. "Some Thoughts on the Old Testament Citations in the Epistle to the Hebrews." *Neotestamentica* 5 (1971): 22–26.

Corwin, V. *St. Ignatius and Christianity in Antioch.* New Haven, Conn.: Yale University Press, 1960.

Costello, Charles J. *St. Augustine's Doctrine on the Inspiration and Canonicity of Scripture.* Washington, D.C.: Catholic University of America Press, 1930.

Coxe, A. Cleveland, ed. *Apostolic Fathers, Justin Martyr, and Irenaeus.* Vol. 1 of *Ante-Nicene Fathers.* Grand Rapids: Eerdmans, 1987.

______. *Hermas, Tatian, Athenagoras, Theophilus, and Clement of Alexandria.* Vol. 2 of *Ante-Nicene Fathers.* Reprint. Grand Rapids: Eerdmans, 1986.

Cranfield, C. E. B. *A Critical and Exegetical Commentary on the Epistle to the Romans.* 2 vols. ICC. Edinburgh: T & T Clark, 1975–79.

Crehan, J. H. *Early Christian Baptism and the Creed.* London: SPCK, 1950.

Cross, F. L. *The Early Christian Fathers.* London: Duckworth and Co., 1960.

______. *The Study of St. Athanasius.* Oxford: Oxford University Press, 1945.

Crouzel, H. "Origen and Origenism." *NCE* 10 (1967): 767–74.

______. *Origene et la philosophie.* Paris: Cerf, 1959.

Culley, R. C. *Studies in the Structure of Hebrew Narrative.* Philadelphia: Fortress, 1976.

Cullman, Oscar. *Heils als Geschichte.* Tübingen: Mohr, 1965.

Cumont, Franz. *Astrology and Religion among the Greeks and Romans.* Reprint. New York: Dover, 1960.

Cunliffe-Jones, H., ed. *A History of Christian Doctrine.* Philadelphia: Fortress, 1978.

Cushman, Robert E. "Faith and Reason." In *A Companion to the Study of St. Augustine,* edited by Roy W. Battenhouse, 290–94. New York: Oxford University Press, 1955.

Daly, R. J. "The Hermeneutics of Origen: Existential Interpretation of the Third Century." In *The Word in the World,* 135–44. Cambridge: Weston College Press, 1973.

Danby, Herbert, ed. *Mishna.* Oxford: Clarendon, 1933.

Daniélou, Jean. *Origen.* Translated by Walter Mitchell. New York: Sheed and Ward, 1955.

______. *The Origins of Latin Christianity.* Philadelphia: Westminster, 1977.

______. *Philon D'Alexandaire.* Paris: Librairie Artheme Fayard, 1958.

______. *The Theology of Jewish Christianity.* London: Darton, Longman and Todd, 1964.

______. "Typologie et allegorie chez Clement d'Alexandrie." *StPat* 4 (1959): 50–57.

Daniélou, Jean, with A. H. Couratin and John Kent. *Historical Theology.* Vol. 2 of *The Pelican Guide to Modern Theology,* edited by R. P. C. Hanson. 3 vols. Middlesex, England: Penguin, 1969.

Daube, David. "Rabbinic Methods of Interpretation and Hellenistic Rhetoric." *HUCA* 22 (1949): 239–64.

Davidson, Richard M. *Typology in Scripture: A Study of Hermeneutical TYPOS Structures.* Andrews University Seminary Doctoral Dissertation Series, 2. Berrien Springs, Mich.: Andrews University Press, 1981.

Davies, W. D. "The Moral Teaching of the Early Church." In *Use of the Old Testament in the New Testament and Other Essays,* edited by James M. Effird. Durham, N.C.: Duke University Press, 1972.

______. *Paul and Rabbinic Judaism.* 4th ed. Philadelphia: Fortress, 1984.

______. *Torah in the Messianic Age and/or the Age to Come.* Cambridge: Cambridge University Press, 1952.

de Roy, O. J-B. "St. Augustine." *NCE,* 1:1041–58.

Delling, Gerhard. *"Stoicheo." TDNT,* 7:666–87.

Dennefeld, L. *Der Alttestamentliche Kanon der antiochischen Schule.* Freiburg: Breisgua, 1909.

Derrida, Jacques. *Of Grammatology.* Translated by Gayatri Chakravorty Spivak. Baltimore: Johns Hopkins University Press, 1974.

______. *Speech and Phenomena.* Edited and translated by D. B. Allison. Evanston, Ill.: Northwestern University Press, 1973.

______. *Writing and Difference.* Chicago: University of Chicago Press, 1978.

Detweiler, Robert, ed. "Derrida and Biblical Studies." *Semeia* 23 (1982): passim.

Devreesse, R. "La methode exegetigue de Theodore de Mopsuestia." *RB* 53 (1946): 207–41.

Dicks, D. C. "The Matthean Text of Chrysostom in His Homilies on Matthew." *JBL* 67 (1948): 365–76.

Diels, H., and W. Kranz, eds. *Die Fragmente der Vorsokratiker.* Berlin: Weidmann, 1960.

Dillon, John. *The Middle Platonists.* London: Duckworth, 1977.

Dilthey, Wilhelm. "The Rise of Hermeneutics." *NLH* 3 (1971–72): 244–51.

______. *Gessammelte Schriften,* vols. 5 and 7. 4th ed. 12 vols. Stuttgart: Teubner, 1964.

Dockery, David S. "The Christological Hermeneutics of Martin Luther." *GTJ* 4 (1983): 189–203.

______. *The Doctrine of the Bible.* Nashville: Convention, 1991.

______. "Typological Exegesis: Beyond Abuse and Neglect." In *Reclaiming the Prophetic Mantle,* edited by G. L. Klein. Nashville: Broadman, 1992.

Dodd, C. H. *According to the Scriptures: The Sub-Structure of New Testament Theology.* London: Nisbet, 1952.

______. *The Apostolic Preaching and Its Development.* Rev. ed. Philadelphia: Westminster, 1963.

______. *The Old Testament in the New.* London: Althone, 1952.

Dods, Marcus, trans. and ed. *The Writings of Justin Martyr and Athenagoras.* Edinburgh: T & T Clark, 1892.

Doeve, J. W. *Jewish Hermeneutics in the Synoptic Gospels and Acts.* Assen: Van Gorcum, 1954.

Donnelly, John Patrick. "Calvinist Thomism." *Victor* 7 (1976): 441–51.

Doty, W. G. *Contemporary New Testament Interpretation.* Englewood Cliffs, N.J.: Prentice-Hall, 1972.

Dowey, Edward A., Jr. *The Knowledge of God in Calvin's Theology.* New York: Columbia University Press, 1952.

Downey, G. *A History of Antioch in Syria.* Princeton, N.J.: Princeton University Press, 1961.

Doyle, A. D. "St. Irenaeus on the Pope and the Early Heretics." *IER* 54 (1939): 298–306.

Drower, Ethel Stefana. "Adam and the Elkasaites." *StPat* 4 (1961): 406–10.

Dudden, F. Homes. *The Life and Times of St. Ambrose.* 2 vols. Oxford: Oxford University Press, 1935.

Duke, J. O. "Pietism versus Establishment: The Halle Phase." *CQ* 72 (1978): 3–16.

Dulles, Avery. *A History of Apologetics.* Theological Resources. Edited by Jaroslav Pelikan and John P. Whalen. New York: Corpus, 1971.

______. *Models of the Church.* Garden City, N.Y.: Doubleday, 1978.

______. *Models of Revelation.* Garden City, N.Y.: Doubleday, 1983.

Dunn, James D. G. *Baptism in the Holy Spirit.* Philadelphia: Westminster, 1977.

______. "Demythologizing—The Problem of Myth in the New Testament." In *New Testament Interpretation,* edited by I. Howard Marshall, 285–307. Grand Rapids: Eerdmans, 1975.

______. "The New Perspective on Paul." *BJRL* 65 (1982–83): 95–122.

______. *Unity and Diversity in the New Testament: An Inquiry into the Character of Earliest Christianity.* Philadelphia: Westminster, 1977.

Duval, Y. M. "Jerome et Origene avant la querrel origeniste." *Aug* 24 (1984): 471–94.

Ebeling, Gerhard. *Introduction to a Theological Theory of Language.* London: Collins, 1973.

Edgar, S. L. "New Testament and Rabbinic Messianic Interpretation." *NTS* 5 (1958): 47–54.

Eichrodt, Walther. *Ezekiel.* Philadelphia: Westminster, 1970.

Elliger, Karl. *Studien zum Habakuk-Kommentar vom Toten Meer.* Tübingen: Mohr-Siebeck, 1953.

Ellis, E. Earle. "Biblical Interpretation in the New Testament Church." In *Compendia Rerum Judaicarum ad Novum Testamentum,* edited by S. Safrai, 2:704–21. 4 vols. Assen: Van Gorcum, 1988.

______. *The Gospel of Luke.* NCB. London: Marshall, Morgan and Scott, 1966.

______. "How the New Testament Uses the Old." In *New Testament Interpretation,* edited by I. Howard Marshall. Grand Rapids: Eerdmans, 1975.

______. "Midrash, Targum and New Testament Quotations." In *Neotestamentica et Semitica,* edited by E. Earle Ellis and M. Wilcox, 61–69. Edinburgh: T & T Clark, 1969.

______. "A Note on Pauline Hermeneutics." *NTS* 2 (1955–56): 131–34.

______. *Paul's Use of the Old Testament.* Grand Rapids: Eerdmans, 1957.

______. *Prophecy and Hermeneutic in Early Christianity.* Grand Rapids: Eerdmans, 1978.

______. "Reading the Gospels as History." *CTR* 3 (1988): 3–15.

Ellison, H. L. "Typology." *EQ* 25 (1953): 158–66.

Ellsperman, C. L. *The Attitude of the Early Christian Fathers towards Pagan Literature and Learning.* Washington, D.C.: Catholic University of America, 1949.

Enslin, M. S. "Irenaeus: Mostly Prolegomena." *HTR* 40 (1947): 137–65.

______. "Puritan of Carthage." *JR* 27 (1947): 197–212.

Erickson, Millard. *Christian Theology.* 3 vols. Grand Rapids: Baker, 1983–86.

Erickson, Richard J. "Linguistics and Biblical Language." *JETS* 26 (1983): 257–63.

Ermoni, V. "Antioche, ecole theologigue." *DTC,* 1:1435–39.

Eusebius of Caesarea. *Ecclesiastical History.* Translated by A. C. McGiffert. Vol. 1 of *Nicene and Post-Nicene Fathers,* 2d series. Grand Rapids: Eerdmans, 1986.

Evans, D. F. "Tradition and Scripture." *RS* 3 (1967): 323–37.

Evans, E. "Tertullian's Theological Terminology." *CQR* 139 (1944–45): 56–77.

Evans, Gillian R. *The Language and Logic of the Bible: The Earlier Middle Ages.* Cambridge: Cambridge University Press, 1984.

______. *The Language and Logic of the Bible: The Road to Reformation.* Cambridge: Cambridge University Press, 1985.

______. "Patristic and Medieval Theology." In *The Science of Theology,* Gillian R. Evans, Alister E. McGrath, and Allan D. Galloway, 1:3–106. In *The History of Christian Theology,* edited by Paul Avis. 3 vols. Grand Rapids: Eerdmans, 1986.

Fahey, Michael Andrew. *Cyprian and the Bible: A Study in Third-Century Exegesis.* Tübingen: Mohr, 1971.

Fairbairn, Patrick. *The Typology of Scripture.* New York: Funk and Wagnalls, 1900.

Fairweather, W. *Origen and the Greek Patristic Theology.* Edinburgh: T & T Clark, 1901.

Farkasfalvy, Dennis. "Theology of Scripture in Irenaeus." *RBen* 78 (1968): 313–19.

Farrar, Frederick W. *History of Interpretation.* London: Macmillan, 1886.

Fee, Gordon D. *The First Epistle to the Corinthians.* NIC. Grand Rapids: Eerdmans, 1987.

Ferguson, Everett. "Irenaeus." *EDT,* 569.

______. "Jerome." *GLCC,* 77–80.

Feyerabend, Paul. *Against Method.* London: Thretford, 1975.

Fiorenza, Elisabeth Schüssler. "Toward a Feminist Biblical Hermeneutics: Biblical Interpretation and Liberation Theology." In *The Challenge of Liberation Theology: A First World Response,* edited by Brian Hahan and C. Dale Richesin, 91–112. Maryknoll: Orbis, 1981.

Fitzmyer, Joseph A. "The Use of Explicit Old Testament Quotations in Qumran Literature and in the New Testament." *NTS* 7 (1961): 297–333.

Flessman-Van Leer, E. *Tradition and Scripture in the Early Church.* Assen: Van Gorcum, 1954.

Florovsky, G. *Bible, Church and Tradition.* Belmont, Md.: Nordland, 1972.

Forster, E. M. *Alexandria: A History and a Guide.* 2d ed. Garden City, N.Y.: Doubleday, 1961.

France, R. T. "The Formula-Quotations of Matthew 2 and the Problem of Communication." *NTS* 27 (1981): 223–51.

______. *Jesus and the Old Testament: His Application of Old Testament Passages to Himself and His Message.* London: Tyndale, 1971.

Freedman, H., and M. Simon, eds. *Midrash Rabbah.* 10 vols. London: Soncino, 1939.

Freemantle, W. H. "Prolegomena to Jerome." *NPNF,* 6:xi–xxxv.

Frege, Gottlob. "On Sense and Reference." In *Translations from the Philosophical Writings of Gottlob Frege,* translated by Peter Geach and Max Black, 56–78. Oxford: Blackwell, 1966.

Frei, Hans W. *The Eclipse of Biblical Narrative.* New Haven, Conn.: Yale University Press, 1974.

Frend, W. H. C. *The Early Church.* Philadelphia: Lippincott, 1966.

Froehlich, Karlfried. "Biblical Hermeneutics on the Move." *Word & World* 1 (1981): 140–52.

______. *Biblical Interpretation in the Early Church.* Philadelphia: Fortress, 1984.

______. "Problems in Lutheran Hermeneutics." In *Studies in Lutheran Hermeneutics,* edited by J. Reumann, 127–41. Philadelphia: Fortress, 1979.

Fuchs, Ernst. *Hermeneutik.* Tübingen: Mohr, 1970.

______. *Marburge Hermeneutik.* Tübingen: Mohr, 1968.

Fuller, Daniel P. "Biblical Theology and the Analogy of Faith." In *Unity and Diversity in New Testament Theology,* edited by R. Guelich. Grand Rapids: Eerdmans, 1978.

______. "History of Interpretation." *ISBE,* 2:863–74.

Gadamer, Hans-Georg. "Martin Heidegger und die Marburger Theologie." In *Zeit und Geeschicte: Dankesgabe an Rudolf Bultmann zum 80,* edited by E. Dinkler, 479–90. Tübingen: Mohr, 1964.

______. "The Problem of Language in Schleiermacher's Hermeneutic." *JTC* 7 (1970): 68–95.

______. *Truth and Method.* Edited by Garrett Borden and John Cumming. New York: Sheed and Ward, 1975.

______. "Von Zirkel des Verstehens." In *Festschrift Martin Heidegger zum Siebzigsten Geburstag,* 24–34. Pfullingen: Neske, 1959.

______. *Warheit und Methode*. Tübingen: Mohr, 1960.

Gallatin, H. K. "John Chrysostom." *EDT*, 228.

Gamble, Richard C. "Brevitas et Facilitas: Toward an Understanding of Calvin's Hermeneutics." *WTJ* 47 (1985): 1–17.

Garrett, Duane A. *Chrysostom's "Interpretation in Isaiam": An English Translation with an Analysis of Its Hermeneutics*. Lewiston, N.Y.: Edwin Mellen, 1992.

Gaston, Lloyd. *Paul and Torah*. Vancouver: University of British Columbia Press, 1987.

Gelven, Michael. *A Commentary on Heidegger's "Being and Time."* New York: Harper and Row, 1970.

George, Timothy. *Theology of the Reformers*. Nashville: Broadman, 1988.

Gerhardsson, Birger. *Memory and Manuscript: Oral Tradition and Written Transmission in Rabbinic Judaism and Early Christianity*. Translated by E. J. Sharpe. Lund: Gleerup, 1961.

______. *The Testimony of God's Son*. Lund: Gleerup, 1966.

Gilbert, G. H. *Interpretation of the Bible*. New York: Macmillan, 1908.

Gill, Jerry H. "Mediated Meaning: A Contextualist Approach to Hermeneutical Method." *ATJ* 43 (1988): 27–42.

Gillespie, Thomas W. "Biblical Authority and Interpretation: The Current Debate on Hermeneutics." In *A Guide to Contemporary Hermeneutic*, edited by Donald K. McKim, 192–219. Grand Rapids: Eerdmans, 1986.

Gilson, E. *The Christian Philosophy of St. Augustine*. New York: Random, 1960.

Goguel, Maurice. *The Birth of Christianity*. New York: Macmillan, 1954.

Gonzalez, Justo L. *A History of Christian Thought*. 3 vols. Nashville: Abingdon, 1970.

Goodenough, E. R. *An Introduction to Philo Judaeus*. New Haven, Conn.: Yale University Press, 1940.

______. *The Theology of Justin Martyr*. 1923. Amsterdam: Philo, 1968.

Goodspeed, E. J., ed. *The Apostolic Fathers: An American Translation*. New York: Harper, 1950.

Goppelt, Leonhard. *Apostolic and Post-Apostolic Times*. Translated by R. Guelich. Grand Rapids: Baker, 1970.

______. *Theology of the New Testament*. Translated by John Alsup. 2 vols. Grand Rapids: Eerdmans, 1982.

______. *"Typos." TDNT*, 9:246–59.

______. *TYPOS: The Typological Interpretation of the Old Testament in the New*. Translated by Donald H. Madvig. Grand Rapids: Eerdmans, 1982.

Gorday, Peter. *Principles of Patristic Exegesis: Romans 9-11 in Origen, John Chrysostom, and Augustine*. New York: Edwin Mellen, 1983.

Gorman, M. M. "A Study of the Literal Interpretation of Genesis." Ph.D. dissertation, University of Toronto, 1975.

Graham, A. A. K. "Their Word to Our Day: IV. Ignatius of Antioch." *ExT* 80 (1969): 100–104.

Grant, Robert M. *After the New Testament.* Philadelphia: Fortress, 1967.

______. "Aristotle and the Conversion of Justin." *JTS* 7 (1956): 246–48.

______. *The Bible in the Church.* New York: Macmillan, 1948.

______. "The Earliest Christian Gnosticism." *CH* 22 (1953): 81–98.

______. *The Formation of the New Testament.* London: SCM, 1965.

______. "From Tradition to Scripture and Back." In *Scripture and Tradition,* edited by Joseph F. Kelly. Notre Dame, Ind.: Fides, 1976.

______. *Gnosticism and Early Christianity.* New York: Oxford University Press, 1960.

______. "Hermeneutics and Tradition in Ignatius of Antioch." In *Ermeneutica e Tradizone,* edited by E. Castelli, 183–201. Rome: Pontifico Institu Biblico, 1963.

______. *Ignatius of Antioch.* Camden, N.J.: Thomas Nelson, 1966.

______. "Irenaeus and Hellenistic Culture." *HTR* 42 (1949): 41–51.

______. *The Letter and the Spirit.* New York: Macmillan, 1957.

______. "Scripture and Tradition in St. Ignatius of Antioch." *CBQ* 25 (1963): 322–35.

______. *A Short History of the Interpretation of the Bible.* New York: Macmillan, 1963.

Grant, Robert M., ed. *Gnosticism: A Source Book of Heretical Writings from the Early Christian Period.* New York: Harper and Row, 1961.

Grant, Robert M., with David Tracy. *A Short History of the Interpretation of the Bible.* Rev. ed. Philadelphia: Fortress, 1984.

Greesnslade, S. L. "Tertullian of Carthage." *ExT* 44 (1932–33): 247–52.

Greer, Rowan A. "The Antiochene Christology of Diodore of Tarsus." *JTS* 17 (1966): 327–41.

______. *The Captain of Our Salvation: A Study in the Patristic Exegesis of Hebrews.* Tübingen: Mohr, 1973.

______. "The Dog and the Mushrooms: Irenaeus' View of the Valentinians Assessed." In *The Rediscovery of Gnosticism,* vol. 1, *The School of Valentine,* edited by Bentley Layton, 146–75. Leiden: Brill, 1980.

______. *Theodore of Mopsuestia: Exegete and Theologian.* London: Faith, 1961. 413–22.

Gregory, Joel C. "The Chiliastic Hermeneutic of Papias of Hierapolis and Justin Martyr Compared with Later Patristic Chiliasts." Ph.D. dissertation, Baylor University, 1983.

Gregory of Nyssa. *Selected Works and Letters.* Vol. 5 of *Nicene and Post-Nicene Fathers.* Translated by William Moore and H. A. Wilson. Reprint. Grand Rapids: Eerdmans, 1983.

Grillmeier, Aloys. *Christ in the Christian Tradition,* volume 1, *From the Apostolic Age to Chalcedon (451).* Translated by John Bowden. 2d ed. Atlanta: John Knox, 1975.

Grobel, Kendrick. "History and Principles of Interpretation." *IDB,* 2:718–24.

Guillet, Jacques. "Les exegeses d'Alexandrie et d'Antioche: conflit ou malentendu?" *Recherches de science religieuse* 34 (1957): 257–302.

Gundry, Robert H. *Matthew.* Grand Rapids: Eerdmans, 1982.

______. *The Use of the Old Testament in St. Matthew's Gospel.* Leiden: Brill, 1967.

Guthrie, Donald. *New Testament Introduction.* Downers Grove, Ill.: InterVarsity, 1970.

______. *New Testament Theology.* Downers Grove, Ill.: InterVarsity, 1981.

Haardt, Robert. *Gnosis: Character and Testimony.* Leiden: Brill, 1971.

Hagner, Donald A. "Interpreting the Epistle to the Hebrews." In *The Literature and Meaning of Scripture,* edited by Morris A. Inch and C. Hassell Bullock, 217–42. Grand Rapids: Baker, 1981.

______. "Paul in Modern Jewish Thought." In *Pauline Studies,* edited by Donald A. Hagner and Murray J. Harris, 143–68. Grand Rapids: Eerdmans, 1980.

______. "Philo." *NDT,* 509–10.

______. *The Use of the Old and New Testaments in Clement of Rome.* Supplement to *Novum Testamentum,* no. 34. Leiden: Brill, 1973.

Haller, E. "On the Interpretive Task." *Int* 21 (1967): 158–66.

Hamell, Patrick J. *Handbook of Patrology.* New York: Alba House, 1968.

Hammond, Charles P. "Philocalia IX, Jerome, Epistle 121, and Origen's Exposition of Romans VII." *JTS* n.s. 32 (1981): 50–81.

Hancher, Michael. "Three Kinds of Intention." *MLN* 87 (1972): 827–51.

Hanson, A. T. *Jesus Christ in the Old Testament.* London: SPCK, 1965.

______. *Studies in Paul's Technique and Theology.* London: SPCK, 1974.

Hanson, R. P. C. *Allegory and Event: A Study of the Sources and Significance of Origen's Interpretation of Scripture.* Richmond: John Knox, 1959.

______. *The Bible as a Norm of Faith.* Durham, N.C.: Duke University Press, 1963.

______. "Biblical Exegesis in the Early Church." In *The Cambridge History of the Bible,* vol. 1, edited by P. R. Ackroyd and C. F. Evans, 412–53. Cambridge: Cambridge University Press, 1970.

______. *Origen's Doctrine of Tradition.* London: SPCK, 1954.

______. "Origen's Interpretation of Scripture Exemplified from His Philocalia." *Hermathena* 63 (1944): 47–58.

______. *Tradition in the Early Church.* London: SCM, 1962.

Hardy, Edward R. *Christology of the Later Fathers.* Library of Christian Classics. Philadelphia: Westminster, 1954.

Harnack, Adolf von. "Das Alte Testament in den paulinischen Briefen und in den paulinischen Gemeinden." In *Sitzungs berichte der Preussischen Akademie der Wissenschaften zu Berlin.* Berlin: de Gruyter, 1928.

______. *History of Dogma.* Translated by Neil Buchanan. 3d. ed. 7 vols. New York: Russell and Russell, 1958.

Harris, J. Rendel. "Genuine and Apocryphal Works of Ignatius of Antioch." *BJRL* 2 (1927): 204–31.

Hatch, Edwin. *The Influence of Greek Ideas and Usages on Christianity.* New York: Harper, 1957.

Hawthorne, Gerald F. "The Role of Christian Prophets in the Gospel Tradition." In *Tradition and Interpretation in the New Testament,* edited by Gerald F. Hawthorne and O. Betz, 119–33. Grand Rapids: Eerdmans, 1987.

Hay, C. "St. John Chrysostom and the Integrity of the Human Nature of Christ." *Franciscan Studies* 19 (1959): 290–317.

Hay, David M. *Glory at the Right Hand: Psalm 110 in Early Christianity.* Nashville: Abindgon, 1973.

Heard, Richard, "The APOMNHMONEYMATA in Papais, Justin and Irenaeus." *NTS* 1 (1954): 130–34.

Hefner, P. "Theological Methodology in St. Irenaeus." *JR* 44 (1964): 294–309.

Heidegger, Martin. *Being and Time.* Translated by John Macquarrie. Oxford: Blackwell, 1962.

______. *On the Way to Language.* Translated by Peter D. Hertz. New York: Harper and Row, 1971.

Heinisch, P. *Der Einfluss Philos auf die alteste christliche Exegese (Barnabas, Justin und Clemens von Alexandria). Ein Beitrag zur Geschichte der allegorisch-mystischen Schriftauslegung im christlichen Altertum.* Munster: Aschendorff, 1908.

Hendricks, William L. "Learning from Beauty." *SWJT* 29(1987): 19–27.

Hengel, Martin. *Between Jesus and Paul.* Translated by John Bowden. Philadelphia: Fortress, 1983.

______. "Zwischen Jesus und Paulus." *ZKT* 72 (1975): 151–206.

Hermeren, Goran. "Intention and Interpretation in Literary Criticism." *NLH* 7 (1975–76): 57–82.

Hesselgrave, David. "Contextualization and Revelational Epistemology." In *Inerrancy and Hermeneutics,* edited by E. Radmacher and R. Preus, 693–764. Grand Rapids: Zondervan, 1984.

Higgins, A. J. B. "Jewish Messianic Belief in Justin Martyr's *Dialogue with Trypho.*" *NovT* 9 (1967): 298–305.

Hill, Robert. "John Chrysostom's Teaching on Inspiration in 'Six Homilies in Isaiah.'" *VC* 22 (1968): 21–37.

Hinchliff, P. "Bishop." *NDLW,* 92–93.

Hirsch, E. D., Jr. *The Aims of Interpretation.* Chicago: University of Chicago Press, 1976.

______. *Validity in Interpretation.* New Haven, Conn.: Yale University Press, 1967.

Hitchcock, F. R. M. "Holy Communion and Creed in Clement of Alexandria." *CQR* 129 (1939): 57–70.

______. "Holy Communion and Creed in Origen." *CQR* 142 (1941): 216–39.

______. *Irenaeus of Lugdunum: A Study of His Teaching.* Cambridge: Cambridge University Press, 1914.

Hoffman, R. Joseph. *Marcion: On the Restitution of Christianity.* Chico, Calif.: Scholars, 1980.

Holmes, Michael W. "Origen and the Inerrancy of Scripture." *JETS* 24 (1981): 221–32.

Homans, Peter, "Psychology and Hermeneutics." *JR* 60 (1975): 327–47.

Hooker, Morna D. *Studying the New Testament.* Minneapolis: Augsburg, 1979.

Hooker, Morna D., and S. G. Wilson, eds. *Paul and Paulinism*. London: SPCK, 1982.

Horton, Susan R. *Interpreting Interpreting*. Baltimore: Johns Hopkins University Press, 1979.

Howard, G. "Hebrews and the Old Testament Quotations." *NovT* 10 (1968): 208–16.

Hoy, David Couzens. *The Critical Circle: Literature and History in Contemporary Hermeneutics*. Berkeley: University of California Press, 1978.

Hulen, A. B. "The Dialogues with the Jews as Sources for Early Jewish Argument Against Christianity." *JBL* 51 (1932): 58–70.

Hunter, A. M. *The Gospel According to John*. Cambridge: Cambridge University Press, 1965.

Hurd, John Coolidge, Jr. *The Origin of 1 Corinthians*. Macon, Ga.: Mercer University Press, 1983.

Irenaeus. *Against Heresies*. Translated by A. Cleveland Coxe. Vol. 1 of *Ante-Nicene Fathers*. Reprint. Grand Rapids: Eerdmans, 1971.

Iser, Wolfgang. *The Act of Reading: A Theory of Aesthetic Response*. Baltimore: Johns Hopkins University Press, 1978.

Jackson, Belford D. "Semantics and Hermeneutics in Saint Augustine's *De doctrina Christiana*." Ph.D. dissertation, Yale University, 1967.

Jackson, Blomfield, and E. G. Richardson, trans. and eds. *Theodoret, Jerome, Gennadius, Rufinius*. Vol. 3 of *Nicene and Post-Nicene Fathers*, 2d series. Reprint. Grand Rapids: Eerdmans, 1983.

Jaeger, W. *Early Christianity and Greek Paideia*. Cambridge: Harvard University Press, 1962.

Jay, P. "Allegoriarum nubilum chez St. Jerome." *REAug* 22 (1976): 82–89.

______. "Saint Jerome et le triple sens de l'Ecriture." *REAug* 26 (1980): 214–27.

Jellicoe, Sidney. *The Septuagint and Modern Study*. Oxford: Clarendon, 1968.

Jenkins, C. "Origen on 1 Corinthians." *JTS* 9 (1908): 235–46.

Jeremias, Joachim. *The Central Message of the New Testament*. Philadelphia: Fortress, 1965.

______. "Paulus als Hillelit." In *Neotestamentica et Semitica*, edited by E. Earle Ellis and M. Wilcox, 88–94. Edinburgh: T & T Clark, 1969.

Jerome. *Commentary on Daniel*. Translated by Gleason L. Archer, Jr. Grand Rapids: Baker, 1958.

______. *Lives of Illustrious Men*. Translated by Ernest C. Richardson. Vol. 6 of *Nicene and Post-Nicene Fathers*, 2d series. Reprint. Grand Rapids: Eerdmans, 1977.

______. *Select Works, Letters*. Translated by W. H. Fremantle, G. Lewis, and W. G. Martley. Vol. 6 of *Nicene and Post-Nicene Fathers*. Reprint. Grand Rapids: Eerdmans, 1983.

Jewett, Paul K. "Concerning the Allegorical Interpretation of Scripture." *WTJ* 17 (1954): 1–20.

Jewett, Robert. "The Agitators and the Galatian Congregation." *NovT* 21 (1968): 241–54.

John Chrysostom. *Homilies on Acts and Romans.* Translated by J. Walker, J. Sheppard, H. Brown, J. B. Morris, and W. H. Simcox. Edited by G. B. Stevens. Vol. 11 of *Nicene and Post-Nicene Fathers,* 2d series. Reprint. Grand Rapids: Eerdmans, 1979.

______. *Homilies on the Epistles of Paul to the Corinthians.* The Oxford Translation. Edited by T. W. Chambers. Vol. 12 of *Nicene and Post-Nicene Fathers,* 1st series. Reprint. Grand Rapids: Eerdmans, 1983.

______. *Homilies on the Epistles of St. Paul the Apostle to the Galatians and Ephesians, Philippians, Colossians, Thessalonians, Timothy, Titus and Philemon.* The Oxford Translation. Edited by Gross Alexander, John A. Broadus, and Philip Schaff. Vol. 13 of *Nicene and Post-Nicene Fathers,* 1st series. Reprint. Grand Rapids: Eerdmans, 1983.

______. *Homilies on the Gospel of John, and Hebrews.* The Oxford Translation. Edited by Philip Schaff with Frederick Gardiner. Vol. 14 of *Nicene and Post-Nicene Fathers,* 1st series. Reprint. Grand Rapids: Eerdmans, 1983.

______. *Homilies on the Gospel of Saint Matthew.* Translated by George Provost. Edited by M. B. Riddle. Vol. 10 of *Nicene and Post-Nicene Fathers,* 1st series. Reprint. Grand Rapids: Eerdmans, 1986.

Johnson, David W. "The Myth of the Augustinian Synthesis." In *Biblical Hermeneutics in Historical Perspective,* edited by Mark S. Burrows and Paul Rorem, 100–114. Grand Rapids: Eerdmans, 1991.

Johnson, Elliot. "Author's Intention and Biblical Interpretation." In *Hermeneutics, Inerrancy and the Bible,* edited by E. Radmacher and R. Preus, 409–29. Grand Rapids: Zondervan, 1984.

______. *Expository Hermeneutics.* Grand Rapids: Zondervan, 1989.

Johnson, R. A. *The Origins of Demythologizing: Philosophy and Historiography in the Theology of Rudolf Bultmann.* Leiden: Brill, 1974.

Johnson, Sherman E. "The Biblical Quotations in Matthew." *HTR* 36 (1943): 135–53.

Johnston, Robert E. C. "Text and Text-Interpretation in the Thought of Paul Ricoeur." Licentiate dissertation, Katholieke Universiteit te Leuven, 1977.

Johnston, Robert K., ed. *The Use of the Bible in Theology.* Atlanta: John Knox, 1985.

Jonas, Hans. *The Gnostic Religion: The Message of the Alien God and the Beginning of Christianity.* Boston: Beacon, 1958.

Jones, A. H. M. "St. John Chrysostom's Parentage and Education." *HTR* 46 (1953): 171–73.

Juel, Donald. *Messianic Exegesis: Christological Interpretation of the Old Testament in Early Christianity.* Philadelphia: Fortress, 1988.

Juhl, P. D. *Interpretation.* Princeton, N.J.: Princeton University Press, 1980.

Justin Martyr. *Dialogue with Trypho and First Apology.* Translated by M. Dods. Vol. 1 of *Ante-Nicene Fathers,* 2d series. Reprint. Grand Rapids: Eerdmans, 1971.

Kaiser, Walter C., Jr. "The Current Crisis in Exegesis and the Apostolic Use of Deuteronomy 25:4 in 1 Corinthians 9:8–10." *JETS* 21 (1978): 3–11.

______. "The Old Promise and the New Covenant: Jeremiah 31:31–34." *JETS* 15 (1972): 11–23.

______. "The Promise to David in Psalm 16 and Its Application in Acts 2:25–33 and 13:32–37." *JETS* 23 (1980): 219–29.

______. "The Single Intent of Scripture." In *Evangelical Roots: A Tribute to Wilbur Smith,* edited by Kenneth A. Kantzer, 3–41. Nashville: Thomas Nelson, 1978.

______. *Toward an Exegetical Theology.* Grand Rapids: Baker, 1981.

______. *Toward an Old Testament Theology.* Grand Rapids: Zondervan, 1978.

______. *The Uses of the Old Testament in the New.* Chicago: Moody, 1985.

Kannengiesser, C. "Athanasius of Alexandria and the Foundation of Traditional Christology." *TS* 34 (1973): 103–13.

Käsemann, Ernst. *Commentary on Romans.* Translated by G. W. Bromiley. Grand Rapids: Eerdmans, 1980.

Kee, Howard Clark. *Community of the New Age: Studies in Mark's Gospel.* Philadelphia: Westminster, 1977.

Keegan, Terence J. *Interpreting the Bible.* New York: Paulist, 1985.

Keifert, Patrick R. "Mind Reader and Maestro: Models for Understanding Biblical Interpreters." *Word & World* 1 (1980): 153–68.

Kelly, J. F., ed. *Perspectives on Scripture and Tradition.* Notre Dame, Ind.: Fides, 1976.

Kelly, J. N. D. *A Commentary on the Epistles of Peter and Jude.* HNTC. New York: Harper, 1969.

______. *Early Christian Doctrine.* New York: Harper and Row, 1960.

______. *Early Christian Doctrines.* 4th rev. ed. San Francisco: Harper and Row, 1978.

______. *Jerome: His Life, Writings and Controversies.* London: Duckworth, 1975.

Kelly, J. N. D., ed. *Early Christian Creeds.* London: Black, 1972.

Kelsey, David H. *The Use of Scripture in Recent Theology.* Philadelphia: Fortress, 1975.

Kepple, Robert J. "An Analysis of the Antiochene Exegesis of Galatians 4:24–26." *WTJ* 39 (1976): 239–49.

Kerr, David W. "Augustine of Hippo." In *Inspiration and Interpretation,* edited by John F. Walvoord, 65–77. Grand Rapids: Eerdmans, 1957.

Kerrigan, Alexander. "The Objects of the Literal and Spiritual Senses of the New Testament according to St. Cyril of Alexandria." *StPat* 1 (1957): 356–66.

______. *St. Cyril of Alexandria: Interpreter of the Old Testament.* Rome: Pontifico Institu Biblico, 1952.

Kettler, Heinrich. *Der ursprungliche Sinn der Dogmatik des Origenes. BZNW* 31. Berlin: Topelmann, 1966.

Kevane, E. "Philosophy, Education and the Controversy on Saint Augustine's Conversion." *Studies in Philosophy and the History of Philosophy* 2 (1963): 61–103.

Kim, K. W. "The Matthean Text of Origen in His Commentary on Matthew." *JBL* 68 (1949): 125–39.

Kim. S. *The Origin of Paul's Gospel.* Grand Rapids: Eerdmans, 1982.

Kistemaker, Simon J. *The Psalm Citations in the Epistle to the Hebrews.* Amsterdam: Van Soest, 1961.

Kittel, G. "*Lego.*" *TDNT,* 4:68–143.

Klauk, Hans-Josef. *Alegorie und Allegorese in Synoptischen Gleichnistexten.* Neutestamentliche Abhandlungen, 19. Munster: Aschendorf, 1977.

Klawiter, Frederick C. "The New Prophecy in Early Christianity: The Origin, Nature, and Development of Montanism, A.D. 165–220." Ph.D. dissertation, The University of Chicago, 1975.

Knox, John. *Marcion and the New Testament.* Chicago: University of Chicago Press, 1942.

Knox, W. L. "Origen's Conception of the Resurrection Body." *JTS* 39 (1938): 247–48.

Koch, H. "War Tertullian Priester?" *HJG* 28 (1907): 95–103.

Koolman, W. J. *Luther and the Bible.* Translated by J. Schmidt. Philadelphia: Muhlenberg, 1961.

Kraeling, C. H. "The Jewish Community of Antioch." *JBL* 51 (1932): 130–41.

Kraus, Hans-Joachim. "Calvin's Exegetical Principles." *Int* 31 (1977): 8–18.

Krause, Martin, ed. *Gnosis and Gnosticism: Papers Read at the Seventh International Conference on Patristic Studies.* Leiden: Brill, 1977.

Krentz, Edgar. *The Historical-Critical Method.* Philadelphia: Fortress, 1975.

Kroeger, Catherine Clark. "Origen." *EDT,* 803.

Kugel, James L., and Rowan A. Greer. *Early Biblical Interpretation.* Philadelphia: Westminster, 1986.

Kuhn, Thomas. *The Structure of Scientific Revolutions.* 2d ed. Chicago: University of Chicago Press, 1970.

Kümmel, W. G. *Introduction to the New Testament.* Nashville: Abingdon, 1975.

______. *The New Testament: The History of the Investigation of Its Problems.* Translated by S. MacLean Gilmour and Howard Clark Kee. Nashville: Abingdon, 1970.

Kunjummen, Raju D. "The Single Intent of Scripture—Critical Examination of a Theological Construct." *GTJ* 7 (1986): 81–110.

LaSor, William Sanford. "The *Sensus Plenior* and Biblical Interpretation." In *Scripture, Tradition and Authority,* edited by W. Ward Gasque and William Sanford LaSor, 260–77. Grand Rapids: Eerdmans, 1978.

Ladd, George Eldon. *The New Testament and Criticism.* Grand Rapids: Eerdmans, 1967.

______. *A Theology of the New Testament.* Grand Rapids: Eerdmans, 1974.

Lake, Kirsopp, ed. *The Apostolic Fathers with an English Translation.* Vols. 24 and 25 of the Loeb Classical Library. Cambridge: Harvard University Press, 1912–13.

Lamb, J. A. "The Place of the Bible in the Liturgy." *The Cambridge History of the Bible.* Vol. 1, edited by P. R. Ackroyd and C. F. Evans, 563–86. Cambridge: Cambridge University Press, 1970.

Lampe, G. W. H., ed. *The Cambridge History of the Bible.* Vol. 2, *The West from the Fathers to the Reformation.* Cambridge: Cambridge University Press, 1969.

______. "Christian Theology in the Patristic Period." In *A History of Christian Doctrine,* edited by Hubert Cunliffe-Jones with Benjamin Drewery. Philadelphia: Fortress, 1978.

______. "The Reasonableness of Typology." *Essays on Typology,* compiled by G. W. H. Lampe and K. J. Woolcombe, 9–38. London: SCM, 1957.

Landais, M. Le. "Deus annees de predication de saint Augustin." In *Etudes Augustiniennes,* edited by H. Rondet, M. Le Landais, A. Lauras, and C. Coutourier, 9–95. Paris: Cerf, 1953.

Langsdorf, Lenore. "Current Paths Toward an Objective Hermeneutic." *CTR* 2 (1987): 145–54.

______. "Husserl on Judging." Ph.D. dissertation, State University of New York at Stony Brook, 1977.

Lawson, John. *The Biblical Theology of St. Irenaeus*. London: Epworth, 1948.

______. *Theological and Historical Introduction to the Apostolic Fathers*. New York: Macmillan, 1961.

Lebeau, Paul. "L'interpretation origenienne de Rom. 8.19–22." In *Kyriakon: Festschrift Johannes Quasten,* edited by Patrick Granfield and Josef A. Jungman, 336–45. Munster: Aschendorff, 1970.

Lebreton, Jules, S. J., and Jacques Zeiller. *Heresy and Orthodoxy*. New York: Collier, 1962.

Lehmann, Paul L. "The Reformers' Use of the Bible." *ThT* 3 (1946): 328–44.

Leith, John H. "Creeds." *WDCT* (1983): 131–32.

______. *An Introduction to the Reformed Tradition*. Richmond: John Knox, 1977.

Lewis, G. *Origen: The Philocalia*. Edinburgh: T & T Clark, 1911.

Lewy, Hans. *Chaldean Oracles and Theurgy: Mysticism, Magic, and Platonism in the Later Roman Empire*. Edited and revised by Michel Tardieu. Paris: Etudes Augustiniennes, 1978.

Lietzmann, Hans. *A History of the Early Church*. Translated by Bertram Lee Woolf. 3 vols. New York: Scribners, 1937–50.

______. *Kleine Schriften II: Studien zum Neven Testament.* Texte und Untersuchungen. 68. Edited by Kurt Aland. Berlin: Akadamie-Verlag, 1958.

Lightfoot, J. B., ed. and trans. *The Apostolic Fathers.* 5 vols. London: Macmillan, 1889–90.

Lilla, R. C. *Clement of Alexandria: A Study of Christian Platonism and Gnosticism*. London: Oxford, 1971.

Lindbeck, George. *The Nature of Doctrine: Religion and Theology in the Postliberal Age.* Philadelphia: Fortress, 1984.

Loewe, R. "The 'Plain' Meaning of Scripture." In *Papers of the Institute of Jewish Studies, London,* edited by J. G. Weiss, 140–85. Jerusalem: Hebrew University Press, 1964.

Longacre, Robert E. "The Discourse Structure of the Flood Narrative." *JAAR* 41 (1979): 89–133.

______. *Grammar of Discourse.* New York: Plenum, 1983.

Longenecker, Richard N. *Biblical Exegesis in the Apostolic Period.* Grand Rapids: Eerdmans, 1975.

______. "Can We Reproduce the Exegesis of the New Testament?" *TB* 21 (1970): 3–38.

______. *Christology of Early Jewish Christianity.* London: SCM, 1970.

______. "On the Concept of Development in Pauline Thought." In *Perspectives on Evangelical Theology,* edited by Kenneth A. Kantzer and Stanley Gundry, 195–207. Grand Rapids: Baker, 1979.

______. *Paul: Apostle of Liberty.* New York: Harper and Row, 1964.

Longman, Tremper, III. *Literary Approaches to Biblical Interpretation.* Grand Rapids: Zondervan, 1987.

Louth, Andrew. *The Origins of the Christian Mystical Tradition: From Plato to Denys.* Oxford: Oxford University Press, 1981.

Lowy, S. "Some Aspects of Normative and Sectarian Interpretation of the Scriptures." *ALUOS* 6 (1966–68): 98–163.

Lubac, Henri de. *Exegese medieval: Les quatres sens de l'ecriture.* Paris: Aubier, 1959.

______. *Historie et Esprit: L'intelligence de l'Ecriture d'apres Origene.* Paris: Aubier, 1950.

______. "'Typologie' et 'allegorisme.'" *RSR* 34 (1947): 180–226.

Luedemann, Gerd. *Early Christianity According to the Tradition in Acts.* Philadelphia: Fortress, 1988.

Lundin, Roger, Anthony C. Thiselton, and Clarence Walhout. *The Responsibility of Hermeneutics.* Grand Rapids: Eerdmans, 1985.

Lyotard, J.-F. *The Post-Modern Condition: A Report on Knowledge.* Translated by G. Bennington and B. Massummi. Minneapolis: University of Minnesota Press, 1984.

Lyonnet, S. "St. Cyrille d'Alexandrie et 2 Cor. 3:17," *Bib* 32 (1951): 25–33.

Lys, Daniel. *The Meaning of the Old Testament.* Nashville: Abingdon, 1967.

Lysa, Colin. "Personal Qualities and the Intentional Fallacy." Vol. 6 of *Philosophy and the Arts,* 194–210. The Royal Institute of Philosophy Lectures. New York: St. Martin's, 1973.

Mack, Burton L. "Exegetical Traditions in Alexandrian Judaism: A Program for the Analysis of the Philonic Corpus." *StPhil* 3 (1974–75): 71–112.

Macky, Peter W. "The Coming Revolution: The Literary Approach to New Testament Interpretation." *TE* 9 (1979): 32–46.

Macleod, C. W. "Allegory and Mysticism in Origen and Gregory of Nyssa." *JTS* n.s. 22 (1971): 362–79.

Macmullen, Ramsay. "Provincial Languages in the Roman Empire." *AJP* 87 (1966): 1–17.

Macquarrie, John. *An Existentialist Theology: A Comparison of Heidegger and Bultmann.* London: SCM, 1955.

Maier, Gerhard. *The End of the Historical-Critical Method.* St. Louis: Concordia, 1977.

Malkowski, J. L. "The Element of the *aikairos* in John Chrysostom's Anti-Jewish Polemic." *StPat* 12 (1975): 222–31.

Mallard, W. "The Incarnation in Augustine's Conversion." *RAug* 15 (1980): 80–98.

Margerie, B. de. *Introduction a l'historie de l'exegese.* Vol. 1. Paris: Cerf, 1980.

Markowicz, Walter A. "Chrysostom's Sermons on Genesis: A Problem." *TS* 24 (1963): 652–64.

Markus, R. A. "Augustine of Hippo." *CHLGEMP,* 341–419.

______. *Saeculum: History and Society in the Theology of St. Augustine.* Cambridge: Cambridge University Press, 1970.

______. "St. Augustine." *EP,* 1:198–99.

Marou, H. I. *A History of Education in Antiquity.* Translated by George Lamb. New York: Sheed and Ward, 1956.

______. *St. Augustine and His Influence through the Ages.* New York: Harper and Row, 1957.

Marsh, H. G. "The Use of 'Mysterion' in the Writings of Clement of Alexandria." *JTS* 37 (1936): 64–80.

Marshall, I. Howard. *Luke: Historian and Theologian.* Grand Rapids: Zondervan, 1970.

Marshall, I. Howard, ed. *New Testament Interpretation: Essays on Principles and Methods.* Grand Rapids: Eerdmans, 1975.

Martin, Ralph P. "Approaches to New Testament Exegesis." In *New Testament Interpretation,* edited by I. Howard Marshall, 220–51. Grand Rapids: Eerdmans, 1975.

______. *Worship in the Early Church.* Grand Rapids: Eerdmans, 1964.

______. *The Worship of God.* Grand Rapids: Eerdmans, 1982.

Mayer, Herbert T. "Clement of Rome and His Use of Scripture." *CTM* 42 (1971): 536–40.

Mayor, J. B. *The Epistle of St. Jude and the Second Epistle of St. Peter.* 1907. Grand Rapids: Baker, 1965.

______. "Tertullian's Apology." *JPhil* 21 (1893): 259–95.

McBrien, Richard P. *Catholicism.* Minneapolis: Winston, 1981.

McCartney, Dan E. "Literal and Allegorical Interpretation in Origen's *Contra Celsum.*" *WTJ* 48 (1986): 281–301.

McCaughey, J. D. "The Nag Hammadi or Chenoboskion Library and the Study of Gnosticism." *JRH* 1 (1960): 61–71.

McCollough, C. Thomas. "Theodoret of Cyrus as Biblical Interpreter and the Presence of Judaism in Later Roman Syria." Ph.D. dissertation, University of Notre Dame, 1984.

McConnell, R. S. *Law and Prophecy in Matthew's Gospel.* Basel: Reinhardt, 1969.

McCoy, Jerry. "Philosophical Influences on the Doctrines of the Incarnation in Athanasius and Cyril of Alexandria." *Encounter* 38 (1977): 362–91.

McCullough, J. C. "The Old Testament Quotations in Hebrews." *NTS* 26 (1980): 363–79.

McDonald, H. D. "Antiochene Theology." *NIDCC,* 49.

McGinley, John. "Heidegger's Concern for the Lived-World in His Dasein-Analysis." *PhT* 16 (1972): 92–116.

McIndoe, John H. "Chrysostom on St. Matthew: A Study in Antiochene Exegesis." S.T.M. thesis, Hartford Seminary Foundation, 1972.

McKenzie, John L. "Annotations on Theodore of Mopsuestia." *TS* 19 (1958): 345–73.

______. "A Chapter in the History of Spiritual Exegesis." *TS* 12 (1951): 365–81.

______. "The Commentary of Theodore of Mopsuestia on John 1:46–51." *TS* 14 (1953): 73–84.

______. "A New Study on Theodore of Mopsuestia." *TS* 10 (1949): 394–408.

______. "Problems of Hermeneutics in Roman Catholic Exegesis." *JBL* 77 (1958): 197–204.

McKim, Donald K. *A Guide to Contemporary Hermeneutics.* Grand Rapids: Eerdmans, 1986.

McKnight, Edgar V. *The Bible and the Reader: An Introduction to Literary Criticism.* Philadelphia: Fortress, 1985.

McLelland, Joseph. *God the Anonymous: A Study in Alexandrian Philosophical Theology.* Cambridge, Mass.: Philadelphia Patristic Foundation, 1976.

McNally, Robert E. *The Bible in the Early Middle Ages.* Westminster, Md.: Newman, 1959.

McNamara, Kevin. "Theodore of Mopsuestia and the Nestorian Heresy." *ITQ* 19 (1952): 254–68.

______. "Theodore of Mopsuestia and the Nestorian Heresy." *ITQ* 20 (1953): 172–91.

______. "Theodoret of Cyrus and the Unity of the Person in Christ." *ITQ* 22 (1955): 313–28.

McQuilkin, J. Robertson. "Problems of Normativeness in Scripture." In *Inerrancy and Hermeneutics,* edited by E. Radmacher and R. Preus, 219–82. Grand Rapids: Zondervan, 1984.

Meeks, Wayne A. "And Rose Up to Play: Midrash and Parenesis in 1 Cor. 10:1–22." *JSNT* 16 (1982): 64–78.

Megivern, James J. *Official Catholic Teachings: Biblical Interpretation.* Wilmington, N.C.: McGrath, 1978.

Meijering, E. D. *Orthodoxy and Platonism in Athanasius: Synthesis or Antithesis?* Leiden: Brill, 1974.

Melancthon, Philipp. *Romerbrief-kommentar, 1532. Melancthon's werke in Auswahle* 5. Edited by R. Stupperich. Guttersloh: Bertelsmann, 1965.

Melito of Sardis. "A New English Translation of the *Paschal Homily.*" In *Current Issues in Biblical and Patristic Interpretation,* edited by Gerald F. Hawthorne. Grand Rapids: Eerdmans, 1975.

Menzies, A., ed. *Peter, Tatian and Commentaries of Origen.* Translated by J. A. Robinson et al. Vol. 10 of *Ante-Nicene Fathers.* Reprint. Grand Rapids: Eerdmans, 1986.

Merlan, Philip. "Greek Philosophy from Plato to Plotinus." *CHLGEMP,* 14–132.

______. "Neoplatonism." *EP,* 6:473–76.

Merrill, E. T. "On Clement of Rome." *AJT* 22 (1918): 426–42.

Michaels, J. Ramsey. "Apostolic Fathers." *ISBE,* 1:203–13.

______. *First Peter.* WBC. Waco: Word, 1988.

Michel, Otto. *Paulus und seine Bibel.* Guttersloh: Bertelsmann, 1929.

Milkolaski, Samuel J. "Arianism." *NIDCC,* 66–68.

Millar, Edward L., ed. *Classical Statements on Faith and Reason.* New York: Random, 1970.

Miller, M. P. "Targum, Midrash and the Use of the Old Testament in the New Testament." *JSJ* 2 (1970): 29–82.

Moeller, B. "Scripture, Tradition and Sacrament in the Middle Ages and in Luther." In *Holy Book and Holy Tradition,* edited by F. F. Bruce and E. G. Rupp. Manchester: Manchester University Press, 1968.

Moffatt, James. "An Approach to Ignatius." *HTR* 29 (1936): 1–38.

______. "Ignatius of Antioch: A Study in Personal Religion." *JR* 10 (1930): 169–86.

Mollard, Einar. "Clement of Alexandria on the Origin of Greek Philosophy." *SO* 25 (1936): 57–85

______. *The Conception of the Gospel in the Alexandrian Theology.* Oslo: Jacob Dybwad, 1938.

Moo, Douglas J. *The Old Testament in the Gospel Passion Narratives.* Sheffield: Almond, 1983.

______. "The Problem of *Sensus Plenior.*" In *Hermeneutics, Authority and Canon,* edited by D. A. Carson and John Woodbridge, 175–211. Grand Rapids: Zondervan, 1986.

Moore, G. F. *Judaism in the First Centuries of the Christian Era.* 2 vols. Cambridge: Harvard University Press, 1950.

Morgan, James. *The Importance of Tertullian in the Development of Christian Dogma.* London: Kegan Paul, Trench, Trubner and Co., 1928.

Moule, C. F. D. *The Birth of the New Testament.* New York: Harper and Row, 1966.

______. *The Origin of Christology.* Cambridge: Cambridge University Press, 1977.

Mounce, R. H. *The Essential Nature of New Testament Preaching.* Grand Rapids: Eerdmans, 1960.

Mueller-Vollmer, Kurt. *The Hermeneutic Reader.* New York: Continuum, 1985.

Muilenburg, James. "Preface to Hermeneutics." *JBL* 77 (1958): 18–26.

Muller, H. "Type." *NIDNTT,* 3: 903–7.

Muller, Richard A. "*Regula Fidei.*" In *Dictionary of Latin and Greek Theological Terms.* Grand Rapids: Baker, 1985.

Mumm, H. J. "Origen as an Exegete of the Fourth Gospel." Ph.D. dissertation, Hartford Seminary Foundation, 1952.

Murphy. F. X., ed. *A Monument to Saint Jerome.* New York: Sheed and Ward, 1952.

Musurillo, H. "Ignatius of Antioch." *TS* 22 (1961): 103–10.

Nash, Henry. "The Exegesis of the School of Antioch." *JBL* 11 (1892): 22–37.

Nash, Ronald H. *The Light of the Mind: St. Augustine's Theory of Knowledge.* Lexington: University Press of Kentucky, 1969.

Neary, Michael. "Philo of Alexandria." *ITQ* 54 (1988): 41–49.

Neill, Stephen. *Chrysostom and His Message.* World Christian Books, 44. New York: Association, 1962.

______. *The Interpretation of the New Testament, 1861–1961.* Oxford: Oxford University Press, 1966.

Neiswander, D. R. "Scripture and Culture in the Early Church." *CT* 22 (November 10, 1967): 7–8.

Neusner, Jacob. *Invitation to Midrash.* San Francisco: Harper and Row, 1989.

Newton-de Molina, David. *On Literary Intention.* Edinburgh: Edinburgh University Press, 1976.

Nicholson, Graeme. *Seeing and Reading.* Atlantic Highland: Humanities, 1984.

Nielsen, J. T. *Adam and Christ in the Theology of Irenaeus of Lyons.* Assen: Van Gorcum, 1968.

Nilson, Jon. "To Whom Is Justin's *Dialogue with Trypho* Addressed?" *TS* 38 (1977): 538–46.

Nock, A. D. *Conversion: The Old and New Religion from Alexander the Great to Augustine of Hippo.* Oxford: Oxford University Press, 1933.

______. *Manhood and Christ. A Study in the Christology of Theodore of Mopsuestia.* Oxford: Oxford University Press, 1963.

Noll, Mark A. *Between Faith and Criticism.* San Francisco: Harper and Row, 1986.

O'Cleirigh, P. M. "The Meaning of Dogma in Origen." In *Jewish and Christian Self-Definition, I: The Shaping of Christianity in the Second and Third Centuries,* edited by J. Sanders, 201–16. Philadelphia: Fortress, 1980.

O'Connell, R. J. *St. Augustine's Confessions: The Odyssey of Soul.* Cambridge: Cambridge University Press, 1969.

O'Donovan, O. *The Problem of Self-Love in St. Augustine.* New Haven, Conn.: Yale University Press, 1980.

O'Malley, T. P. *Tertullian and the Bible: Language—Imagery—Exegesis.* Utrecht: Dekker and Van de Vegt N. V. Nijmegen, 1967.

O'Meara, J. J. *The Young Augustine.* London: Longmans, Green, 1954.

Oden, Thomas C. *Agenda for Theology: Recovering Christian Roots.* San Francisco: Harper and Row, 1979.

______. *The Living God: Systematic Theology.* Vol. 1. San Francisco: Harper and Row, 1987.

Ogden, Shubert M. *Christ without Myth.* New York: Harper and Row, 1961.

Origen. *Commentary on John.* Translated by Allan Menzies. Vol. 10 of *Ante-Nicene Fathers.* Reprint. Grand Rapids: Eerdmans, 1974.

______. *Commentary on the Song of Songs.* Translated by R. P. Lawson. Vol. 26 of *Ancient Christian Writers.* Westminster, Md.: Newman, 1957.

______. *An Exhortation to Martyrdom, Prayer, First Principles: Book IV. Prologue to the Commentary on the Song of Songs. Homily XXVII on Numbers.* Translated by Rowan A. Greer. New York: Paulist, 1979.

______. *On First Principles, and Contra Celsum.* Translated by Frederick Crombie. Vol. 4 of *Ante-Nicene-Fathers.* Reprint. Grand Rapids: Eerdmans, 1976.

Osborn, Eric F. *Justin Martyr.* Beitrage zur Historischen Theologie, 47. Tübingen: Mohr, 1973.

______. *The Philosophy of Clement of Alexandria.* Cambridge: Cambridge University Press, 1975.

Osborne, Grant. *The Hermeneutical Spiral: Meaning and Significance.* Downers Grove, Ill.: InterVarsity, 1991.

Otis, B. "Cappadocian Thought as a Coherent System." *Dumbarton Oaks Papers 12* (1958): 95–124.

Ottley, R. L. *Studies in the Confessions of St. Augustine.* London: Macmillan, 1919.

Outler, Albert C. "Origen and the *Regula Fidei.*" *CH* 8 (1939): 212–21.

______. "The Platonism of Clement of Alexandria." *JR* (1940): 217–39.

Owens, Virginia Stem. "Fiction and the Bible." *RJ* 38 (July 1988): 12–15.

Pagels, Elaine H. *The Gnostic Paul: Gnostic Exegesis of the Pauline Letters.* Philadelphia: Fortress, 1975.

______. "Origen and the Prophets of Israel: A Critique of Christian Typology." *JANESCU* 5 (1973): 335–44.

Palmer, R. E. *Hermeneutics.* Evanston, Ill.: Northwestern University Press, 1969.

Pannenberg, Wolfhart. "Hermeneutics and Universal History." In *History and Hermeneutics,* edited by R. W. Funk. Tübingen: Mohr, 1967.

Parker, T. D. "The Interpretation of Scripture: A Comparison of Calvin and Luther on Galatians." *Int* 17 (1963): 60–69.

Parsons, Michael. "Being Preceded Act: Indicative and Imperative in Paul's Writings." *EQ* 50 (1988): 99–129.

Parsons, Mikeal C. "'Allegorizing Allegory': Narrative Analysis and Parable Interpretation." *PRS* 15 (1988): 147–64.

Patrick, J. *Clement of Alexandria.* Edinburgh: T & T Clark, 1914.

Patte, Daniel M. *Early Jewish Hermeneutics in Palestine.* SBLDS 22. Missoula, Mont.: Scholars, 1975.

Payne, Philip B. "The Fallacy of Equating Meaning with the Human Author's Intention." *JETS* 20 (1977): 243–52.

Pelikan, Jaroslav. *The Christian Tradition. A History of the Development of Doctrine,* vol. 1, *The Emergence of the Catholic Tradition (100–600).* Chicago: University of Chicago, 1971.

______. *Development of Christian Doctrine.* New York: Yale University Press, 1969.

______. *Historical Theology: Continuity and the Change in Christian Doctrine.* Washington: Corpus, 1971.

______. *Luther the Expositor: Introduction to the Reformer's Exegetical Writings.* St. Louis: Concordia, 1959.

______. *The Preaching of Chrysostom: Homilies on the Sermon on the Mount.* Philadelphia: Fortress, 1967.

Pepin, J. *Mythe et allegorie: Les origines grecques et les contestations judeo–chretiennes.* Rev. ed. Paris: Etudes Augustiniennes, 1976.

Perler, Othmar. "Das Vierte Makkabaeerbuch Ignatius von Antiochien und die aeltesten Martyrer berichte." *Rivista di Archeologia Cristiana* 25 (1949): 47–72.

Perumal, A. C. "Are Not Papias and Irenaeus Competent to Report on the Gospels?" *ExT* 91 (1980): 332–37.

Philip, T. V. "Authority of Scripture in the Patristic Period." *IJT* 23 (1974): 1–8.

______. "Authority of Scripture in the Patristic Period." *IJT* 23 (1974): 39–55.

Pike, Kenneth L, and Evelyn G. Pike. *Grammatical Analysis.* SIL Publications in Linguistics 53. Dallas: Summer Institute of Linguistics and University of Texas at Arlington Press, 1977.

Pincherle, A. "The 'Confessions' of St. Augustine." *AugSt* 7 (1976): 119–33.

Pinnock, Clark. *The Scripture Principle.* San Francisco: Harper and Row, 1985.

Pirot, L. *L'Oeuvre Exegetigue de Theodore de Mopsueste.* Rome: Pontifico Institu Biblico, 1973.

Polhill, John B. *Acts.* NAC. Nashville: Broadman, 1992.

Polman, A. D. R. *The Word of God According to St. Augustine.* Translated by A. J. Pomerans. Grand Rapids: Eerdmans, 1961.

Polycarp. *Two Epistles to the Philippians.* Edited by P. N. Harrison. Cambridge: Cambridge University Press, 1936.

Portalie, E. *A Guide to the Thought of St. Augustine.* Chicago: Regnery, 1960.

Postgate, J. P. "On the Text of the *Stromateis* of Clement of Alexandria." *CQ* 8 (1914): 237–47.

Powell, Douglas, "Tertullianists and Cataphrygians." *VC* 29 (1975): 33–54.

Poythress, Vern. "Analysing a Biblical Text: Some Important Linguistic Distinctions." *SJT* 32 (1979): 113–37.

______. "Divine Meaning of Scripture." *WTJ* 48 (1986): 241–79.

______. "God's Lordship in Interpretation." *WTJ* 50 (1988): 27–64.

______. *Science and Hermeneutics.* Grand Rapids: Zondervan, 1988.

______. *Symphonic Theology: The Validity of Multiple Perspectives in Theology.* Grand Rapids: Zondervan, 1987.

Prestige, G. L. *Fathers and Heretics.* London: SPCK, 1954.

______. *St. Basil the Great and Apollinaris of Laodicea.* London: Hodder and Stoughton, 1956.

Preus, James Samuel. *From Shadow to Promise: Old Testament Interpretation from Augustine to the Young Luther.* Cambridge: Harvard University Press, 1969.

______. "Luther on Christ and the Old Testament." *CTM* 43 (1972): 490–93.

Quasten, Johannes. *Patrology.* 4 vols. Reprint. Westminster, Md.: Christian Classics, 1984.

Quasten, Johannes, and J. C. Plumpe, eds. *Ancient Christian Writers: The Works of the Fathers in Translation.* Multiple vols. Westminster, Md.: Newman, 1946.

Quinn, Jerome D. "St. John Chrysostom on History in the Synoptics." *CBQ* 24 (1962): 140–47.

Rabil, A. *Erasmus and the New Testament: The Mind of a Christian Humanist.* San Antonio: Trinity University Press, 1972.

Rabinowitz, Isaac. "Pesher/Pittaron: Its Biblical Meaning and Its Significance in the Qumran Literature." *RevQ* 8 (1973): 219–32.

Ramm, Bernard. *Protestant Biblical Interpretation: A Textbook of Hermeneutics.* 3d rev. ed. Grand Rapids: Baker, 1970.

Ramsbothan, A. "The Commentary of Origen on the Epistle to the Romans: Part 1."*JTS* 13 (1912): 209–24.

______. "The Commentary of Origen on the Epistle to the Romans: Part 2." *JTS* 13 (1912): 357–68.

______. "The Commentary of Origen on the Epistle to the Romans: Part 3." *JTS* 14 (1913): 10–22.

Ramsey, I. T. *Models and Mystery.* New York: Oxford University Press, 1964.

______. *Religious Language.* New York: Macmillan, 1963.

Ravel, Suresh. *Metacriticism.* Athens, Ga.: University of Georgia Press, 1981.

Reardon, B. M. G. "The Relation of Philosophy to Faith in the Teaching of St. Augustine." *StPat* 2 (1957): 288–94.

Rees, D. A. "Platonism and the Platonic Tradition." *EP,* 6:337–40.

Reid, J. K. S. *The Authority of Scripture: A Study of Reformation and Post-Reformation Understanding of the Bible.* London: Methuen, 1962.

Reine, F. J. *The Eucharist Doctrine and Liturgy of the Mystagogical Catecheses of Theodore of Mopsuestia.* Washington, D.C.: Catholic University of America Press, 1942.

Rendall, R. "The Method of the Writer to the Hebrews in Using Old Testament Quotations." *EQ* 27 (1955): 214–20.

Renwick, A. M. "Gnosticism." *ISBE,* 2:487–91.

Reuss, J. "Cyrill von Alexandrien und sein Kommentar zum Johannes-Evangelium." *Bib* 25 (1944): 201–9.

Richardson, Alan. "Manichaeism." *WDCT,* 344.

Richardson, Cyril C. *The Christianity of Ignatius of Antioch.* New York: Columbia University Press, 1935.

______. "The Condemnation of Origen." *CH* 6 (1937): 50–64.

Richardson, Cyril C., ed. *Alexandrian Christianity.* Philadelphia: Westminster, 1953.

______. *Early Christian Fathers.* Vol. 1 of The Library of Christian Classics. Philadelphia: Westminster, 1953.

Ricoeur, Paul. *The Conflict of Interpretations: Essays in Hermeneutics.* Studies in Phenomenology and Existential Philosophy. Edited by Paul D. Ihde. Evanston, Ill.: Northwestern University Press, 1974.

______. *Essays on Biblical Interpretation.* Edited by L. S. Mudge. Philadelphia: Fortress, 1980.

______. *Hermeneutics and the Human Sciences.* Translated and edited by John B. Thompson. Cambridge: Cambridge University Press, 1981.

______. *Hermeneutics and the Human Sciences.* Edited and translated by John B. Thompson. Cambridge: Cambridge University Press, 1986.

______. *Interpretation Theory: Discourse and the Surplus of Meaning.* Fort Worth: Texas Christian University Press, 1976.

Riesenfeld, H. "Reflections on the Style and the Theology of St. Ignatius of Antioch." *Texte und Untersuchungen* 79 (1961): 312–22.

Rigaux, B. *The Letters of St. Paul.* Chicago: Franciscan Herald, 1968.

Riley, Hugh M. *Christian Initiation: A Comparative Study of the Interpretation of Baptismal Liturgy in the Mystagogical Writings of Cyril of Jerusalem, John Chrysostom, Theodore of Mopsuestia, and Ambrose of Milan.* Washington, D.C.: Catholic University of America Press, 1974.

Rist, J. M. "Augustine on Free Will and Predestination." *JTS* n.s. 20 (1969): 420–47.

Robbins, Gregory Allen. "*PERI TON ENDIATHEKON GRAPHON:* Eusebius and the Formation of the Christian Bible." Ph.D. dissertation, Duke University, 1986.

Roberts, Alexander, and James Donaldson, eds. *Ante-Nicene Fathers.* 10 vols. Reprint. Grand Rapids: Eerdmans, 1971–79.

Roberts, R. C. *Rudolf Bultmann's Theology.* Grand Rapids: Eerdmans, 1977.

Roberts, Robert G. *The Theology of Tertullian.* London: Epworth, 1924.

Robinson, J. A. "The Armenian Capitula of Irenaeus *Adversus Haereses,* IV." *JTS* 32 (1930): 71–74.

Robinson, James M., ed. *The Beginnings of Dialectic Theology.* 2 vols. Richmond: John Knox, 1968.

______. "Hermeneutics Since Barth." In *The New Hermeneutic,* edited by James M. Robinson and John B. Cobb, Jr. New Frontiers in Theology, 2. New York: Harper and Row, 1964.

______. *The Nag Hammadi Library in English.* San Francisco: Harper and Row, 1977.

Robinson, James M., and John B. Cobb, Jr. *The Later Heidegger.* New York: Harper and Row, 1967.

Rogers, Jack B., and Donald K. McKim. *The Authority and Interpretation of the Bible: An Historical Approach.* Grand Rapids: Eerdmans, 1979.

Rogerson, John, Christopher Rowland, and Barnabas Lindars. *The Study and Use of the Bible.* Vol. 2 of *The History of Christian Theology,* edited by Paul Avis. 3 vols. Grand Rapids: Eerdmans, 1988.

Rossiter, Francis S. "Messianic Prophecy According to Theodoret of Cyrus and Antioche *Theoria.*" Ph.D. dissertation, Pontifical Gregorian University, Rome, 1949.

Rubinkiewicz, R. "Psalm LXVIII.19 (= Ephesians IV.8): Another Textual Tradition or Targum." *NovT* 17 (1975): 218–29.

Ruether, R. R. *Gregory of Nazianzus: Rhetor and Philosopher.* Oxford: Oxford University Press, 1969.

Runia, Klaas. *The Present-Day Christological Debate.* Downers Grove, Ill.: InterVarsity, 1984.

Russell, D. S. *The Method and Message of Jewish Apocalyptic.* London: SCM, 1964.

Ryken, Leland, *Words of Delight: A Literary Introduction to the Bible.* Grand Rapids: Baker, 1987.

______. *Words of Life: A Literary Introduction to the New Testament.* Grand Rapids: Baker, 1988.

Rylaarsdam, J. Coert. "The Problem of Faith and History in Biblical Interpretation." *JBL* 77 (1958): 26–32.

Sailhamer, John H. "Exegesis of the Old Testament as a Text." In *A Tribute to Gleason Archer,* edited by Walter C. Kaiser and Ronald Youngblood, 279–96. Chicago: Moody, 1986.

Sanders, E. P., ed. *Jewish and Christian Self-Definition.* Vol. 1, *The Shaping of Christianity in the Second and Third Centuries.* Philadelphia: Fortress, 1980.

______. *Paul and Palestinian Judaism: A Comparison of Patterns of Religion.* Philadelphia: Fortress, 1977.

______. *Paul, the Law, and the Jewish People.* Philadelphia: Fortress, 1983.

Sanders, James A. *Canon and Community.* Philadelphia: Fortress, 1984.

______. *From Sacred Story to Sacred Text.* Philadelphia: Fortress, 1985.

______. *Torah and Canon.* Philadelphia: Fortress, 1972.

Sandmel, Samuel. *Philo of Alexandria.* New York: Oxford University Press, 1979.

Sandys, John Edwin. *A History of Classical Scholarship.* 3d ed. 3 vols. Cambridge: Cambridge University Press, 1921.

Sang, Barry Ray. "The New Testament Milieu: The Inheritance and the Heir." Ph.D. dissertation, Drew University, 1983.

Scalise, Charles J. "Allegorical Flights of Fancy: The Problem of Origen's Exegesis." *GOTR* 32 (1987): 69–88.

Schaff, David Schley. "St. Augustine as an Exegete." *NPNF,* 6:xi–xx.

Schaff, Philip. *History of the Christian Church.* 6th ed. 7 vols. New York: Scribners, 1894–1907.

______. "The Life and Work of St. John Chrysostom." *NPNF,* 9:3–23.

Schaublin, Christoph. *Untersuchungen zu Methode und Herkunft des antiochenischen Exegese.* Theophaneia 23. Cologne-Bonn: Peter Hanstein, 1974.

Schleiermacher, F. E. D. *Hermeneutics: The Handwritten Manuscripts.* Edited by H. Kimmerle. Translated by James Duke and H. J. Forstman. Missoula, Mont.: Scholars, 1977.

Schmithals, Walter. *Paul and the Gnostics.* Translated by John E. Steeley. Nashville: Abingdon, 1971.

Schneider, H. P. "Some Reflections on the *Dialogue with Trypho* in Justin Martyr." *SJT* 15 (1962): 164–75.

Schneiders, Sandra M. "Faith, Hermeneutics and the Literal Sense of Scripture." *TS* 39 (1978): 719–36.

Schnucker, R. "Origen." *NIDCC,* 733–34.

Schodde, G. H. "Allegory." *ISBE,* 1:95.

Schoedel, W. R. *Ignatius of Antioch.* Philadelphia: Fortress, 1985.

______. "Theological Method in Irenaeus." *JTS* (1984): 31–49.

Schoeps, Hans Joachim. *Theologie und Geschichte des Judenchristentums.* Tübingen: Mohr, 1949.

Scholem, Gershom Gerhard. *Jewish Gnosticism, Merkabah Mysticism and Talmudic Tradition.* New York: Jewish Theological Seminary, 1960.

Scholer, David M. "Issues in Biblical Interpretation." *EQ* 88 (1988): 5–22.

Schurer, Emil. *The Jewish People in the Age of Jesus Christ (175 B.C.–A.D. 135).* Revised and edited by Geza Vermes and Fergus Millar. Edinburgh: T & T Clark, 1973.

Schweizer, Eduard. "Diodore von Tarsus als Exeget." *ZNW* 40 (1941): 33–75.

Scott, Walter. *Hermetica: The Ancient Greek and Latin Writings which Contain Religious or Philosophic Teachings Ascribed to Hermes Trismegistus.* 2 vols. Oxford: Clarendon, 1924–25.

Scott-Muncrief, P. D. "Gnosticism and Early Christianity in Egypt." *CQR* 69 (1909): 64–83.

Seeberg, R. *Textbook of the History of Doctrines.* Translated by C. E. Hay. 2 vols. Grand Rapids: Baker, 1977.

Seebohn, Frederick. *The Oxford Reformers: John Colet, Erasmus and Thomas More.* London: Longmans, Green and Co., 1896.

Seisdedos, Alvarez. "Le 'teoria' antioguena." *Estudios Biblicos* 11 (1952): 31–67.

Sellers, R. V. *Eustathius of Antioch and His Place in the Early History of Christian Doctrine.* Cambridge: Cambridge University Press, 1928.

______. *Two Ancient Christologies: A Study in the Christological Thought of the Schools of Alexandria and Antioch in the Early History of Christian Doctrine.* London: SPCK, 1954.

Selwyn, E. G. *The First Epistle of St. Peter.* 2d ed. London: Macmillan, 1947.

Semple, Witt. "St. Jerome as Biblical Translator." *BJRL* 48 (1965–66): 227–43.

Shelton, Raymond Larry. "Martin Luther's Concept of Biblical Interpretation in Historical Perspective." Ph.D. dissertation, Fuller Theological Seminary, 1974.

Shepherd, M. H., Jr. "Clement, Epistles of." *IDB,* 1:467.

Shotwell, Willis A. *The Biblical Exegesis of Justin Martyr.* London: SPCK, 1965.

Sider, R. D. "Approaches to Tertullian: A Study of Recent Scholarship." *SC* 2 (1982): 228–60.

Siegfried, Carl. *Philo von Alexandria als Ausleger des Alten Testaments an sich selbst und nach seinem geschichtlichen Einfluss betractet, nebst Untersuchungen uber die Graecitaet Philos.* Jena: Duft, 1875.

Silberman, Lou H. "Unriddling the Riddle: A Study in the Structure and Language of the Habakkuk Pesher." *RevQ* 3(1961): 323–64.

Silva, Moisés. *Has the Church Misread the Bible?: The History of Interpretation in Light of Current Issues.* Grand Rapids: Zondervan, 1987.

______. "The New Testament Use of the Old Testament." In *Scripture and Truth,* edited by D. A. Carson and John Woodbridge, 143–65. Grand Rapids: Zondervan, 1983.

Skarsaune, Oskar. "The Conversion of Justin Martyr." *ST* 30 (1976): 53–74.

______. *Proof from Prophecy: A Study in Justin Martyr's Proof-Text Tradition.* Leiden: Brill, 1987.

Skinner, Quentin. "Conventions and the Understanding of Speech Acts." *PQ* 20 (1970): 118–38.

______. "Hermeneutics and the Role of History." *NLH* 7 (1975): 209–32.

______. "Meaning and Understanding in the History of Ideas." *HT* 8 (1969): 3–53.

______. "Motives, Intentions and the Interpretation of Texts." *NLH* 3 (1971–72): 393–408.

______. "On Performing and Explaining Linguistic Action." *PQ* 21 (1971): 1–21.

Sloan, Robert B. "The Use of the Old Testament in the New Testament." In *Reclaiming the Prophetic Mantle,* edited by G. L. Klein. Nashville: Broadman, 1992.

______. "Signs and Wonders: A Rhetorical Clue to the Pentecost Discourse." *EQ* 63 (1991): 225–40.

Slomivic, Elieser. "Toward an Understanding of the Exegesis in the Dead Sea Scrolls." *RevQ* 7 (1969): 3–15.

Smalley, Beryl. "The Bible in the Middle Ages." *The Church's Use of the Bible Past and Present,* edited by D. E. Nineham. London: Macmillan, 1960.

______. *The Study of the Bible in the Middle Ages.* 2d ed. Oxford: Blackwell, 1952.

Smith, Clyde C. "Valentinus." *NIDCC,* 1008.

Smith, Harold. *Ante-Nicene Exegesis of the Gospels.* Vol. 1. New York: Macmillan, 1925.

Smith, J. P. "Res Bibliographicae: Some Sources for the History of Exegesis." *Bib* 33 (1952): 529–32.

______. *St. Irenaeus: Proof of the Apostolic Preaching.* New York: Paulist, 1952.

Smith, John E. *The Analogy of Experience.* New York: Harper and Row, 1973.

Smith, R. G. "Tertullian and Montanism." *Theology* 46 (1943): 127–39.

Snodgrass, Klyne. "The Use of the Old Testament in the New Testament." In *New Testament Criticism and Interpretation,* edited by David Alan Black and David S. Dockery. Grand Rapids: Zondervan, 1991.

Soskice, Janet Martin. *Metaphor and Religious Language.* Oxford: Clarendon, 1985.

Soulen, Richard N. *Handbook of Biblical Criticism.* Atlanta: John Knox, 1976.

Sparks, H. F. D. "Jerome as Biblical Scholar." In *The Cambridge History of the Bible,* vol. 1, edited by P. R. Ackroyd and C. F. Evans, 510–40. Cambridge: Cambridge University Press, 1970.

Spicq, C. "Le philonisme de l'Epitre aux Hebreaux." *RB* 56 (1949): 542–72.

______. "Le philonisme de l'Epitre aux Hebreaux." *RB* 57 (1950): 212–42.

______. *L'Epitre aux Hebreaux.* 2 vols. Paris: Gabalda, 1952–53.

Staehl, Karl. *Die Zahlenmystik bei Philon von Alexandreia.* Leipzig and Berlin: Verlag und Druck von B. G. Teubner, 1931.

Stahlin, G. "*Mythos.*" *TDNT,* 4:762–95.

Staniforth, Maxwell, ed. *Early Christian Writings: The Apostolic Fathers.* Penguin Classics. Baltimore: Penguin, 1968.

Stein, K. J. "Philip Jacob Spener's Hope for Better Times: Contribution in Controversy." *CQ* 73 (1979): 3–20.

Stein, Robert H. "'Authentic' or 'Authoritative': What Is the Difference?" *JETS* 24 (1981): 127–30.

______. "The Criteria for Authenticity." In *Gospel Perspectives: Studies of History and Tradition in the Four Gospels,* edited by R. T. France and David Wenham, 225–63. Sheffield: JSOT, 1980.

______. "The Interpretation of the Parable of the Good Samaritan." In *Scripture Tradition and Interpretation,* edited by W. Ward Gasque and William Sanford LaSor, 278–95. Grand Rapids: Eerdmans, 1978.

______. "What Is Redaktiongeschichte?" *JBL* 88 (1969): 45–56.

Steinmetz, David C. "The Superiority of Precritical Exegesis." *ThT* 27 (1980): 27–38.

Stendahl, Krister. "Contemporary Biblical Theology." *IDB,* 1:418–32.

______. "Implications of Form Criticism and Tradition Criticism for Biblical Interpretation." *JBL* 77 (1958): 33–38.

______. *The School of St. Matthew and Its Use of the Old Testament.* Philadelphia: Fortress, 1968.

Stephens, William R. W. *St. John Chrysostom: His Life and Times.* London: John Murray, 1880.

Stewardson, Jerry, "The Christology of Theodoret of Cyrus According to His Eranistes." Ph.D. dissertation, Northwestern University, 1972.

Story, Cullen I. K. *Nature of Truth in "The Gospel" and in the Writings of Justin Martyr: A Study of the Pattern of Orthodoxy in the Middle of the Second Century.* Leiden: Brill, 1970.

Strack, Hermann L., and Paul Billerbeck. *Kommentar zum Neuen Testament aus Talmud und Midrasch.* 4 vols. Munich: Beck, 1922–28.

Strawley, J. H., ed. *The Epistles of St. Ignatius, Bishop of Antioch.* London: SPCK, 1935.

Stuhlmacher, Peter. *Historical Criticism and Theological Interpretation: Toward a Hermeneutics of Consent.* Translated by R. A. Harrisville. Philadelphia: Fortress, 1977.

Suhl, Alfred. *Die Function der alttestamentlichen zitate und Anspielungen im Markusevangelium.* Guttersloh: Mohr, 1965

Sullivan, F. A. *The Christology of Theodore of Mopsuestia.* Rome: Gregorian University Press, 1956.

______. "Notes on Theodore of Mopsuestia." *TS* 20 (1959): 264–79.

Surburg, R. F. "The Significance of Luther's Hermeneutics for the Protestant Reformation." *CTM* 24 (1954): 241–61.

Swete, Henry B. *Patristic Study*. New York: Longmans, Green and Co., 1902.

______. *Theodori Episcopi Mopsuestia in Epistolas B. Pauli Commentarii*. 2 vols. Cambridge: Cambridge University Press, 1982.

Tabbernee, William. "Early Montanism and Voluntary Martyrdom." *Colloquium* 17 (1985): 33–43.

Talbert, Charles H. *Reading Corinthians*. New York: Crossroad, 1987.

Tasker, R. V. G. "The Text of St. Matthew Used by Origen in His Commentary on St. Matthew." *JTS* 38 (1937): 60–64.

______. "The Text of the Fourth Gospel Used by Origen in His Commentary on John." *JTS* 37 (1936): 146–55.

Tate, J. "The Beginnings of Greek Allegory." *CR* 41 (1927): 214–15.

______. "On the History of Allegorism." *CQ* 28 (1934): 105–14.

______. "Plato and Allegorical Interpretation, 1." *CQ* 23 (1929): 142–54.

______. "Plato and Allegorical Interpretation, 2." *CQ* 24 (1930): 1–10.

Te Selle, Eugene. *Augustine the Theologian*. New York: Random, 1970.

______. *Augustine's Strategy as an Apologist*. Villanova, Penn.: Villanova University Press, 1974.

Ternant, Paul. "La *Theoria* d'Antiochene dans le cadre des sens de l'Ecriture." *Bib* 34 (1953): 135–58, 354–83, 456–86.

Tertullian. *Apologetical Writings, Against Marcion, and Ethical Writings*. Translated by Peter Holmes and S. Thelwell. Vol. 3 of *Ante-Nicene Fathers*. 2d series. Reprint. Grand Rapids: Eerdmans, 1973.

Theodore of Mopsuestia. *Commentary on the Minor Epistles of St. Paul*. Edited by Henry B. Swete. 2 vols. Cambridge: Cambridge University Press, 1880–82.

______. *Le commentaire de Theodore de Mopsueste sur les Psaumes*. Edited by R. Derreese. Studia Testi 93. Vatican City: Biblioteca apostolica vaticaina, 1939.

______. *Pauluskommentare aus der greichischen Kirche*. Edited by K. Staab. Neutestamentliche Abhandlungen 15. Munster: Aschendorff, 1933.

______. *Commentarius in Evangelium Johannis Apostoli*. Edited by J. M. Voste. Paris: Typographe Republicae, 1940.

Theophilus of Antioch. *Ad Autolycum*. Edited by Robert M. Grant. Oxford: Oxford University Press, 1970.

Thiselton, Anthony C. "The New Hermeneutic." In *New Testament Interpretation*, edited by I. Howard Marshall, 308–33. Grand Rapids: Eerdmans, 1975.

______. "The Parables as Language-Event." *SJT* 23 (1970): 437–68.

______. *Two Horizons: New Testament Hermeneutics and Philosophical Description*. Grand Rapids: Eerdmans, 1980.

______. "Understanding God's Word Today." In *Christ the Lord*, edited by John R. W. Stott. London: Collins Fontana, 1977.

______. "The Use of Philosophical Categories in New Testament Hermeneutics." *Churchman* 87 (1973): 87–100.

Thomas, K. J. "Old Testament Citations in Hebrews." *NTS* 11 (1965): 303–25.

Thompson, J. Alexander. "Alexandria." *ISBE,* 1:89–94.

Thurley, Geoffrey. *Counter-Modernism in Current Critical Theory*. New York: St. Martin's, 1983.

Tigcheler, J. *Didyme l'areugle et l'exegese allegorigue*. Nijmegen: Dekker and Van de Vegt, 1977.

Timothy, H. B. *The Early Christian Apologists and Greek Philosophy*. Philosophical Texts and Studies. Assen: Van Gorcum, 1973.

Tixeront, J., trans. *A Handbook of Patrology*. St. Louis: Herder, 1920.

Tollinton, R. B. *Selections from the Commentaries and Homilies of Origen*. London: SPCK, 1929.

Toon, Peter. *The Development of Doctrine in the Church*. Grand Rapids: Eerdmans, 1979.

Torjesen, Karen Jo. "Hermeneutical Procedure and Theological Structure in Origen's Exegesis." Ph.D. dissertation, Claremont Graduate School, 1982.

______. "Origen's Interpretation of the Psalms." *StPat* 18 (1982): 144–58.

Torrance, James. "Interpretation and Understanding in Schleiermacher's Theology: Some Critical Questions." *SJT* 21 (1968): 268–82.

Torrance, T. F. "Hermeneutics according to Schleiermacher." SJT 21 (1968): 257–67.

Tracy, David. *Plurality and Ambiguity: Hermeneutics, Religion, Hope*. San Francisco: Harper and Row, 1987.

Trigg, Joseph Wilson. *Origen: The Bible and Philosophy in the Third-Century Church*. Atlanta: John Knox, 1983.

Turner, H. E. W. *The Pattern of Christian Truth: A Study of the Relations Between Orthodoxy and Heresy in the Early Church*. London: Mobray, 1954.

Tyconius. *The Book of Rules*. Edited by F. C. Burkitt. In *Texts and Studies* 3:1, edited by J. A. Robinson. Cambridge: Cambridge University Press, 1894.

Tying, D. "Theodore of Mopsuestia as an Interpreter of the Old Testament." *JBL* 50 (1931): 298–303.

Unnik, W. C. van. "Is *1 Clement* 20 Purely Stoic?" *VC* 4 (1950): 181–89.

Vaccari, A. "I fattori della esegesi geronomiana." *Bib* 1 (1920): 457–66.

______. "La *Theoria* nella Scouola esegetica di Antiochia." *Bib* 1 (1920): 3–36.

Vallee, G. "Theological and Non-Theological Motives in Irenaeus's Refutation of the Gnostics." In *Jewish and Christian Self-Definition,* edited by S. Sanders, 174–85. Philadelphia: Fortress, 1980.

Van Steenberghen, F. *Aristotle in the West: The Origins of Latin Aristotelianism*. Translated by Leonard Johnston. Louvain: E. Nauwelaerts, 1955.

Van Winder, J. C. M. *An Early Christian Philosopher*. Leiden: Brill, 1971.

Vermes, Geza. "The Qumran Interpretation of Scripture in Its Historical Setting." *ALUOS* 6 (1966–68): 90–97.

Visser, A. J. "A Bird's Eye View of Ancient Christian Eschatology." *Numen* 14 (1967): 4–22.

Vos, Arvin. *Aquinas, Calvin and Contemporary Protestant Thought: A Critique of Protestant Views on the Thought of Thomas Aquinas.* Grand Rapids: Eerdmans, 1985.

Wagner, Walter. "Another Look at the Literary Problem in Clement of Alexandria's Major Writings." *CH* 37 (1968): 251–62.

______. "The Paideia Motif in the Theology of Clement of Alexandria." Ph.D. dissertation, Drew University, 1968.

Walenbach, John R. "John Calvin as Biblical Commentator: An Investigation into Calvin's Use of John Chrysostom as an Exegetical Source." Ph.D. dissertation, University of Pittsburgh, 1974.

Walgrave, J. H. *Unfolding Revelation: The Nature of Doctrinal Development.* Philadelphia: Westminster, 1981.

Wallace, Mark I. "The New Yale Theology." *CSR* 17 (1987): 154–70.

Wallace-Hadrill, D. S. *Christian Antioch.* Cambridge: Cambridge University Press, 1982.

Waltke, Bruce K. "A Canonical Process Approach to the Psalms." In *Tradition and Testament,* edited by J. S. Feinberg and P. D. Feinberg, 3–18. Chicago: Moody, 1981.

Wand, J. W. C. *A History of the Early Church to A.D. 500.* London: Methuen, 1937.

Wells, David F. *The Person of Christ.* Westchester, Ill.: Crossway, 1984.

Wenham, John W. *Christ and the Bible.* Downers Grove, Ill.: InterVarsity, 1973.

Wessel, Walt W. "Ebionites." *ISBE,* 2:9–10.

Wickert, Ulrich. "Die Personlichkeit des Paulus in den Pauluskommentaren Theodors von Mopsuestia." *ZNW* 53 (1962): 51–66.

______. *Studien zu dem Paulus kommentaten Theodors von Mopsuestia als Beitrag zum Verstandnis der antiochenischen Theologie.* Biehefte 27 zur Zeitschrift für die neutestamentliche Wissenschaft und die Kunde der alteren Kirche. Berlin: Topelmann, 1962.

Wikgren, A. "Patterns of Perfection in the Epistle to the Hebrews." *NTS* 6 (1960): 159–67.

Wilder, A. N. *Early Christian Rhetoric.* London: SCM, 1964.

Wiles, Maurice F. *The Divine Apostle: The Interpretation of St. Paul's Epistles in the Early Church.* Cambridge: Cambridge University Press, 1967.

______. "Origen as Biblical Scholar." In *The Cambridge History of the Bible,* vol. 1, edited by P. R. Ackroyd and C. F. Evans, 454–88. Cambridge: Cambridge University Press, 1970.

______. *The Spiritual Gospel.* Cambridge: Cambridge University Press, 1960.

______. "Theodore of Mopsuestia as Representative of the Antiochene School." *CHB,* 1:489–509.

Wiley, John Heston. *Chrysostom: The Orator.* Cincinnati: Jennings and Graham, 1906.

Wilken, Robert L. *John Chrysostom and the Jews: Rhetoric and Reality in the Late Fourth Century.* Berkeley: University of California Press, 1983.

______. *Judaism and the Early Christian Mind.* New Haven, Conn.: Yale University Press, 1971.

______. "Toward a Social Interpretation of Early Christian Apologetics." *CH* 39 (1970): 437–58.

______. "Tradition, Exegesis and the Christological Controversies." *CH* 34 (1965): 123–45.

Williams, C. Peter. "Lucian of Antioch." *NIDCC,* 607.

Williams, David John. *Acts.* GNC. New York: Harper and Row, 1985.

Williamson, Clark M. "The *Adversus Judaeos* Tradition in Christian Theology." *Encounter* 39 (1978): 273–96.

Williamson, R. *Philo and the Epistle to the Hebrews.* Leiden: Brill, 1970.

______. "Platonism and Hebrews." *SJT* 16 (1963): 415–24.

Willis, G. G. *St. Augustine and the Donatist Controversy.* London: SPCK, 1950.

Wilson, R. McL. *The Gnostic Problem and Gnosis and the New Testament.* London: Mowbray, 1958.

______. "Philo and the Fourth Gospel." *ExT* 65 (1953): 47–49.

Wilson-Kastner, P. "Grace as Participation in the Divine Life in the Theology of Augustine." *AugSt* 7 (1976): 135–52.

Wimsatt, William K., and Monroe C. Beardsley. "The Intentional Fallacy." In *The Verbal Icon: Studies in the Meaning of Poetry.* Lexington: University of Kentucky Press, 1954.

Wingren, G. *Man and the Incarnation: A Study in the Biblical Theology of Irenaeus.* Philadelphia: Muhlenberg, 1959.

Witt, R. E. "The Hellenism of Clement of Alexandria." *CQ* 25 (1931): 195–204.

______. *Isis in the Graeco-Roman World.* Ithaca, N.Y.: Cornell University Press, 1971.

Wolfson, Harry A. "Clement of Alexandria on the Generation of the Logos." *CH* 20 (1951): 3–11.

______. *Philo I.* Cambridge: Harvard University Press, 1968.

______. *Philo: Foundations of Religious Philosophy in Judaism, Christianity and Islam.* 3d rev. ed. 2 vols. Cambridge: Harvard University Press, 1962.

______. *The Philosophy of the Church Fathers.* Cambridge: Harvard University Press, 1956.

Wood, A. Skevington. *Captive to the Word: Martin Luther's Doctrine of Sacred Scripture.* Grand Rapids: Eerdmans, 1969.

______. "Luther as Interpreter of Scripture." *CT* 3 (November 24, 1958): 7.

______. *Luther's Principles of Biblical Interpretation.* London: Tyndale, 1960.

______. *The Principles of Biblical Interpretation as Enunciated by Irenaeus, Origen, Augustine, Luther and Calvin.* Grand Rapids: Zondervan, 1967.

Wood, Charles M. *The Formation of Christian Understanding: An Essay in Theological Hermeneutics.* Philadelphia: Westminster, 1981.

Woolcombe, K. J. "The Biblical Origins and Patristic Development of Typology." In *Essays on Typology,* compiled by G. W. H. Lampe and K. J. Woolcombe, 39–75. London: SCM, 1957.

Wratislav, A. H. "Origen's Exegesis of Romans VIII: 18–25." *JSL* 12 (1861): 410–20.

Wright, A. G. *The Literary Genre Midrash.* Staten Island, N.Y.: Alba House, 1968.

______. "The Literary Genre Midrash." *CBQ* 28 (1966): 105–38.

Wright, David F. "Christian Faith in the Greek World: Justin Martyr's Testimony." *EQ* 54 (1982): 77–87.

______. "Theodore of Mopsuestia." *NIDCC,* 964–65.

______. "Why Were the Montanists Condemned?" *Themelios* 2:1 (1977): 15–22.

Yamauchi, Edwin M. "Gnosticism." *NIDCC,* 416–18.

______. *Pre-Christian Gnosticism: A Survey of the Proposed Evidences.* London: Tyndale, 1973.

Yoder, John Howard. "The Authority of the Canon." In *Essays in Biblical Interpretation.* Elkhart, Ind.: Institute of Mennonite Studies, 1984.

Young, Francis M. "Antiochene Theology." *WDCT,* 28.

______. *From Nicea to Chalcedon.* London: SCM, 1983.

Zeller, E. *A History of Greek Philosophy from the Earliest Period to the Time of Socrates.* Translated by S. F. Alleyne. 2 vols. London: Longmans and Green, 1881.

Ziegler, Joseph, ed. *Septuaginta Vol. XIV: Isaias.* Gottingen: Vandenhoeck und Ruprecht, 1967.

Zollig, A. *Die Inspirationslehre des Origenes.* Freiburg: Strassburger Theologische Studien, 1902.

Zuharapoulos, Dimitri Z. "Theodore of Mopsuestia's Critical Methods in Old Testament Study." Ph.D. dissertation, Boston University, 1964.

Index

220.601
D6371
c.1

8622

LINCOLN CHRISTIAN COLLEGE AND SEMINARY

220.601 D6371 c.1
Dockery, David S.
Biblical interpretation then
and now

DEMCO